D1562932

Greater China in an Era of Globalization

Challenges Facing Chinese Political Development

Series Editor: Sujian Guo, Ph.D.
San Francisco State University

In an attempt to reflect the rapidly changing political environment of the People's Republic of China, editor Sujian Guo has assembled a book series to present specialized areas of research in current Chinese political studies. Incorporating theoretical, empirical, and policy research on contemporary Chinese politics both domestically and internationally, this series contemplates the Chinese past, present, and future by utilizing interdisciplinary perspectives to approach issues related to Chinese politics, economy, culture, social development, reform, the military, legal system, and foreign relations. Aimed at bringing a greater understanding of the current Chinese political climate to Western audiences, this series is focused on the emerging voices of Chinese scholars and their perspectives on the ever-changing Chinese diaspora.

Recent titles in the series are:

Challenges Facing Chinese Political Development, edited by Sujian Guo and Baogang Guo

New Dimensions of Chinese Foreign Policy, edited by Sujian Guo and Shiping Hua

The Dragon's Hidden Wings: How China Rises with Its Soft Power, by Sheng Ding

"Harmonious World" and China's New Foreign Policy, by Sujian Guo and Jean-Marc F. Blanchard

China in Search of a Harmonious Society, edited by Sujian Guo and Baogang Guo

Greater China in an Era of Globalization, edited by Sujian Guo and Baogang Guo

Toward Better Governance in China, edited by Baogang Guo and Dennis Hickey

Dynamics of Local Governance in China during the Reform Era, edited by Tse-Kang Leng and Yun-han Chu

Greater China in an Era of Globalization

Edited by Sujian Guo and Baogang Guo

LEXINGTON BOOKS
A division of
ROWMAN & LITTLEFIELD PUBLISHERS, INC.
Lanham • Boulder • New York • Toronto • Plymouth, UK

Published by Lexington Books
A division of Rowman & Littlefield Publishers, Inc.
A wholly owned subsidiary of The Rowman & Littlefield Publishing Group, Inc.
4501 Forbes Boulevard, Suite 200, Lanham, Maryland 20706
http://www.lexingtonbooks.com

Estover Road, Plymouth PL6 7PY, United Kingdom

British Library Cataloguing in Publication Information Available

Library of Congress Cataloging-in-Publication Data

Greater China in an era of globalization / edited by Sujian Guo and Baogang Guo.
        p. cm.
     Includes bibliographical references and index.
     ISBN 978-0-7391-3534-1 (cloth : alk. paper) -- ISBN 978-0-7391-3536-5 (electronic)
     1.   China--Foreign economic relations. 2.   Globalization--China. I. Guo, Sujian, 1957-
II. Guo, Baogang, 1960-
     HF1604.G563 2010
     337.51--dc22   2009032444

⊖™ The paper used in this publication meets the minimum requirements of American
National Standard for Information Sciences—Permanence of Paper for Printed Library
Materials, ANSI/NISO Z39.48-1992.

Printed in the United States of America

Contents

List of Figures

List of Tables

Contributors

Thomas Cieslik, Lecturer in International Relations at the Institute for Political Science and Social Research of University of Würzburg (Germany). From 2002 to 2007 he taught as assistant professor at the Tecnologico de Monterrey, Mexico-City. His areas of specialty are Comparative Foreign Policy, International Migration, and International Regimes. Recent publications include *Immigration—A Documentary and Reference Guide* (Westport: Praeger-Greenwood, 2008), "Mexikos künftige Energiepolitik nach den Präsidentschaftswahlen 2006: Zwischen Privatisierungswillen und politischem Widerstand," *Lateinamerika-Analysen*, German Institute of Global and Aera Studies, Institute of Latin American Studies, Hamburg, No.16 (2007), 149-168, *Beyond the wall: Perspectives and Proposals on Migration* (Mexico-City: Friedrich Naumann Foundation, 2007).

Edward Friedman, Hawkins Chair Professor of Political Science at University of Wisconsin, Madison. His teaching and research interests include democratization, Chinese politics, international political economy, evolution, and the comparative study of transitions in Leninist States. His most recent books *Political Transitions in Dominant Party Systems* (2008); *Asia's Giants: Comparing China and India* (2006); *China's Rise, Taiwan's Dilemmas and International Peace* (2006); *Revolution, Resistance and Reform in Village China* (2005); *International Cooperation and Its Enemies in Northeast Asia* (2005); *What if China doesn't Democratize? Implications for War and Peace* (2001); *National Identity and Democratic Prospects in Socialist China* (1995); *The Politics of Democratization: Generalizing the East Asian Experience* (1994); and *Chinese Village, Socialist State* (1991).

Baogang Guo, Associate Professor of Political Science at Dalton State College, and president of the Association of the Association of Chinese Political Studies. He is associate editor of the *Journal of Chinese Political Science* and research associate in China Research Center in Atlanta, GA. His research interests include comparative public policy, political culture and political legitimacy, and Chinese and Asia politics. He is an associate editor of *China Today* (Greenwood Press, 2005), and author of nine book chapters and eleven peer reviewed journal articles. His recent publications appeared on *Asian Survey, Journal of Chinese Political Science, Modern China Studies, Journal of Comparative Asian Development, Twenty-first Century,* and *American Journal of China Studies.*

Sujian Guo, Distinguished Professor of Fudan University and Associate Dean of National Institute of Advanced Study in Social Sciences at Fudan University, Professor in the Department of Political Science and Director of Center for U.S.-China Policy Studies at San Francisco State University, Editor-in-Chief of the *Journal of Chinese Political Science*, Series Editor of Rowman & Littlefield-Lexington's Chinese political studies, and former President of Association of Chinese Political Studies (2006-08). He received his MA degree from Peking University and Ph.D. from the University of Tennessee. His research interests include Chinese/Asian politics, U.S.-China relations, communist and post-communist studies, democratic transitions, and the political economy of East and Southeast Asia. He has published more than 30 academic articles both in English and Chinese. His authored and edited books include *Harmonious World and Chinese New Foreign Policy* (2008); *China in Search of a Harmonious Society* (2008); *Challenges Facing Chinese Political Development* (2007); *New Dimensions of Chinese Foreign Policy* (2007); *China in the Twenty-First Century: Challenges and Opportunities* (2007); *The Political Economy of Asian Transition from Communism* (2006); *China's 'Peaceful Rise' in the 21st Century: Domestic and International Conditions* (2006); and *Post-Mao China: From Totalitarianism to Authoritarianism?* (2000).

James C. Hsiung, Professor of Politics at New York University, and author and editor of 18 books on Pacific Asian international relations, U.S. Asian relations, Chinese foreign policy, and international law. His current research interest is in sea power and the twenty-first century. At NYU, he teaches comparative politics of China and Japan, international relations of Asia, international law, and international governance.

Antonio C. Hsiang, Associate Professor at Chihlee Institute of Technology in Taiwan, and editor of *Preventing a Perfect Storm in the Taiwan Strait*. He has written extensively on both Latin American and China/Taiwan affairs.

Jerome S. Hsiang, an attorney at the Shiang Law Firm, P.C. in Los Angeles, California. He has contributed to and edited a number of works regarding Taiwan's involvement in the global arena.

Wenshan Jia, Senior Associate Professor of the Department of Communication Studies at Chapman University, California. His published areas of research are primarily communication theory, intercultural communication, and Chinese culture and communication. He has published half a dozen books and two dozen scholarly articles and book chapters. Three of these books hit on the list of "Outstanding Academic Book" in *Choice*, a magazine of American Library Association. He has won multiple research awards such as Early Career Award granted biannually by International Academy for Intercultural Research and Wang-Fradkin Professorship (2005-2007), the highest faculty research award given by Chapman University. Jia is Consulting Editor for *International Journal* *for Intercultural Relations* and on the editorial board of *Global Media Journal* (the Chinese edition) published by Tsinghua University, China. Jia has been interviewed on his expertise by various local, national and international media. He is former Chair of Department of Communication Studies at Chapman University as well as former Chair of Faculty Personnel Council at Chapman University.

Jing Men, the InBev-Baillet Latour Chair and Professor of EU-China relations at the College of Europe. She is also Assistant Professor of Vesalius College and senior researcher at the Brussels Institute of Contemporary China Studies of Vrije Universiteit Brussel. She is specialized in Chinese foreign policy and EU-China relations. Her most recent publications include: "China's Rise and Its Relations with Other Major Powers: Competitors or Partners," in Sujian Guo and Jean-Marc F. Blanchard (eds.), *Harmonious World and China's New Foreign Policy* (Lanham: Rowman & Littlefield-Lexington, 2008), pp. 83-103; "Crisis across the Taiwan Strait," in Stanley Crossick and Etienne Reuter (eds.) *China-EU: A Common Future* (World Scientific Publishing Co Ltd of Singapore, 2007), pp. 81-92; "Changing Ideology in China and Its Impact on Chinese Foreign Policy," in Sujian Guo and Shiping Hua (eds.), *New Dimensions of Chinese Foreign Policy* (New York/Lexington: Rowman & Littlefield Publishers, 2007), pp. 7-39; *European Integration: Decision-Making and External Relations of the European Union* [Ouzhou yitihua jincheng: Oumeng de juece yu duiwai guanxi], (Beijing: China Renmin University Press, 2007, 237pp (written together with Youri Devuyst and published in Chinese); "The Construction of the China-ASEAN Free Trade Area: A Study of China's Active Involvement," *Global Society: Journal of Interdisciplinary International Relations*, Vol. 21, No. 2 (April 2007), pp. 249-268; and "Chinese Perception of the European Union: A Review of Leading Chinese Journals," *European Law Journal*, Vol. 12, No. 6 (November 2006), pp. 788–806.

Xiaoyang Tang, Ph.D. Candidate in the Philosophy Department at the New School for Social Research. He is also lecturing at New York University and the City University of New York. His teaching and research interests include practical philosophy, ethics, political economics, Chinese modern society and China's global engagement. He has published several papers on Chinese engagement in Africa and on innovation systems in China and India. His current project is to compare Chinese and Western philosophical traditions and their roles in politics. He got his B.A. in management from Fudan University and his M.A. in philosophy and law from Freiburg University in Germany.

William Vlcek, Lecturer in International Politics at the Institute of Commonwealth Studies, University of London when this chapter was written. His research interests include global political economy, offshore finance as economic development, and global financial governance, particularly the campaigns against money laundering and terrorist financing. The author of *Offshore Finance and Small States: Sovereignty, Size and Money* (Palgrave,

2008), he has published articles on offshore financial centers and international campaigns against money laundering and terrorist financing in a number of journals including the *British Journal of Politics and International Relations, International Journal of Politics, Culture and Society,* and *Journal of International Relations and Development.*

Marion Chyun-Yang Wang, Associate Professor of International Studies in the Graduate Institute of Political Science at the National Sun Yat-sen University, Kaohsiung. Her research in Chinese, English and German are focused on China studies, area studies in Asia and Europe. Her major publications *Groter China als drijvende kracht van de regionale integratie in Oost-Azië* (2005); *Greater China: Powerhouse of East Asian Regional Cooperation* (2004); *The Chinese Role in Asia-Pacific Regional Cooperation* (2002); *The Linkage of the ROC's Mainland China Policy and Foreign Policy* (2000); *Die Rolle der Bundesrepublik Deutschland in der EG/EPZ vom Amtsantritt der Regierung Kohl/Genscher bis Ende 1983* (1991).

Katja Weber, Associate Professor in the Sam Nunn School of International Affairs at Georgia Tech and, during fall semester 2008, was Visiting Research Scholar at the Graduate School of Law and Politics at the University of Tokyo. Her research interests include international relations theory, transatlantic and East Asian security issues, theories of integration, and German foreign policy. She is the author *of Hierarchy Amidst Anarchy: Transaction Costs and Institutional Choice* (SUNY Press, 2000), co-author (with Paul Kowert) of *Cultures of Order: Leadership, Language, and Social Reconstruction in Germany and Japan,* (SUNY Press, 2007), and co-editor (with Michael Baun and Michael Smith) of *Governing Europe's Neighborhood: Partners or Periphery?* (Manchester University Press, 2007).

Acknowledgments

This book is a collection of papers from an Association of Chinese Political Studies (ACPS) conference entitled "Greater China in an Era of Globalization" from July 14–15, 2008 at Chinese University of Hong Kong. The conference was hosted and co-sponsored by the Hong Kong Institute of Asia-Pacific Studies at Chinese University of Hong Kong, the College of Behavioral and Social Sciences at San Francisco State University, the Mr. and Mrs. S. H. Wong Foundation Ltd. Hong Kong, International Relations Research Association and Roundtable Social Science Network in Hong Kong. The authors would like to thank the above organizations for their generous funding for the conference. In addition, the authors want to thank Ms. Jessica Yother for her help in producing this manuscript.

Introduction

Greater China in an Era of Globalization

Baogang Guo & Sujian Guo*

INTRODUCTION

In three decades, China has transformed herself from one of the world's most closed economies to an open and free market one. As one commentator says, "It would be no exaggeration to say that China's rise is a watershed event that will change the global landscape and that is on par with the ascent of the United States of America as a global economic, political, and military power a century earlier."[1] China's transition takes place in an era of rapid globalization. The impact of this process on China's rise is twofold. On the one hand, globalization has enabled China to have easy access to Western technologies and the global trading system, and this in turn has helped China's economic and military modernization. On the other hand, globalization has promoted the integration of the once disconnected Chinese societies, thanks to the roles Chinese in Hong Kong, Taiwan and Macao have played as bridges and gateways between the East and the West. As countries have become more interdependent and homogenized, so are the economies of greater China region.

China has always been vigilant about the potential negative impact of globalization and deemed it a double-edged sword. While trying to take full advantage of all the opportunities an integrated world economy can offer, Chinese have also tried hard not to become victimized by it. Though China's economic success has benefited from its embracement of free market principles, Chinese leaders in Beijing have managed to maintain a high level of control over the process of opening up and the pace of integration with other economies. Because of this measured incorporation, China was able to stay out of the Asian financial crisis of the 1990s, and has been able to minimize the impact of the global financial meltdown that began in 2008 on the Chinese economy

Nevertheless, the surge of protectionism and the worldwide labor resistance of globalization have put China and the economies in greater China region in a defensive position. The environment greater China is in now has become all the time more hostile. The wave of protectionism against Chinese made products in recent years has cast a shadow over the region's strategic reliance on export. The increasing number of anti-dumping measures used against Chinese products has damaged the images of China and the region as a whole. A sharp down turn in global demands has put the economies in the region into disarray. The rapid expansion of Internet and other communication technologies has undermined the ability of political leaders in Beijing to manage the political and economic development in that country. Furthermore, the relations among the political entities in greater China remain unsettling. The recent political and military tensions across the Taiwan Strait provoked by the pro-independent leader Chen Shui-bian in Taiwan and the legal controversy over a security law in Hong Kong in 2003 highlight the potential conflicts that may lie ahead among key players in greater China region.

This edited book is based on an international conference, titled "Greater China in an Era of Globalization," co-sponsored by the Association of Chinese Political Studies (ACPS) and the Hong Kong Institute of Asia-Pacific Studies (HKIAPS) at Chinese University of Hong Kong, held between July 13 and 15, 2008. The contributors to this volume are China scholars and experts from the U.S. and other parts of the world. Their insightful contributions will help students of this academic field understand Chinese globalization and its implications for greater China and the rest of the world, and how greater China will influence the economic and political development of China in years to come.

In this book, we will examine critical issues such as how China's globalization has influenced greater China and how China has been influenced by it? What is the role of greater China in Chinese globalization, and what are the major challenges and issues facing China's own integration and unification? How to understand the new role China is playing in the greater China region and in places like Africa and Latin America? What is the implication of a more closely integrated greater China? Will the rise of China and the greater Chinese region alter the course of the Western-dominated globalization process and the balance of power in the Asia-Pacific region or the world?

THE EMERGENCE OF A GREATER CHINA

The term "greater China" used in this book refers to geographic territories of mainland China, Taiwan, Hong Kong and Macao. Scholars sometimes also treat areas that have a high concentration of ethnic Chinese population as part of greater China. Singapore, for instance, is predominantly a Chinese community. But China has no territorial claim over that country, and there is no issue of political reunification. Taiwan, Hong Kong, and Macao, however, are claimed by mainland China as parts of its territory. Taiwan remains to be unified with mainland China, according to mainland Chinese leaders. Hong Kong and Macao, both former colonies, have already reunited with China after the handover of the sovereignty by the British and the Portuguese governments at the end of the 1990s.

The concept of a greater China appeared first in the 1970s, and became fashionable term in the 1980s and 1990s.[2] It grew out of the need of business communities to avoid the political sensitivities over the sovereignty disputes between the two political rivals in China, namely, the People's Republic of China (PRC) on the mainland, and the Republic of China (ROC) in Taiwan. The term has been used frequently today due to the rapid integration of the four economies. The combined GDP of the four economies in 2007 was about 4 trillion U.S. dollars, or 1/3 of the U.S. economy. But if measured by the PPP, the share of greater China in the world economy makes about 12% of the world total and 2/3 of the U.S. economy in the same period.[3] With the continued high-speed economic growth on the Chinese mainland, it is projected that China's economy may surpass the United States around 2020. Some even predicted that by 2050, China's GDP will be 75% larger than that of the U.S.[4]

The interconnectivity among the four economies did not come easily. For decades, the antagonism between the Chinese Communist Party (CCP) and the Kuomintang (KMT) prevented the two sides from having any direct contact or trade with each other. After the CCP initiated the new reform and opening-up policy in late 1978, the mainland proposed to Taiwan to establish three direct links across the Taiwan Strait (trade, postal, and communication links). The KMT did not respond to the proposal until the mid-1980s. Since then, the trade between the two sides has grown steadily. Taiwan's parliament lifted a fifty-year-long ban on direct trade and transport links with China in 2000, but only on a limited scale. It only allowed routes between a handful of offshore islands and mainland China but still banned direct links between the mainland and Taiwan Island. Between 1981 and 2002, Taiwan's trade with the Chinese mainland increased 134 fold. Since 1993, China has become Taiwan's third largest trading partner, after the United States and Japan. In 2002, mainland China became Taiwan's largest export market for the first time and has remained so ever since.[5] The bilateral trade surpassed 100 billion U.S. dollars by 2008, with more than 750,000 Taiwanese living in the mainland. Taiwanese business people invested a total of 439 billion U.S. dollars in over 71,847 projects on the mainland. Over fifty million Taiwanese visits to the mainland were recorded by 2007.[6]

More remarkable changes have taken place since the KMT regained power in 2008. The three direct links were finally opened in that year. In his speech made on December 31, 2008, CCP Chairman Hu Jintao called for the normalization of the Cross-Strait relations, and an end to the hostility and military confrontations between the two sides that had existed for more than six decades. It sent a clear signal to Taipei that the mainland was ready to do business with the new leaders in Taipei. If the focus of the mainland's Taiwan policy before Taiwan's presidential election in 2008 was stability and anti-separation, now the new focus set by Hu is peace and development. But differences remain. While Taiwanese leaders want to keep economic relations as their main focus, their counterparts want to raise the bar higher, and are eager to push for more political breakthroughs in the bilateral relations, including the signing of a peace agreement.

Compared with Taiwan, Hong Kong and Macao are much smaller economies. But the importance of the two cities should not be underestimated.

Hong Kong has always played a multifaceted role in China's opening up to the outside world. It has served not only as a transport hub and a gateway for China's foreign trade but also a bridge between China and the West. The share of China's merchandise trade, shipping, tourism, investment, and foreign loans handled by Hong Kong increased rapidly. In 1989, China-Hong Kong trade and trans-shipment accounted for 58% of China's total exports and 42% of total imports. In recent years, these numbers have declined somewhat due to the growth of port facilities in mainland China. However, Hong Kong has continued to play a major role as a contact point and channel for foreign information, and a window for technology transfers for China. [7] After Hong Kong's handover to Chinese sovereignty by the British in 1997, the territory has become increasingly integrated with mainland China through trade, tourism, and financial links. The mainland is Hong Kong's largest trading partner, accounting for 46% of Hong Kong's total trade by value in 2006. In the same year, 13.6 million mainland tourists visited Hong Kong. More and more mainland Chinese companies have gone to Hong Kong to raise capital. By September 2007 mainland companies accounted for one-third of the firms listed on the Hong Kong Stock Exchange (HKSE), and more than half of the Exchange's market capitalization. [8]

Macao is a small city with a population of less than a half million. Although the significance of Macao is not nearly as important as Hong Kong, Macao has served as a useful gateway for connecting China with Portuguese-speaking countries in the world. Macao is also known as "the Monte Carlo of the Orient." Macao's gaming industry has attracted millions of mainlanders and Hong Kong gamblers. International conglomerates have poured in billions in building new casinos in Macao after Macao government liberalized the gambling industry. The revenues of Macao's gaming industry surpassed Las Vegas in 2006 for the first time. [9]

In order to attract foreign capital and technology know-how, China created Shenzhen Special Economic Zone (SEZ) next to Hong Kong, and Zhuhai Special Economic Zone next to Macao in 1979. Today both places have thrived. The story of Shenzhen's rise from a small fishing village to a world-class metropolis is beyond anyone's imagination, thanks to the critical role Hong Kong has played in the development of this super modern city. The development of Shenzhen has produced a ripple effect and led to the phenomenal growth of the whole Pearl River delta region. To keep the momentum going, on January 8, 2009, China unveiled a 2008-2020 development plan for the southern Pearl River delta region. This proposed economic region includes cities of Guangzhou, Shenzhen, Zhuhai, Foshan, Jiangmen, Dongguan, Zhongshan, Huizhou and Zhaoqing in south China's Guangdong Province. [10] To facilitate further integration of this region with Hong Kang and Macao, a super-bridge between the east and west banks of the Pearl River delta area, with an estimated cost of 5.47 billion U.S. dollars, is currently under construction. The mega-project is seen by economists as a great chance to turn the Pearl River delta area into a super-development zone on a global scale. It will encourage deeper economic integration between Hong Kong and the area, promote the socioeconomic development of the Pearl River West, and strengthen Hong Kong's position as the logistics center. To be sure, the integration among greater China is still at its preliminary stage. Based on the European Union's experience, a total integration involves five criteria or phrases: Free Trade Agreement (FTA, provide for free trade), Custom Union (CU, provides for common policy on tariff), Common Market (CM, provides for free mobility of goods and services), Economic Union (EcU, provides for common currency), and Political Union (PU, provides for shared governance).[11] Measured by these criteria, greater China still has a long way to go. The four parties have not yet reached any bilateral free trade agreements, making it lag even behind many other integrated economic zones such as ASEAN, EU, and NAFTA.

However, with the continued march of globalization, the four economies may see more reasons to speed up the process of economic integration in order to protect their mutual economic interests and prevent excessive dependency on the international markets. With its still largely untapped market, the mainland can serve as a great outlet for products, capital, and professional services from Taiwan, Hong Kong and Macao. To help Hong Kong survive the economic difficulties in 2003, the mainland and Hong Kong signed a "Closer Economic Partnership Agreement (CEPA)" in June of that year. Under the agreement, all goods of Hong Kong origin importing into the mainland enjoy tariff free treatment, upon applications by local manufacturers and upon the CEPA rules of origin (ROOs) being agreed upon and met, and all service suppliers enjoy preferential treatment in entering into the mainland market in various service areas.[12] This one-way free trade agreement is designed primarily to benefit Hong Kong. According to officials in Hong Kong, this agreement opens up a huge market for Hong Kong goods and services, greatly enhancing the already close economic cooperation and integration between the mainland and Hong Kong.[13]

In October 2003, the mainland extended CEPA to Macao. Under the CEPA, 272 Macau products are exempted from import customs, which help promote the development of manufacturing and tourism industries in Macao and reduce its reliance on the gambling industry. The mainland also proposed to Taiwan authorities to sign a similar agreement with Taiwan in September 2008.[14] However, being worried about falling into some kind of unification trap, Taiwan has turned a cold shoulder to this idea so far. CEPA may sound attractive, but some Taiwanese leaders prefer to negotiate the terms of free trade within the framework of the World Trade Organization (WTO).[15] According to Kao Koong-lian, the deputy chairman of the Straits Exchange Foundation (SEF), it is more pragmatic for Taiwan to ink a Trade and Investment Framework Agreement (TIFA) with China than a CEPA.[16] However, TIFA is normally negotiated between sovereign countries, and the mainland will not be able to come to terms on this with Taiwan. The newly elected Taiwanese President, Ma Ying-jeou, is reportedly in favor of a "cross-Taiwan Strait common market," a concept first proposed by his vice president Vincent C. Siew in 2001. It was basically modeled on the example of the EU, with a hope that the economic integration will gradually lead to political integration.[17] The relaxation of tensions between the two sides since 2008 has brought new hope about a peaceful reunification between the two sides in the long run.

Regardless of the continued political mistrust among all sides, the integration of greater China region will go on, but the scope and the velocity of the integration will largely depend on the direction of next wave of globalization. The economic slow down since 2008 may have some lasting impact on the future of the current wave of globalization process. If the U.S. does not recover soon enough, it may put an end to the U.S.-dominated globalization. The question is who will lead the next wave of globalization? The rapid ascendance of China in world affairs may provide some answers.

GLOBALIZATION WITH CHINESE CHARACTERISTICS

Although no one doubts that we are living in an era of unprecedented globalization, the interpretation of the meaning of this new development varies greatly. Sociologist Anthony Giddens links globalization with the march of modernity, capitalism, and global civil society.[18] Roland Robertson believes that the globalization means a coming age of a culturally compressed world within which the comparison and confrontation of worldviews are bound to produce new cultural conflicts.[19] One thing in common in these theories is the strong influence of the mirror image of the Western society in their study of globalization. This is also reflected in the so-called Washington Consensus, which celebrates the universal victory of neo-liberalism based on free market, privatization, and invisible.

For many Chinese, the concept of globalization implies a two-way street. On the one hand, globalization means China's acceptance of the existing norms and rules and behavior in accordance with its international roles and obligations. On the other hand, globalization can also help spread Chinese influences and cultural norms and establish a new world order within which China can play a more constructive role. Many Chinese consider the existing world system to be unfair and unjust and believe that China was victimized by it over the course of the last two centuries. They prefer a globalization with distinctive Chinese characteristics. Joshua Cooper Ramo, a British economist, conceptualizes this new vision as "Beijing Consensus." Ramo believes that the "Beijing Consensus" will serve as a new model for developing. According to Ramo,

> China is marking a path for other nations around the world who are trying to figure out not simply how to develop their countries, but also how to fit into the international order in a way that allows them to be truly independent, to protect their way of life and political choices in a world with a single massively powerful centre of gravity. I call this new centre and physics of power and development the Beijing Consensus.[20]

Ramo claims that the "Washington Consensus," which was promoted to developing countries at the end of the Cold War, was a hallmark of Western arrogance; it left a trail of destroyed economies and bad feelings around the globe. On the other hand, "China's new development approach is driven by a desire to have equitable, peaceful high-quality growth, critically speaking, it turns traditional ideas like privatization and free trade on their heads." [21]

The notion of "Beijing Consensus" also reflects the resilience of Chinese culture and history. Chinese always learn from other cultures but have resisted being adsorbed by them. Traditionally, many Chinese viewed China as a Middle Kingdom or the center of the universe. Chinese rulers tried throughout history to expand China's influence militarily and culturally. But the insurmountable geographic barriers such as deserts, mountains, plateaus, and oceans blocked their ambitions. The impressive navy expedition led by Zheng He in the Ming Dynasty did not end in conquest and expansion, but instead in China's disengagement and disassociation with the rest of the world for the next four millennia. What followed were three waves of globalization dominated by several Western powers, starting with the Columbus discovery of the New World in 1492. During the same period of time, China remained a strong power in the world, and continued its Sino-centric tribute-trade system in Asia. By the late 19th century and the early 20th century, China began its decay due to domestic turmoil and the assaults of Western colonialism and imperialism. Though China managed to retain its independence, she gradually became what Mao Zedong characterized as "a semi-feudal and semi-colonial society." After the communist took over China, China regained its full sovereignty and territorial integrity. But the isolation from the Western trading system prevented China from being incorporated by the U.S. dominated world system after 1949.

While the other players in greater China region were gradually incorporated into the world system, the real impact globalization had on mainland China was not present until 1978. The reform leader Deng Xiaoping launched his open-door policy and economic reform at the end of that year. He clearly saw that it was to her best interest to liberalize its economy and to integrate with the contemporary capitalist world economic system. China fought a long and hard battle to join the World Trade Organization (WTO). After experiencing some up and downs, China was finally admitted to the WTO in 2001. While many developed countries wage a protectionist war against globalization, China, ironically, has now become a strong advocate for free trade and market economy.

We believe that the success of the market-oriented economic reform in China will push China to take a lead in the next wave of globalization. According to some scholars, "The contemporary economic expansion in East Asia, beginning with Japan, then in the East Asian NICs and now apparently also in coastal China, may spell the beginnings of a return [to a world system] in which parts of Asia again play a leading role in the future as they did in the not so distant past." [22] However, the next wave of globalization is going to be very different from the current U.S.-dominated globalization.

In order to respond to this optimistic view of Asia's rise, we need to reexamine the meaning of globalization more closely. The theory of globalization suggests that globalization means the infiltration of Western technologies and culture into the rest of the world. For obvious reasons, some refer to the current wave of globalization as Westernization or Americanization. To them, globalization has become a process whereby non-Western societies come under or adopt the Western culture in areas such as industry, technology, law, politics, economics, lifestyle, religion or values. According to Immanuel Wallerstein's world system theory, the globalization has only made the countries at the peripheral regions more dependent on the capitalist core. But this assumption of permanent unequal position in the new world system has been challenged by the experience of the newly industrialized economies. Countries can overcome the barriers of the core-peripheral separation. Some of the former economies in the peripheral areas have now joined the core and become Newly Industrialized Economies (NIEs). But one thing Wallerstein is right about is that the strong nations have always played a dominant role in the formation of world systems, and been able to put their own mark on the globalization process. The question now becomes: Will China come under the same pressure to be westernized? Will China lose its cultural identity in embracing globalization?

Mark A. Jones observed in his book *Flowing Waters Never Stale* that "various cultures of China, rather than being diluted by foreign imports, are instead thriving on it, for the Chinese have a long history of integrating foreign ideas, products and technologies into their lives, though in ways that are culturally specific, enabling them to modernize while still retaining their 'Chinese characteristics'."[23] He challenged the commonly held assumption that the 'traditional' cultures of China were somehow being seriously diluted or destroyed by the processes of globalization. According to Jones, the willingness of Chinese people to appropriate what is foreign and new is perhaps the most enduring of all Chinese characteristics.[24] Although Western influence is apparent everywhere in China, the resilience of Chinese culture will prevent China from losing its cultural identities. As a matter of fact, the opposite may be true. Everywhere in China we see a strong revival of Chinese civilization, which includes many of its traditional cultures and values. Instead of seeking wisdom from Western cultures, more and more Chinese turn their eyes to their ancient ancestors. For example, to counter Western liberalism, CCP Chairman Hu Jintao has aggressively promoted the ancient idea of "put people first" (以民为本).[25]

Perhaps a more important Chinese characteristic is a peculiar universalistic view Chinese have long held, namely, the "one-world philosophy "or "*datong*" (great harmony) idea. This somewhat utopian idea is not based on conquest but on morality and Confucian universalism. One may find this noble idea in many Chinese writings. Sun Yat-sen, for instance, interpreted the Chinese tradition of "governing the states and pacifying the world" (治国平天下) as a Chinese moral obligation to unify the world with Chinese moral foundations. However, he considered the restoration of the Chinese nation to be a necessary precondition for spreading this kind of Chinese universalism. "If we want China to rise to power," Sun said, "we must not only restore our national standing, but we must also assume a great responsibility towards the world."[26] That responsibility is to "unify the world and [to create the Great Commonwealth— *added, originally omitted by this translation*] based upon the foundation of our ancient morality and love of peace, and bring about a universal rule of equality and fraternity."[27] As one scholar points out, "In his turn Sun Yat-sen was unify the peoples of the entire world. He wanted to procure the welfare of his people as well as of other peoples; he wanted to give peace within and without . . ."[28] What is implied in Sun Yat-sen's political thinking is that China cannot lead the world by force; instead, it should lead the world by higher morality and universal values.

It is far from clear how China can influence the process of globalization by spreading Chinese values. Many Chinese political thinkers like Kang Youwei and Mao Zedong share this sentiment of historical responsibility and obligation to spread the Chinese value of universal love and brotherhood.[29] Though many contemporary Chinese leaders may share this Sino-centric view of China's role in the world, they have been reluctant to play a more assertive role in world affairs. After all, soft power alone cannot sustain China's influence. Without a strong economy and military, China will be unable to fulfill its ambition to revive its ancient glory and to become a leading power in the 21st century.

What China has done so far is to use its soft power to expand China's cultural and diplomatic influence globally. But its main goal seems to mainly at fighting the negative impact of the so-called "China threat theory," and to ease the anxiety of the world community over an increasingly powerful China. China has indeed increased its support for cultural and economic exchanges with foreign countries in recent years. China has sent more and more doctors and teachers to work abroad, welcomed more and students from other nations to study in China, and sponsored Confucian Institutes in many countries to teach Chinese language and Chinese culture. China received more than 190,000 overseas students in 2007. It is expected that number will reach a half million by 2020.[30] In Southeast Asia, Chinese culture, cuisine, calligraphy, cinema, curios, art, acupuncture, herbal medicine, and fashion fads have been revived due to strong cultural influences of Taiwan and Hong Kong in the region. In Latin America, the Chinese government has negotiated more than 400 trade and investment deals in recent years and invested more than $50 billion in the region. In Africa, China has forgiven more than $1 billion debts owed by some of the African countries, provided training for more than 100,000 African students in Chinese universities and military institutes, and sent more than 900 doctors to work across the African continent. China has also built roads, hospitals, sports stadiums, and bridges in many countries.[31]

Can there be a Sino-centric globalization? Will China lead the next wave of globalization? Will that attempt collide with the American-dominated globalization process? If Thomas Friedman's assumption about the escalating speed of globalization is true, will there be an inevitable clash between the U. S. and China? [32] Can China's peaceful rise ever be possible? This book will not be able to answer all these questions. We hope our researches will shed light on these important issues, and provoke more discussions and debates in the field.

CHAPTER OUTLINES

This book is organized into two parts. The first part includes a theoretical inquiry about Sino-centric globalization and politics and policies of the four political entities in greater China region. The second part includes many case studies of the expanding Chinese ties with the developing countries and growing Chinese influence throughout the world.

In the first chapter, Wenshan Jia raised some provocative issues about the next wave of Globalization. He argued that what the world has been witnessing about China since the beginning of the new millennium is the beginning of a new wave of globalization which he calls "Chiglobalization." He identified three waves of globalization which differs from some of unconventional analyses. According to Jia, while the Silk Road, originating from Chinese culture in the pre-modern times, represented the first wave of a prototype of globalization, Anglobalization, significantly built upon the Silk Road (even though this is not sufficiently recognized by the West due to Eurocentrism), is the second wave of globalization. Ameriglobalization, the third wave, has grown out of Anglobalization. Chiglobalization, the fourth wave, is emerging out of the synchronic and diachronic interplay among Ameriglobalization, Anglobalization and the Silk Road. In the several decades ahead of us, the world will most likely be shaped, transformed and reconstructed by the tensions and interactions between Ameriglobalization and Sino-centric globalization, a dual process of ever deepening communication and reconstruction of the global reality. With Sino-centric globalization becoming more independent from Ameriglobalization in several decades, the mutual and global influence of the Eastern culture and the Western culture will, in most likelihood, break even. As a consequence, humanity will most probably have a global fusion of the East and the West and will acquire a bicultural identity for the first time in the history of mankind. This global bicultural identity would entertain an internal balance between self and other, individual and group at a level unprecedented in the history of mankind. With the global bicultural identity, the global village would enjoy a much higher level of consensus over common challenges to humanity, whether internal or external.

The second chapter is James C. Hsiung's "The Age of Geoeconomics, China's Global Role, and Prospects of Cross-Strait Integration." This chapter explores China's global role in the age of geoeconomics. In the globalizing world, geoeconomics rivals geopolitics as a determinant of national interests and policy choices. It re-defines power and its balance in international relations. Survival of a nation hinges on its economic security, which, in turn, depends on an aggregate of requisites including access to vital natural resources, economic competitiveness, participation in key FTAs and super trading blocs. China ranks high on all these measures and is internationally well-connected. Taiwan with a much poorer showing is marginalized and isolated from key international economic networking structures, such as ASEM, the ASEAN-China FTA, etc. The resource-deficient island will soon realize that a rational choice for its survival in the geoeconomic age is closer integration with, not separatism from, mainland China.

In the third chapter, "Empire, Nation, State, and Marketplace: China's Complex Identity and Its Implications for Geopolitical Relationships in Asia," Xiaoyang Tang examines China's changing identities in an era of globalization. Within a century China has evolved from an ancient empire to a struggling nation, further to a modern absolutist state and finally a huge open marketplace. The earlier stages were not simply replaced, but have precipitated to become the under-layers of China's new appearance. As a result, not only China's engagement with other countries is a mixture of these elements, other countries also have a complicated attitude towards China. The multiple identities affect the communication and relationship between China and other countries, make it difficulty to predict actions and reactions of each other, and can cause problems to the regional stability if the gap of understanding is not appropriately filled.

This chapter divides China's complex identity into four major sources and identifies the features of each source. This analysis will help understand the tensions within China's foreign politics and the related paradoxical phenomena in Asia-Pacific region, e.g. intense economic and cultural exchange in contrast with fierce political and public antagonism. This also raises the question of the functioning pattern of multiple identities: when, where and in which way one kind of identity will dominate or compromise with other kinds. Such a discussion may eventually lead to the control, coordination and convergence of these identities and the related interests.

In the fourth chapter, entitled "Globalization and Cross-Strait Relations," Jing Men argues that globalization, in particular economic globalization, has introduced a new factor to the traditional understanding of international relations. Economic development has joined political and security concerns to become high politics issues. Globalization has also brought new dimensions to the analysis of the Cross-Strait relations. China takes the opportunity of economic globalization to realize its peaceful rise. The deepened economic interdependence between China and the others has not only strengthened bilateral cooperation, but also increased China's influence in international politics. Unification of Taiwan is the ultimate goal of Beijing. Apart from diplomatic and political efforts, Beijing has encouraged economic interdependence across the Taiwan Strait. The deepened economic connections between the two sides may probably lay an important foundation for the unification of the two sides in the future.

Antonio C. Hsiang and Jerome S. Hsiang, in the fifth chapter, "Democratic Peace across the Taiwan Strait," observe that on the National Day of 2007, Chinese Premier Wen Jiabao called on Taiwan to resist moving toward formal independence. At the same time, Taiwan reportedly was deploying long-range missiles against China. Based on the Democratic Peace Theory, this chapter will investigate the crisis in the Cross-Strait relations during the latest two presidents, Lee Teng-hui and Chen Shui-bian. The study shows that the more Taiwan's democracy develops the closer Taiwan steps into war with the mainland because of the rising nationalism and competition for popular support. This observation is consistent with the research of Edward D. Mansfield and Jack Snyder. According to them, "Statistical evidence covering the past two centuries shows that in this transitional phase of democratization, countries become more aggressive and war-prone, not less . . ."

The chapter has two focuses. First, it focuses on how Taiwan's democracy has been negatively developed in a populist way in the last decade. Moreover, it also discusses how Taiwan's domestic calculations may drive U.S.-Taiwan relations, not to mention U.S.-China ties, into unwelcome and dangerous territory. Second, it focuses on the role of nationalism played in the Cross-Strait relations. Both the Democratic Progress Party (DPP) and the KMT asserted that the precondition for unification with Beijing is for China to become a democracy. However, the quicker China is democratizing, the higher the possibility that its nationalism will increase. Consequently, the confrontation of two democracies in transition may eventually lead to what Ian Buruma called "the clash between Taiwan's new nationalism and China's old nationalism."

In the sixth chapter, "China's Policy on Regional Cooperation in East Asia," written by Marion Chyun-Yang Wang, the whole picture of China shaping a new order in East Asia and the U.S. factor in this context will be examined. In the era of globalization, the Chinese leadership hopes to create a multi-polar world in which the major powers can develop friendly ties with each other and non-zero-sum games are the norm. The emergence of regional powers and regional organizations in the developing world will help to bring about a multi-polar order. The new wave of regional cooperation in East Asia, which is based on open regionalism and led by the nations from within, is shaping a new arrangement of power in this region. As an internal regional power, China *per se* pushes a multilateral strategy of regional cooperation in East Asia, i.e., China would put Greater China *via* CEPA for Hong Kong and Macao, and the PPRD, as well as the newly proposed CECA and Cross-Strait Economic Zone as the consequences of "Three Links" for Taiwan, as the core to drive ASEAN+1, ASEAN+3, and BFA as well as other multilateral mechanics to set agendas for the cooperation in this region. With China's comprehensive engagement in the regional cooperation and the steady move of the cooperation in East Asia, Greater China, ASEAN+1 and ASEAN+3 are run materially under the framework of China's macro economic control policy. The *status quo* shaped by the U.S. is therefore continually revised.

The seventh chapter is Edward Friedman's "How Economic Superpower China Could Transform Africa." Against the conventional wisdom that Chinese involvement in Africa cannot transform Africa's economy for the better so as to end much of the poverty and also to spark high-speed growth, this chapter finds that China is already in the process of transforming Africa. While the conventional wisdom sees corrupt regimes and weak state capacity in Africa frittering away Africa's opportunity to rise by plugging into Chinese dynamism, China is found in this paper already to be exporting entrepreneurial talent to Africa and to be dynamiting the African economy through East Asian practices. Chinese can bring industry to Africa much as Japan brought it to Southeast Asia in the 1960s and 1970s. Africa could therefore be incorporated into Asian economic dynamism.

In the eighth chapter, "The Role of Greater China in Latin America," Thomas Cieslik argues that within the global integration of national economies, greater China is gaining gradually more influence in all regions of the world. This chapter focuses on PRC's influence in Latin America, especially of its political and economical resource market strategy to establish deeper trade relations with Brazil, Argentina, Chile, Cuba, Mexico and Venezuela. After the failure of the Free Trade Agreement of the Americas, promoted by the United States, the Latin American nations are looking for alternative strategic associations from the United States in order to diversify their political and economical international relations. This form of emancipation and independence has culminated into new diplomatic activities. In that context the paper reflects the new actors of the left wing populists in Venezuela, Ecuador or Bolivia in transforming the continent into the socialism of the 21st century. Within this question this chapter defines PRC's role and its political will to form a deeper political cooperation beyond the classical "South-South" rhetoric.

Apart from the influence of the People's Republic in Latin America, the paper analyzes also the struggle of diplomatic recognition. Twelve states from Latin America and the Caribbean still have diplomatic ties with the so-called renegade province, the "Republic of China," and not with Beijing: Belize, Dominican Republic, El Salvador, Guatemala, Haiti, Honduras, Nicaragua, Panama, Paraguay, St. Kitts and Nevis, St. Lucia, St. Vincent and the Grenadines. Costa Rica broke off with Taipei on June 7, 2007, in favor of the People's Republic. The paper discusses the future of the "diplomatic struggle" in Latin America in the context of development aid and economic cooperation. Finally, it evaluates the strategy of both the People's Republic and Taipei in the long run and defines the new form of interdependence of greater China and Latin America within the model of multipolarism in the 21st century.

The ninth chapter is Katja Weber's "Greater China and Its Neighbors in Comparative Perspective: Lessons from Europe?" Recognizing that Asia is not Europe, this paper argues that the process of European integration, nevertheless, provides useful lessons for China and its neighbors. Specifically, the chapter identifies four factors that were instrumental in bringing about regional security, peace, and prosperity on the European continent since the end of World War II and suggests that these are also likely to aid regional integration in East Asia. First, there is a need for remembrance and reconciliation to help transcend historical legacies. Similar to German efforts to bring about reconciliation with France, Poland, and Israel via remembrance, restitution and apology, East Asians need to deal more effectively with their troubled past. Second, due to the multifaceted nature of security threats, increased emphasis should be placed on conflict prevention via financial and technical assistance, trade agreements, etc. Clearly, it is in everyone's interest to agree on basic rules (non-interference in domestic affairs; respect for sovereignty) and create an incentive structure (see EU enlargement and the European Neighborhood Policy) to bring about cooperative behavior. Third, to decrease uncertainty regarding future behavior, it is essential to institutionalize trust on multiple levels. As the European case readily shows, the creation of a complex web of governance over half a century not only has brought prosperity to the continent but also has led to a change of identity and interests that has made war between EU members inconceivable. Fourth, much like it has done in Europe, the United States needs to promote multilateral/multi-layered cooperation in the Pacific Rim. In addition to its "hub-and-spoke" alliances, it must encourage cooperation on multiple levels and, given the strategic instability in the region, persuade East Asians to include their most likely adversaries in cooperative arrangements. If Europe is any indication, by transcending historical divisions and removing remaining obstacles to cooperation, China and its neighbors should reap the fruits of greater integration.

The tenth and final chapter is William Vlcek's "Development—Great and Small: 'Greater China,' Small Caribbean Islands and Offshore Finance." A fact frequently highlighted in examinations of China's development is the increasing quantity of foreign direct investment (FDI) attracted to China over the past two decades. At the present time small islands from the Caribbean and the Pacific are prominently placed on the list of leading sources of FDI to China, together with Hong Kong, the leading financial center in greater China region. This chapter analyzes the pivotal role performed by the offshore financial centers (OFCs) in the economic development of greater China. Initially established as a development strategy on the part of small island territories, OFCs grew in both number and size parallel to the financial globalization in the late twentieth and early twenty-first centuries. Frequently represented as 'tax havens' in the media and academic literature, the OFC offers a variety of financial services beyond the minimization of taxation. Of particular interest here is the use of international business companies (IBCs) registered in OFCs that are used as conduits for FDI to China. The chapter develops an understanding for the relationship between OFCs and China with a brief historical presentation of the offshore sector and the emergence of Hong Kong as an OFC for China. An indeterminate amount of domestic capital is embedded in the flows of FDI after making a round trip journey in order to return as foreign capital. This situation distorts comparative studies analyzing the role and function of FDI for developing economies between China and other states. A concluding assessment on the experience for greater China with the offshore world considers future implications for Chinese direct investment abroad, as well as possible consequences arising from further financial liberalization in China.

These chapters briefly summarize main ideas of the research on some important issues in the emergence of a greater China, and investigate the effects of China's rise on greater China in an era of globalization, as well as the impact of its emergence on the rest of the world. We hope the insights of the contributors of this volume will shed some light on the understanding of this topic, and promote further exploration of the issues and effects of the emergence of China and a greater China in the 21st century.

NOTES

* We would like to thank Dr. George Jones, Professor Emeritus at Dalton State College for his proofreading of this introduction chapter.

[1] Oded Shenkar, *The Chinese Century: the Rising Chinese Economy and Its Impact on the Global Economy, Balance of Power, and Your Job* (Philadelphia: Wharton School Publishing, 2007), 161.

[2] Harry Harding, "The Concept of 'Greater China': Themes, Variations and Reservations," *The China Quarterly* no.136 (1993): 660-686.

[3] World Bank, "Key Development Data and Statistics," 2007, www.worldbank.org (accessed on February 2, 2009).

[4] Jeffery Sachs, "Welcome to the Asian century by 2050, China and maybe India will overtake the U.S. economy in size," *Fortune Magazine*, January 12, 2004.

[5] Chen-yuan Tung, "Trade Relations between Taiwan and China." In *China Today: An Encyclopedia of Life in the People's Republic*, ed. Jing Luo (Westport, CT: Greenwood Press, 2005), 625-628.

[6] Taiwan Affairs Office, State Council, "Mainland China-Taiwan Trade Statistics," http://www.gwytb.gov.cn/lajmsj.htm; Ralph Jennings, "Taiwan, China ties grow with direct links," www.reuters.com (accessed on December 15, 2008).

[7] Yun-wing Sung, *The China-Hong Kong Connection: The Key to China's Open Door Policy* (Cambridge, UK: Cambridge University Press, 1991), 4.

[8] CIA, *The World Factbook: Hong Kong*, https://www.cia.gov/library/publications/the-world-factbook/geos/hk.html (accessed on December 15, 2008).

[9] *Los Angeles Times*, January 24, 2007.

[10] "China's Ambitions for Pearl River Delta Region by 2020," http://www.chinaview.cn (accessed on January 8, 2009).

[11] A. Elgraa, *The European Union: Economics and Politics* (Cambridge, UK: Cambridge University Press, 2007), 2.

[12] Hong Kong Trade and Industry Department, "What is CEPA," http://www.tid.gov.hk/english/cepa/cepa_overview.html (January 12, 2009); for assessment of the impact of CEPA on Hong Kong's economy, please see Hong Kong Legislative Council Panel in Commerce and Industry, "Impact of the First Three Phases of CEPA on the Hong Kong Economy," LC Paper No. CB(1)1849/06-07(04), http://www.tid.gov.hk/english/cepa/statistics/statistics_research.html (accessed on January 12, 2009).

[13] Hong Kong Trade and Industry Department, http://www.tid.gov.hk/english/cepa/cepa_ overview.html (accessed on January 14, 2009).

[14] Philip Liu, "Ranking Chinese Official Proposes Cross-Strait CEPA," *Taiwan Economic News*, September 9, 2008, http://news.cens.com/cens/html/en/news/news_inner_ 24569.html (accessed on January 12, 2009).

[15] "Political motivated CEPA unacceptable to Taiwan: Scholars," AsiaPulse News, April 29, 2005. http://goliath.ecnext.com (accessed on January 12, 2009).

[16] Luis Yu, "Cross-strait trade agreement more practical than CEPA," December 31, 2008, http://www.taiwannews.com.tw (accessed on January 14, 2009).

[17] Vincent Siew, "A Cross-Strait Common Market—Working Together to Build Prosperity in the Asia-Pacific Region," http://www.crossstrait.org/version3/subpage4/ sp4-3.htm (accessed on January 31, 2009).

[18] "The Second Globalization Debate: a Talk with Anthony Giddens," http://www.edge. org/3rd_culture/giddens/giddens_index.html (accessed on February1, 2009).

[19] Roland Robertson, "The Globalization Paradigm: Thinking Globally." In *Religion and Social Order* (Greenwich: JAI Press, 1991), 207-24.

[20] Joshua Cooper Ramo, *The Beijing Consensus: Notes on the Physics of Chinese Power* (London: Foreign Policy Center, 2004), 3-4.

[21] Ibid., 4.

[22] Barry Gills and Andre G. Frank (1994). "The Modern World System under Asian Hegemony: The Silver Standard World Economy 1450-1750." University of Newcastle Department of Politics Research Paper, 1995, 6-7.

[23] Mark Anthony Jones, "Globalization with Chinese Characteristics," posting on http://bbs.chinadaily.com.cn/viewthread.php?tid=621659 (January 12, 2009).

[24] Mark Anthony Jones, *Flowing Water Never Stale: Journeys through China* (Queensland: Zeus Publications, 2008).

[25] Baogang Guo, "Rethinking Chinese Political Culture in *Political Civilization and Modernization in China,*" ed. Zhong Yang and Shiping Hua (World Scientific Press, 2006), also Baogang Guo, "Political Legitimacy and China's Transition Towards a Market Economy." In *China's Deep Reform: Domestic Politics in Transition* ed. Lowell Dittmer and Guoli Liu (Lanham, MD: Rowman & Littlefield Publishers, 2005).

[26] Sun Yat-sen, *Three Principles of the People* (Taipei: China Cultural Service, 1992), 82.

[27] Ibid. 84.

[28] Chai Winberg, *The Political Thought of Kang You-wei: a Study of Its Origin and Its Influences*, Ph.D. thesis, (New York University, 1968), 188.

[29] Baogang Guo, "Utopias of Reconstruction: Chinese Utopianism from Hong Xiuquan to Mao Zedong," *Journal of Comparative Asian Development* 2, no. 2 (2003): 197-210.

[30] Wang Ying, "Foreign student quota to expand," *China Daily*, July 29, 2008.

[31] Esther Pan, "China's Soft Power Initiative," May 18, 2006, Council on Foreign Relations, http://www.cfr.org/publication/10715/ (accessed on January 14, 2009).

[32] Thomas L. Friedman, "The Dell Theory of Conflict Prevention." *Emergin: A Reader.* Ed. by Barclay Barrios (Boston: Bedford: St. Martins, 2008), 49.

Chapter 1

Chiglobalization? A Cultural Argument

Wenshan Jia

INTRODUCTION

Given her global rise to great power status and future development potential, China has been more and more of a hot topic among global public opinion shapers/leaders and policy advisors. While some view China as a potential global trend setter or a re-maker of the new world order, others hope that China will become a potential follower of the existing world order. As a scholar of global/intercultural communication, I have been observing China and analyzing emergent discourses on China over the past twenty years. I tend to reach a conclusion based on my observations and analyses that China's ascension to the superpower status is inevitable just as the United States inevitably replaced the United Kingdom as the new superpower more than half a century ago. I call this ascension a form of reverse globalization-Chiglobalization. Chiglobalization is a creative fusion of the strengths of all the other globalizations—Ameriglobalization, Anglobalization and the Silk Road which I regard as the first wave of globalization originating from China.

LITERATURE REVIEW

The global contour of contemporary discourse on China is varied and multidirectional. The first strand is the China Collapse Discourse marked significantly by Gordon Chang.[1] an associate of Jamestown Foundation, a neoconservative think tank in the United States. The second strand is the China Threat Discourse marked by various groups of personalities such neoconservatives as Donald Rumsfield and Paul Wolfwitz as well as neoliberals such as Peter Navarro.[2] The concept of Chindia, the unity between China and India, could have been created out of this fear. The third one is the China Opportunity Discourse marked by former Deputy Secretary of State Robert Zoelick who is the architect for the China as a stakeholder policy, Joshua Roma's Beijing Consensus,[3] Bijian Zheng's China's peaceful rise[4] and the related concept of "the Chinese model" or "zhongguo muoshi" initially described by Justin Yifu Lin,[5] currently Vice-President and the Chief Economist of the World Bank are all strong staples of this strand of discourse. China's own awareness of her rise as a global power and her effort to get ready to assume a global leadership are lavishly illustrated by CCTV (the major television station controlled by the Chinese Government) airing a 12 TV documentaries on the rise and fall of all the nine great powers (*DaGuoJueQi*) during the past five hundred years of the global history. Finally, Niall Ferguson's concept of Chimerica,[6] the idea of interdependence between and a shared destiny by the U.S. and China, pushes the China Opportunity Discourse to a new level.

While the China Opportunity discourse seems to be on the upper hand, all the above discourses underlie a common realization: China is on the rise. In the meantime, The U.S. decline-ism discourse, having been hovering around for the past 20 years while China has been on the rise, is picking up heat again with the current breakout of the biggest financial crisis in the American history. Paul Kennedy, a Yale historian, has been a leading voice in announcing[7] and reiterating this hypothesis.[8] Joining him are leading opinion leaders such as Fareed Zakaria who argues that humanity has entered into the Post-America era[9] and Thomas L. Friedman who sighs that the U.S. has lost her grove as the global superpower.[10] Ferguson, a Harvard historian, articulates the concepts of Anglobalization and Ameriglobalization[11] and chronicles the shift from the former to the latter, but fails to see a new shift taking place from Ameriglobalization to another wave of globalization which I term as "Chiglobalization". However, in the concept of Chimerica he coined, he seems to have seen a twin-globalization process or a confluence of two concurrent waves of globalizations-Ameriglobalization and Chiglobalization taking place. However, this shift seems to have been detected by a group of consultants of Boston Consulting Group who, in their book Globality,[12] articulates that globalization as we know it has reached its peak and what is happening is reverse globalization. Are they suggesting that Ameriglobalization has reached its peak and emergent economies are new sources of reverse globalization? I am sure that they have not excluded China as one of such sources of reverse globalization. If the above scholars and pundits are reluctant to recognize this trend fully, G. John Ikenberry, a Princeton professor of political science, in *Foreign Affairs*,[13] has already stated it almost as a new fact that China will inevitably take over the U.S. and warned the West that they should make sure China will follow the already established world order shaped by the West once China becomes the next superpower. If Ikenberry does not state it clearly enough, it has taken an Asian, an Indian-Singaporean, Kishore Mahbubani, a former senior diplomat of Singapore and Dean of the Lee Kuan Yew School of National University of Singapore, to state this possibility bluntly:

History teaches us that leadership in any era is provided by emerging powers. For example, when America replaced the UK as the world's leading power, it moved naturally to providing global leadership. By the same logic,

China should eventually take over the mantle of global leadership from America. In its own way, it is providing global inspirations, if not leadership.[14]

This paper, significantly informed by and built upon the above ideas, joins in the China debate and makes a more elaborate cultural argument above and beyond the current debate: China is engineering another wave of globalization which I call Chiglobalization. However, what does Chiglobalization look like? How is it different from Ameriglobalization? More specifically, what are the unique features of Chiglobalization? Furthermore, how could Chiglobalization be more advanced than all the other globalizations in human history? What benefits could Chiglobalization bring to the global village? Finally, what should other countries, especially the U.S., do to respond to Chiglobalization? I hope to answer these questions in the following pages.

CHIGLOBALIZATION DEFINED

I define Chiglobalization as the increasing global relevance, global presence, global influence, and global leadership of China in generating a fresh global vision for humanity, in creating a new model for economic development, in forging an alterative model of global and domestic governance, in creating a new model for science and technology development, and in creating a truly cosmopolitan culture characterized by multiculturalism, interculturalism and pragmatism. Chiglobalization refers to a process of China-led global search for and a global enlightenment by an alternative mode of life for humanity on the basis of, but above and beyond, the Eurocentric model. The nature of Chiglobalization is bicultural and intercultural. It is bicultural in that it is based on an emerging model called "the Chinese model" or "zhongguo muoshi" as sketched by Joshua Ramo in his essay "the Beijing Consensus" after China's creative fusion of the Eastern and the Western cultures. This project of intercultural fusion was initiated by some Chinese intellectuals and Chinese officials during the 1850s when the Opium War occurred and has been eventually substantiated by contemporary China over the past three decades. More specifically, Chiglobalization, which I regard as the fourth wave of globalization in recorded human history, is emboldened by the first wave of globalization engineered by China dating back a 1,000 years during the Tang Dynasty. This globalization is known as the Silk Road. Chiglobalization, spurred by Anglobalization, has been inspired, invigorated and empowered by Ameriglobalization. It is intercultural in that Chiglobalization is both a process of opening China up to other human cultures and a process of identifying with and integrating all other cultures such as Latin American cultures and African cultures besides Western culture. This is illustrated by a typical sign in a public square in any major city in today's China which reads: Let China communicate with the whole world; let the whole world communicate with China.

THE UNIQUE FACTORS SHAPING CHIGLOBALIZATION

Chiglobalization is growing out of Ameriglobalization. During the past thirty years, especially since 1992, the U.S. has become a social, cultural and economic model for China. The U.S. has been not only a major consumer market for goods made in China up until the current Wall Street financial crisis, but also a major source of foreign direct investment in China. It has been not only a major source of ideas and strategies for China's development, but also a major source of inspiration for China. To a great extent, the American dream has been exported to China and has become the Chinese dream.

More importantly, Chiglobalization is engineered, empowered and sustained by a non-Western civilization-the Chinese civilization. While it shares some fundamental values with Ameriglobalization such as free flow of capital, free flow of goods and free flow of ideas and information, Chiglobalization is defined by a set of unique values which radically differ from Ameriglobalization and Anglobalization. It marks another tectonic shift in the course of human history. This shift is bound to be more massive and more profound than the shift from Anglobalization to Ameriglobalization primarily because there are much more shared values and experiences between Ameriglobalization and Anglobalization than between Chiglobalization and Ameriglobalization. Chiglobalization, while being deeply rooted in Chinese culture and increasingly identifying herself with the Anglobalized and Ameriglobalized world, makes the contemporary Chinese way of life a new global model for development fitting the nature of the global village.

There are eight unique factors shaping Chiglobalization which I sketch as follows on condition that China overcomes both internal challenges such as corruption, power succession and external challenges such as containment:

First, size matters. China is not only four times as big as that of the U.S. in population, but also twice as big in terms of labor force and is almost as big in terms of consumption power. In fact, in terms of her domestic purchasing power, China's annual GNP is roughly the same size as that of the United States. If it tries to continue building herself in the image of the U.S., it will inevitably make herself into a super-sized America.

Second, work ethic matters. Most Chinese are industrious, including students from K-12 to Ph.D. students as well as other sectors of the society. They work with a level of intensity and commitment above and beyond their comfort level. In contrast, while most Americans are industrious, more and more Americans are reluctant to work at the level of intensity and commitment above and beyond their comfort level. The fact that fewer and fewer American students are willing to major in science and technology is very telling of this trend. As a result, the U.S. is depending more and more on foreign immigrants for science and high-tech needs. Coupled with industry is mad growth of business entrepreneurship in China which has already sent dozens of emerging global Chinese companies onto the list of Fortune 500 global companies.

Third, frugality matters. Two trillion U.S. dollars savings is a colossal amount, especially in terms of savings rate which is as high as 45%. In contrast, the U.S. has zero savings rate. China's strength of frugality shines through especially in the current global financial crisis. China is spending almost half a trillion U.S. dollars of her surplus to stimulate her economy to reap a possible 7-8% rate of growth in 2009 whereas the U.S. is spending almost a trillion U.S. dollars more into debt to stimulate her economy to save her economy from a deepening recession. While frugality is propelling and sustaining an economic boom for China, reckless spending is creating and the economic stimulus plan is deepening an economic recession for the United States.

The fourth factor is China's openness. China's bicultural and intercultural experience for the past 150 years since the Opium War has yielded a unique working model based on the profound integration of multiple cultures, especially the Eastern culture and the modern Western culture at all levels-intellectual, political, economic, social and cultural. No classics of the Western culture, science and technology have not been translated and published in Chinese and studied in Chinese schools and universities. As many as 300 million Chinese, an equivalent of the total American population, are relatively proficient in English. Chinese leaders of all levels, including the nine-member Political Bureau led by Chinese Communist Party Boss Hu Jintao, attended periodical training sessions on a broad range of current topics from international affairs to internet, from philosophy to finance. The nine-member Political Bureau had already attended 38 monthly training sessions chaired by Hu Jintao and conducted by related experts.[15] Their goal is to create a learning government and create an innovation-based economy. Jiang Zemin's directive "Evolve with the changing times" (Yushi jujin) says it all. It is new common sense that Chinese know much more about the Americans than Americans know about China. While China is becoming more and more pragmatic, the U.S. seems to be becoming more and more insular and fails to see and refuses to acknowledge the sea change taking place in China. While China has been benefiting tremendously from opening herself up to the rest of the world, the U.S. has been withering from the superiority complex. While taking classes on the English language and cultures is commonplace in Chinese universities, it is still very difficult to recruit students to take classes on Chinese language and culture in many American universities.

The fifth factor is China's internal unity and external diversity. While she emphasizes cultural homogenization more than diversity domestically, China respects cultural diversity more than commonality globally. While internal unity gives China more power, external diversity gives China more leverage. In contrast, the United States, while valuing domestic diversity, has been largely ethnocentric towards the diverse and rich cultures outside the U.S. As a result, people of other countries feel alienated, including European cultures which were a major cradle of the Anglo-Saxon-based American culture.

The sixth factor is China's enormous capacity for imitation and innovation. China has profited a lot from legal or illegal copying during the past several decades. However, this is just short-term. China is looking for long-term sustainability of her economic growth by creating her own cultural, scientific and technological innovations. Her investment in education and research and development has been close to the U.S. in quantity. China has the world's largest education system. The number of doctoral degrees China has graduated annually has already outnumbered the U.S. Most importantly, China has sent our 1.2 million students overseas during the past 30 years. One third of them have already returned to China. Recently, China has started a five-year campaign to attract more of such talent back to China. Top scientists such as Yao Qizhi, a leading mathematician from Princeton University, have already returned to China and he is leading the Advanced Research Institute of Tsinghua University which Chen Ning Yang, Nobel-laureate in Physics originally from SUNY Stony Brook, helped establish.

The seventh factor is China's value of long-term relationship with countries and peoples in diplomacy. This is based on the Confucian principle of interpersonal relationship. It is characterized by benevolence and loyalty, among many others. This humanized diplomacy is in stark contrast with the rationalist model of the American diplomacy motivated by short-term self-interest wrapped in the rhetoric of moral superiority. While they tend to maintain good relations with the U.S. out of their need for security, countries and peoples tend to do so with China out of emotional satisfaction. This Chinese diplomatic practice is widely chronicled by Joshua Kurlantzick.[16]

The eighth factor is the Chinese leadership's proposal for "the construction of the harmonious world" as a new global vision for humanity. This vision, rooted in the Chinese value of mutual understanding, mutual benefit and mutual relational satisfaction and co-humanity, incorporates some fundamental Western values such as peace, justice, freedom and democracy.[17] Now that the world has become a global village, the vision of harmony is expected to humanize this village. The vision of peace, justice, freedom and democracy provided by the modern Western culture to the world, while being the ultimate goals of humanity during the pre-global village era, could used as effective instruments in cultivating harmony in this global village. Peace, justice, freedom and democracy are all positive values. However, they are all rooted in individualism and are thus insufficient in making this global village livable and sustainable on their own. Harmony, a concept incorporating both self and other, subjectivity and objectivity, strives for the golden mean and thus has the potential to make this global village more sustainable.

It is not one or a combination of a few factors on the list above that are making China a likely successor as the next superpower. It is a combination of all the above and more that is making China become the next superpower. It is not that the United States, or European Union or India does not possess some or most of the above qualities. It is the sheer size, velocity and long-term ambition and plan that are making China the most likely candidate.

According to China Academy of Science Report,[18] by 2050, China will reach the first stage of cultural modernization. By 2100, China will lead the world in the second stage of cultural modernization marked by innovation. Currently, China's cultural influence has been ranked No. 7 in the world. Just this past summer, China became No. 1 in winning Olympic Gold Medals, surpassing the United States. However, economically, China has already surpassed Germany as the world's No. 3 economic power. It is predicted that China will surpass the United States by 2025 as No. 1 economy in the world. All of these and other achievements are largely attributed to a creative combination of the above eight factors.

WHAT SHOULD THE UNITED STATES DO?

When I state that Chiglobalization is on the rise, it does not necessarily mean that Ameriglobalization has completely ended. For a several decades, in my prediction, Ameriglobalization will still sustain itself if it is managed intelligently. In this sense, Chiglobalization and Ameriglobalization will probably go hand in hand. However, when Chiglobalization becomes more mature, it will inevitably overshadow Ameriglobalization and become single-handed globalization running its own course during the second half of the 21st century.

In order to prolong Ameriglobalization, the U.S. should try to be truly and genuinely multicultural and intercultural globally to tap the best talent available regardless of differences and because of differences. The election of the first African American President Barack Obama is a good start. Being genuinely multicultural and intercultural could not only help make the U.S. more open-minded, but also make the U.S. more powerful.

The United States is also advised to learn to be followers as well as leaders in global governance. Mainstream Americans have learned to be a follower when the United States has elected and accepted Barack Obama as the first non-Caucasian and first African-American president. Since Americans have elected a non-Caucasian President of the United States, Americans will probably also become ready to accept a non-Western civilization such as China as the next superpower. After all, China is the home for the first wave of a prototype of globalization-the Silk Road. However, having been a superpower and the sole global leader for more than half a century herself, it would be psychologically challenging for the United States to share global power or to be a follower of another superpower. However, since the United Kingdom graciously shared the global leadership with the United States first and later accepted the global leadership of the United States when the U.S. replaced U.K. as the superpower, the U.S. should also graciously learn to share the global power with China now and learn to accept the global leadership of China when history propels China into such a position. In fact, the U.S. is learning to share the global power with China using the China as a global stakeholder policy. Therefore, the best strategy for the U.S. to deal with Chiglobalization should be both guidance and accommodation. Guidance here means that the U.S. is advised to help China inherit some of the fundamental values, principles and institutions of global governance which benefit both the industrialized and emerging economies. Accommodation means that the U.S.-led industrialized countries should try to understand and embrace the legitimate needs and wants as well as the new vision and leadership for global governance of China-led emerging powers. By both guiding and accommodating, the U.S. will be able to maximize both her own interest while respecting the interest of the rest of the world.

CONCLUSION

It is neither Chinese culture alone nor the American culture alone that has been propelling China into the status of a global superpower with increasing possibility to overtake the U.S. in the next half of this century. It is the creative fusion of the Chinese culture and the American (Western) culture, or, to use Ramo's words, Chinese culture's capability for localizing foreign cultures which has made China the top contender for the status of the next superpower in the 21st century. In ancient China, Buddhism was introduced to China, became localized or was deeply integrated into Chinese culture. The spirit of individualism rooted in the Western culture has been well localized and integrated into the Chinese culture of collectivism as in the case of China's successful hosting of the Beijing Olympic Games. If China does become the next superpower, it is neither for individualism alone nor collectivism alone, neither freedom alone nor discipline alone which makes it happen. It is a healthy balance between individualism and collectivism, freedom and discipline, capitalism and socialism, stability and change which makes it happen. If the U.S. loses her status of the superpower, it is because it loses this healthy balance between individualism and collectivism. If the U.S. would like to maintain her superpower status, the U.S. should think hard on how to cultivate a balance between the two seemingly polar opposites and should stop thinking in the either-or and black-white mentality. To use both guidance and accommodation in dealing with China's rise is an example of such new thinking. Perhaps this could be the grand strategy which the Barack Obama Administration could use in harnessing her smart power. The smartest use of smart power could lie in allowing for an emerging Confucian model of global leadership outlined by Chung-ying Cheng[19] which centers on the use of moral power-the power of harmonization, the power of humanization and the power of moralization constituted by the five Confucian principles-*ren* (benevolence), *yi* (justice and righteousness), *li* (propriety), *zhi* (knowledge), and *xin* (trust). Moral power is perhaps the smartest of all types of power.

NOTES

[1] Gordon Chang, *The Coming Collapse of China* (New York, NY: Random House, 2001).

[2] Peter Navarro, *The Coming China Wars* (USA: F T. Press, 2008).

[3] Joshua C. Ramo, *The Beijing Consensus* (UK: The Foreign Policy Centre, 2004), from http://fpc.org.uk/publications/123 (accessed on January 20, 2008).

[4] Bijian Zheng, (September/October, 2005). "China's "peaceful rise" to great power status." *Foreign Affairs*, September/October, 2005, pp. 18-24.

[5] Yifu Lin, *Zhongguo de qiji: Fazhan Zhanlue and Jinji Gaige (China's Miracle: Development Strategies and Economic Reform)* (Shanghai, China: Shanghai People's Press, 1994).

[6] Nial Ferguson, "What 'Chimerica' as wrought?" from http://www.the-american-interest.com/ai2/article.cfm?Id=533&MID=23 (accessed on January 26, 2009).

[7] Paul Kennedy, *The Rise and Fall of the Great Powers* (New York, NY: Vintage Books, 1987).

[8] Paul Kennedy, "The American power is on the wane," *Wall Street Journal*, January 14, 2009, A 13.

[9] Fareed Zakaria, *The Post-America World* (USA: W. W. Norton & Co., 2008).

[10] Thomas L. Friedman, *Hot, Flat and Crowded* (USA: Farrar, Straus & Giroux, 2008).

[11] Nial N. Ferguson, *Empire: The Rise and Demise of the British World Order and the Lessons for Global Power* (New York, NY: Basic Books, 2002).

[12] Hal Sirkin, Jim Hemerling, and Arindam Bhattacharya, *Globality: Competing with Everyone from Anywhere for Everything* (USA: Business Plus, 2008).

[13] G. John Ikenberry, "The Rise of China and the Future of the West," *Foreign Affairs*, 87 (1), January/February, 2008.

[14] Kishore Mahbubani, *The New Asian Hemisphere-The Irresistible Shift of Global Power to the East* (New York, NY: Public Affairs, 2008), pp. 237-238.

[15] Changfa Cui and Mingshan Xu Eds, *Gaoceng Jiangtan: Shiliuda Yilai Zhongyang Zhengzhiju Jiti Xuexi de Zhongda Keti* (CCP Political Bureau's Group *Learning Topics of Significance since the CCP Sixteenth Party Congress*) (Beijing, China: the *Hongqi* Publisher, 2007).

[16] Joshua Kurlantzick, *Charm Offensive: How China's Soft Power is Transforming the World* (New Haven, CT: Yale University Press, 2007).

[17] Wenshan Jia,. " The Chinese perspective on harmony: an evaluation of the harmony and peace paradigms," *China Media Research, 4,* no 4 (2008): 25-30.

[18] Xinhua News Agency, "China Academy of Sciences: China's cultural influenced is ranked No 7 in the world." *(zhonguo kexueyuan: zhongguo wenhua yinxiangli gaozhi shijie deqi from* http://newsxinhuanet.com/politics/2009-01/18/content_10676004.htm (accessed on January 19, 2009).

[19] Chung-ying Cheng. "Confucian global leadership: Classical and contemporary from both historical and philosophical points of view." presented at the 10th Anniversary Meeting of the International Leadership Association, Los Angeles, California, USA, November 13, 2008.

Chapter 2

The Age of Geoeconomics, China's Global Role, and Prospects of Cross-Strait Integration

James C. Hsiung[*]

In contrast to all previous eras, geoeconomics has risen to rival geopolitics as a strategic desideratum for a country's national interest and policy choices. As will be explained below, power in the age of geoeconomics is defined very differently; so is the balance of power played out by very different rules. This crucial change has come about not just because of the end of the Cold War—although it did help—but, more important, because of the globalization of the world economy beyond the stage of complex interdependence that Keohane and Nye addressed.[1]

GEOECONOMICS AND POWER IN THE GEOECONOMIC AGE

Despite its by now rather wide usage, the term "geoeconomics" is nowhere clearly defined, except in my 1997 work.[2] Let me summarize that formulation for the sake of our discussion of its relevance to China's role in the globalized world order, with particular reference to the prospects of its reunification with Taiwan.

On the macro level, in the geoeconomic age, matters pertaining to manufacturing, marketing, financing, and research and design (R&D) are transnationalized, ultimately globalized. On the micro level, on the other hand, national power is no longer measured mainly by a state's military might as before. And, economic security has eclipsed (though not displaced) military security on the scale of strategic importance to a country's national interest. National power in this context is measured by an aggregate of a number of components such as human and technological resources, exportable capital, efficient production of modern goods, percentage share of the global economy, influence over global economic decision-making, and the will to mobilize one's economic capability for national ends.[3]

This formulation, which combines both a change in macro-level economic power management and the new era's micro-level implications for the system's actors in the shifting global power game, captures the essence of the age of geoeconomics. It points up the paramountcy of geoeconomic calculations in the concerns of nations in their policy calculus. Equally, as we will see below, this holds direct implications for the strategic choice confronting a resource-scarce and increasingly isolated Taiwan regarding its relations with mainland China. Let us first dwell on an example of how geoeconomic desiderata may shape a nation's policy priorities, by looking at the experience of Japan during the Persian Gulf crisis of 1990-1991, as triggered off by Iraq's invasion and occupation of Kuwait. That event taught the Japanese a lesson in national security in the geoeconomic age: It drove home their nation's vulnerability arising from its near-total dependency on extra-regional supplies of vital resources, because access to these supplies could be disrupted at any flare-up of a crisis in a far-off place. Even more than before, Japan learned to appreciate the strategic value of closer-to-home sourcing of the natural resources vital to its economy. Thus, while the world's industrial countries were enforcing their post-Tiananmen sanctions against Beijing, Japan began in the fall of 1990—during the height of the Gulf crisis—to switch gears and to be the first industrial nation to return to China, in a deliberate effort to uplift its ties with the Chinese. Breaking ranks with the rest of the G-7,[4] Japan not only resumed bilateral trade but even extended to China U.S.\$54 billion in credits.[5] In fact, during the next five years, 1991-1995, Japanese trade with China witnessed a double-digit increase over the already high pre-1989 level.[6]

BALANCE OF POWER IN THE AGE OF GEOECONOMICS

I do not want to leave the impression that geoeconomics has replaced geopolitics in world politics. It has not. The implication is simply that in the age of geoeconomics, for instance, Switzerland or Turkey, in deciding about some business question about which Germany and France disagree, will not necessarily decide in favor of Germany simply because it has a larger GNP than France. But the fact both Germany and France are in a strong enough economic position to help or to hurt other countries is a crucial fact that, more than ever before, neither Switzerland nor Turkey, nor any other country, can afford to ignore or subsume under any consideration based on other factors.[7]

But, the most distinct shift brought on by the age of geoeconomics is in the way in which balance of power is played out. If we can extrapolate from the rich literature on geopolitics, the two most important ingredients—other than power itself—guiding the traditional geopolitical balance of power reflex of nations, are geography and ideology.[8] In a geoeconomic balance of power game, in contrast, a lot is determined by a player's strategic autonomy linked to a number of conditions, viz.: (a) self-sufficiency in or access to basic natural resources, such as energy and steel; (b) relative freedom from long-term dependency on overseas markets; and (c) control of an inexhaustible, inexpensive, and relatively reliable labor force.[9] Unlike its geopolitical counterpart, the geoeconomic balance of power is a game between super-trading blocs, rather than between individual states (or groups of states). It is also a non-zero-sum game, which is another difference from the past, as will become clear below.

Confusion between the two perspectives may befuddle one's ability to distinguish between rivals and partners. Precisely for this reason, China is alternately viewed by some in Washington as a "threat" and as a "stake-holder," depending on whether it is perceived from a geopolitical or geoeconomic point of view. Likewise, Japan may remain a geopolitical ally of the United States in the post-Cold War era, but may have the potential of being a geoeconomic rival in the event of a bilateral trade war. Failure to grapple with the geoeconomic factor will obfuscate one's understanding of the trends in 21st-century international relations. Among the many international-relations (IR) experts forecasting the future directions of world politics on the eve of the new century, Hans Binnendijk[10] foresaw a return to a new kind of "bipolarity," which he identified as a recurrent pattern in the five major periods (hence, five systems) he identified in world history since Westphalia. Each of the previous systems, he found, had a life cycle: "[T]here was a tendency for fluidity, and multipolarity to turn into rigidity and bipolarity, with that bipolarity in turn resulting in large scale conflict (or a Cold War) and the demise of the existing international system."[11]

On the basis of this recurrent pattern, Binnendijk foresaw the gestation of a sixth system in which the end of the Cold War bipolarity will be followed by a brief period (the "first decade") of relative fluidity, until a new bipolarity is in place. The line of division will be between a U.S.-EU-Japan alliance, on the one side, and a coalition of Russia, China, and the rogue states, on the other. What determines this division is the criterion of market democracies, which Binnendijk called "dominant actors," because, in his words, "[t]heir ideology has become the global model and by the end of the decade [1990s], 117 of the world's 191 nations are characterized as democracies."[12]

Now well into the second decade of the post-Cold War era, it is time to review the validity of Binnendijk's forecast of a new bipolarity to emerge in the sixth system. Instead of his projected U.S.-EU-Japan alliance, we find a clear rift separating the United States from its key former European allies (perhaps with the sole exception of Tony Blair's Britain), although the U.S.-Japan bond remains strong.[13] And, there is no sign that Russia, China, and the rogue states are hatching a coalition in opposition. All indications are that a bipolar contention is very unlikely to emerge, from the vantage point of 2008. If history does not repeat itself by the pattern that Binnendijk identified in all the five preceding systems he examined, it is because he failed to factor in the way geoeconomics is reshaping world politics like never before. In his analysis, the key measure of things was traditional geopolitics based on ideology (hence, his measure of "market democracies"). What he failed to take into account was that in the age of geoeconomics, balance of power follows a totally different set of rules, as spelled out above. Moreover, he also missed out on a new hybrid of market economy and socialist polity such as is found in a re-rising China, a pattern unknown to all the previous periods of international relations since Westphalia.

Instead of a return of bipolarity, albeit of a different sort from what prevailed during the U.S.-Soviet Cold War of the second half of the 20th century, the world today sees the interactions among three super trading blocs. The first is the European Union (EU) composed of 27 European states integrated into a single market and polity with its own governance structure. Next is the North American Free Trade Association (NAFTA) joining the United States, Canada, and Mexico into a competing sub-continental free trade area, potentially extendable to other nations in the Western Hemisphere. And, the third super trading bloc is in the Asia Pacific. While the ultimate 16-nation Asian Free Trade Association is in the final stages of gestation, it will be built upon the existing infrastructure of the 10-state Association of Asian Nations (ASEAN). When conjoined with the projected ASEAN+3 (i.e., China, South Korea, and Japan), plus another three members (Australia, New Zealand, and India), the end result will be the 16-nation Asian FTA. A distinct feature of this emergent regional free trade bloc is the absence (or exclusion) of the United States. When it materializes, it will spell the decline of the existing 21-member APEC, the Asian Pacific Economic Cooperation forum that includes the United States and Taiwan. In sum, balance of power in the 21st century age of geoeconomics will be played out among the three regional super trading blocs just outlined.

GEOECONOMICS IN THE RISE OF THE SUPER TRADING BLOCS AND THE ACCENT ON FREE TRADE REGIMES

To fully appreciate the role played by geoeconomics, we need to heed to the often missed point about the timing of the arrival of APEC, NAFTA, and even the World Trade Organization (WTO), all being created within a few years between 1989 and the early 1990s. In addition, the initial negotiations for a Free Trade Area of the Americas (FTAA) also began from the late 1980s on. The common impetus was the adoption in 1986 of the Single Europe Act (SEA) by the European Community, announcing that its 12 members (with three additional states to join later) were scheduled to build a single integrated market in 1992 (known as EC-1992). The news shocked the world. The first to feel the pinch calling for reaction was Australia, which would lose the preferential treatment for its wool and other exports to Britain as a member of the British Commonwealth, following EC-1992. Prime Minister Bob Hawk saw the signs on the walls and heralded the idea of a reactive regional banding together as a protective measure. When promptly responded to by the United States and other nations across the Pacific, the idea materialized into the Asia Pacific Economic Cooperation (APEC) forum, which was established in 1989 with an initial 12 members, eventually growing to 21.

In 1994, or two years after EC-1992, the United States joined hands with Canada and Mexico to form the NAFTA as a means to fend off the challenge posed by a single-market integrated Europe. In the same year (1986) as the SEA was adopted by the European Community, the United States initiated the Uruguay Round of the GATT to examine the future of the governance of global commerce in the face of mounting pressures for regionalism, especially the acceleration of the movement toward European integration. The final decision to establish a new World Trade Organization appears, in retrospect, to have been a U.S. success in making a multilateral system, encompassing the integrated Europe, as the cornerstone of the international trade regime. [14] But, if Washington was hoping that the WTO regime, in addition to the NAFTA, would be adequate to keep European regionalism in check, it was soon to be disappointed when the Europeans began to link up with Pacific Asian nations in a move that literally linked their two super trading blocs together, threatening the U.S.-led North American regional trade bloc.

In 1994, the same year that NAFTA was launched, the EU adopted a resolution on "Towards a New Strategy for Asia," which was published by the European Commission. It stressed the importance of modernizing EU's relationship with Asia. In November, Singapore and France proposed that an EU-Asia summit meeting be held, to consider how to build a new partnership between the two regions. As a result, EU's 15 members and 10 Asian states met in Bangkok in March 1996, for the first ASEM Summit. The goal was to build a "strong partnership" in trade and investment. The summit was the first step to more ambitious joint undertakings, including the establishment of more institutions, such as the Asian-Europe Environmental Technology Center in Thailand, and the Asia-Europe Foundation in Singapore. Other measures include an Asia-Europe university program and links integrating a trans-Asian railway network with the trans-European railway network. [15]

The cooperation between the two supertrading blocs is significant for theory in a number of ways. First, it confirms a collecitivist proclivity, including a reliance on institutions—at least those of the most successful economies. Second, it was an obvious snub to the United States, as the meeting's "mutual respect" motto turned out to mean noninterference in the internal affairs of other countries, a veiled criticism of the U.S. policy of making trade with Asian countries dependent on progress in combating child labor, improving worker-safety conditions, and allowing the formation of labor unions. [16] Third, the combined total GDP of ASEM members—consisting of EU-15 and Asia-10—is 55% (30% + 25%) of the world's total, as compared with NAFTA's 34%. [17] This conforms to the traditional balance of power rules deducible from state practices since Westphalia, in which the second largest and the smallest would align against the largest in a group of three actors or blocs. But, in terms of trade as a share of global trade, the combined 48% share from combining EU-15's 23% and Asian-10's 25% of the total world trade is bigger than NAFTA's 13%. Hence, when measured by GDP, the ASEM is an alliance between the largest (Asian-10) and the second largest (EU-15) against the smallest (13%) component of the group of three.

The ASEM Summit has since developed into a biennial event, alternating between a meeting site in Europe and Asia, supplemented by more frequent ministerial meetings and regular meetings of senior officials. At the ASEM

Summit-5 meeting in Hanoi (2004), the participants had expanded to 39, including EU's 25 members, plus the European Commission, and 13 Asian states.[18] In 2006, at its meeting in Helsinki, ASEM Summit-6 already had 45 participants.[19] ASEM's "partnership building" goal was not just rhetoric. During the Asian financial crisis of 1997-1999, for instance, ASEM established the Asian Financial Crisis Response Trust Fund, to replace the failed AMF (Asian Monetary Fund) proposed initially by the International Monetary Fund, but collapsed after the United States balked at lending a hand. The Trust Fund provided technical advice and training on financial sector and policy reforms, making a positive contribution to the speedy recovery of the region.

In view of the developments surrounding the growth of the ASEM and the U.S. attempt to build a cross-Atlantic economic partnership by creating a Trans-Atlantic Economic Council,[20] we can draw a number of lessons bearing on balance of power in the geoeconomic age.

First, unlike in all previous centuries since Westphalia, balance of power in the age of geoeconomics is not a zero sum game. Hence, the ASEM alignment, drawing European Union and Pacific Asian countries into a mammoth economic community, does not rule out the possibility of a cross-Atlantic economic entity featuring cooperation between the U.S.-led NAFTA and the European single market.

Secondly, in this geoeconomic game, both Europe and the U.S.-led NAFTA are competing for a close partnership with the Asian region for the same reason, namely: the latter's success in rapid and sustained growth. In 2000, EU identified Pacific Asia (East and Southeast Asia) as the growth engine of the world and hence the center of EU's policy toward Asia. For its part, the United States placed before the APEC at its 2006 annual meeting in Hanoi a proposal to build a cross-Pacific super free trade area extending from China to Chile. If materialized, this move and the concomitant U.S. endeavor to fashion a cross-Atlantic economic zone would give Washington an added advantage over all competing trading partners and blocs. For the United States would be the only country that is a member—hence has unimpeded access and influence—in all the three regional super trading blocs (NAFTA, Europe, and Asia) by dint of the two cross-regional linkups.

Thirdly, with its sustained, strong economy, China plays a special role in the global geoeconomic game, as witnessed in two episodes. The first is the ability of China to withstand the Asian Financial Crisis of 1997-99 and emerge unscathed with a sturdy 9% annual growth, when all the region's other high-performance economies fell tumbling down. The second is the shelving of the U.S.-initiated cross-Pacific super free trade area, as a result of China's objection, despite the support of all the other targeted members on the Pacific Rim.

THE PROSPECT OF CHINA'S RESURGENCE

In addressing the resurgence of China, we need to pay equal attention to (a) its economic clout and potential, and (b) the role it will consequently play on the world stage. In this section, we will look at a few indicators why China is on its way back up.

- By 2002, according to WTO data, China had already become the world's fourth largest trading nation, next to the U.S., Germany, and Japan. A report in the New York Times (October 18, 2003) foresaw China to emerge as the biggest trading partner with members of the Association of Southeast Asian Nations (ASEAN) in two years.
- In 2004, China's GDP inched forward to become the world's fourth largest, following the U.S., Japan, and Germany.
- According to statistics made available in 2004 by the Japanese Economic and Trade Organization (JETRO), China was Japan's largest trading partner.
- China in 2005 became the world's largest consumer nation in five categories (i.e., basic foods, industrial goods, meats, steel and iron; and energy), according to data from the Earth Policy Institute, a think tank in Washington, D. C.
- In 2006, China replaced Japan as the holder of the largest foreign reserves, totaling $1.5 trillion, over Japan's $846 billion.
- In the first half of 2006, China was the second largest exporter nation, reported the Wall Street Journal (April 12, 2007), citing data released by the WTO. In the same report, China was expected to surpass Germany as the largest exporter nation in 2008.

The next question is: Will China's economic growth be sustainable? If not, then China might duplicate the experience of Japan, which became an economic superpower by the 1980s only to find its economy hamstrung by a nearly two-decade recession and economic doldrums, from which Japan has yet to fully recover.

    Carsten A. Holz, an economist at the Hong Kong University of Science and Technology, probably has done more than anyone else that I know, in delving into this question in search of an answer. The following is a summary of his analyses and findings. First, relying on tools of transition economics, he looks at the diverse factors contributing to China's rapid growth:

- Jettisoning of the pre-reform planning system eliminated inefficiencies;
- Agricultural and industrial reforms unleashed incentives and thereby caused an immediate increase in output;
- Competition between enterprises, increasingly under private management, led to cost-cutting and innovation;
- The Chinese diaspora (overseas Chinese, plus those from Taiwan and Hong Kong, etc.) helped with management techniques, finance, and knowledge of foreign markets.[21]

For analyzing China's future economic growth, Holz employs a different set of tools, from development economics. He examines the shifts of labor from agriculture to industry and services. In this regard, China shows a different pattern, and thus potential, from other Asian economies. In South Korea and Taiwan, for example, the agricultural share in the total employment showed drastic declines: from 63% (1963) down to 9% (2003) in one case; and from 46% (1965) down to 7% (2003), in the other case. China, however, does not have a similar labor-supply problem as its growing industrial and service sectors demand an ever expanding labor force. In China, agriculture accounted for 71% of employment in 1978, and 49% in 2003. In other words, in 24 years, there was a 22% shift of labor, hence less than 1% per year. Calculated on the basis of an average 1% shifting of labor out of agriculture every year, China is looking forward to another 40 years of agricultural change, or a steady labor supply to the growing industrial needs in that duration.[22]

This matters, because productivity in industry is seven times larger than in agriculture, and three to four times larger in the service sector. At 1% of the labor force moving out of agriculture every year, he continues, this shift alone signifies an approximately 4% to 5% GDP growth a year. Structural change, as such, will remain a major source of China's economic growth in the next two to three decades.[23]

In short, unless the 1% shift of labor from agriculture to industry and services encounters insurmountable obstacles, and barring other unforeseen circumstances, the answer to whether China's growth is sustainable is positively in the affirmative.

CHINA'S BANDWAGONING & CHANGING DEBATES ON THE CHINA THREAT ISSUE

At the turn of the century, after its robust economy had withstood the Asian Financial Crisis of 1997-1999 unscathed, while all other economies in the region were tumbling down, China became the envy, and fear, of many in the West. More scary were forecasts by respectable pundits that China was poised to catch up with the United States economically by 2005 and militarily by mid-century.[24] Hence, the cries of the "China threat" took off relentlessly.

Following the same cue, scholarly warnings of an emerging Chinese hegemony swarmed the literature, to an extent unmatched since the erstwhile warnings of the Soviet threat during the Cold War. The best known, and most blunt, example was probably the mega opus by John Mearsheimer at the University of Chicago. Writing in the *Foreign Affairs*,[25] Mearsheimer called for reversal of America's engagement policy, and suggested that U.S. interests would be best served by keeping China down and encouraging Japan to build up its military capability, to help cope with the China threat.[26]

If Meirsheimer was speaking for the mainstream realist international-relations (IR) scholars at the time, there, however, has been an unforeseen change in the intellectual climate. To wit, there has been a discernible shift away from the realist paradigm, a shift that can in part be traced to the fact that Chinese international behavior has been perceived as at variance with what most realists divined. Kenneth Waltz,[27] arguably the best known spokesman for the realist school since Hans Morgethau, for example, had predicted that secondary states such as China, Japan, and Russia would seek to balance U.S. power in the post-Cold War era. His view was shared by other realists including Christopher Lane. It certainly jived with Mearsheimer's thinking that a rising China would seek dominance at the expense of the United States, the world's prevailing hegemon.

However, from observing that China has not tried to balance the United States but is instead bandwagoning—such as playing a supporting role in brokering the six-nation talks on the denuclearization of the Korean Peninsula, and cooperating on the anti-Terrorism fight after 9/11—Peter Van Ness,[28] at the Australian National University, for one, speculates that the stiff hierarchy in the present system may provide an answer why the realist view is not borne out empirically. Following the same vein, David Kang[29] (Dartmouth College) also raises a question as to why Thailand and other Asian secondary states are not balancing China in the region in "the same way that the United States balanced the Soviet Union." Extrapolating from his earlier studies of six centuries of East Asian international relations, Kang finds bandwagoning, not balancing, to be the typical behavior of secondary states in a steep hierarchy.[30]

The return of scholarly interest in hierarchy, which David Lake (UC-San Diego) calls "one of the dead horses" in IR literature[31] calls into question the adequacy of the realist paradigm, which is purely based on the premise of anarchy (i.e., lack of a supranational authority over the states). Picking up the theme of hierarchy as a structure of international relations, Lake develops a derivative point regarding the importance of (moral) authority in the conduct of hegemonic foreign policy, if the United States is going to lead. Applying this framework to future East-West relations, he sees that conflict with rising powers, especially China, is not "foredoomed." By building authority, rather than relying purely on brute power, he explains, the United States will have enough followings in the world, when it has to face a future Chinese superpower. The U.S., he adds, "might even succeed in locking China into an American-dominated international order."[32]

Similarly tweaked by a curiosity about the prospect of a rising China, many other scholars also began to do some rethinking about IR theory. For example, Jacek Kugler[33] (Claremont Graduate University) who collaborated with the late Alfred Organski in developing the "power transition" theory, steps forward to fine-tine, or clarify, the theory itself. According to the original "power transition" theory, as is generally understood by most IR students, war is most likely when power is roughly equal. Kugler is now emphasizing what has been said only in find print, but often overlooked, in the theory as it was formulated on the basis of historical examples, namely: that "such a war is likely only when the parties fundamentally disagree about the status quo."[34] Thus, an advice he offered is that the United States should focus on Asia far more than on the Global War on Terror. "The path to international peace," he stressed, "can be ensured if action is taken to enhance satisfaction by China and other growing giants in Asia."[35]

Another challenge to the realist reflex on the China threat is from Richard Rosecrance,[36] an IPE expert at Harvard, who weighs in by calling attention to the transformation of the Westphalian system as a result of the post-Cold War economic globalization. Thanks to globalization, China will enter a world market in which "many of the spoils have already been appropriated."[37] In the world of 1914, he adds, great powers (i.e., Britain, France, Germany, etc.) were not dependent upon the commercial ties forged among them. Those ties could be replaced by other suppliers and markets. Foreign direct investments (FDI) did not flow between the major powers, but from the metropole to the colonies, even then in small amounts.

In the world of the 21st century, however, Chinese industries, although growing rapidly, may often be subsidiaries (or joint-venture partners) of major world corporations located elsewhere, he points out. In the age of what Rosecrace calls "vulnerability interdependence,"[38] not even the United States can boast of having attained unipolarity of economies, despite its overwhelming military might. For the Chinese, it means their country will be studded with foreign firms—including U.S., Japanese, European firms—contributing the needed technology for its development.[39] Hence, it is unlikely that China will be so insane as to seek self-destruction by trying to destroy the existing system.

CORRESPONDING CHANGE IN THE U.S. POLITICAL CLIMATE REGARDING CHINA

Consistent with the changing intellectual climate noted above, there has been a corresponding change in the political climate surrounding the official thinking on China. Elsewhere I have dealt with this subject, and I shall only briefly note some noticeable indications of change in both Congress and the Bush Administration. In Congress, for example, a China Caucus was formed in mid-June 2005, shortly after Representatives Randy Forbes (Republican-VA) and Ike Skelton (Democrat-MO) returned from a Congressional trip to China. Forbes was usually very negative toward China and in 2004 he voted against the Chinese oil company CNOOC's bid to acquire Unocal, a U.S. oil company. But after his trip, he was concerned that China knew far more about the United States than the U.S. about China. He deplored that neither the executive branch nor Congress had mechanisms in place that allowed for comprehensive analysis of how the U.S. should deal with a supercharged China. The Caucus idea was like removing blinders from Congress.

Soon afterwards, a House U.S.-China Working Group was also formed, under the leadership of Congressmen Mark Kirk (Republican-IL) and Rick Larsen (Democrat-WA). While security is among the chief concerns of the more formal Caucus, the Working Group is less formal and its purpose is to educate congressional members about U.S.-China relations issues by promoting in-depth discussions of these issues away from the flour of the House.

Within the Bush Administration, there has been a progressive change in its conceptualization of the role the rising China is expected to play. From its initial characterization of China as a "strategic competitor," to a "strategic partner" after 9/11, and finally to a "common stake-holder," the Administration has gradually outgrown its earlier fright bred by a Cold-War mentality that reflected the influence of the neocons in the Administration, such as Vice President Dick Cheney and Donald Rumsfeld, the Secretary of Defense. The more positive change came in Bush's second term. During a November 2005 visit to Beijing, for example, President Bush spoke of the many common opportunities for the United States and China to cooperate in meeting many of the challenges of the 21st century, including the fight on terror, nuclear proliferation, and pandemics like SARS.[40]

References to China as a "stake-holder" began with a speech by Richard Zoellick, Deputy Secretary of State, on September 21, 2005, to the National Committee on U.S.-China Relations, a private organization in New York.[41] In more concrete terms, he named a number of areas (or "opportunities") in which China could be a responsible stakeholder, such as energy, the Korean peninsula, and larger Asian security (provided it can resolve its differences with Taiwan peacefully). Shortly after, Secretary of State Condoleezza Rice repeated the same theme, even going beyond it, during an interactive videoconference with the World Economic Forum in Davos, Switzerland, on January 26, 2006. When asked about the rise of China, Rice replied: "[W]e believe there is an obligation by all of he powers, but perhaps particularly the United States, to engage in policies that will encourage the rise of the second China [sic] about which you spoke, [to be] the responsible stakeholder China."[42] She went further to say that in the six-party talks on North Korea, defense of peace and security of the world (not just Asia), assuring the proper function of the rule-based WTO system, etc., China has a constructive and responsible role to play.[43]

As if not to be left behind, Secretary of Defense Rummsfeld, despite his usual hawkish reputation, also called China an "important stateholder in Asia," when attending an international security conference in Singapore, known as The Shangrila Dialogue, on June 2-4, 2006. Sponsored by the London-based International Institute for Strategic Studies (IISS), the conference was attended by 250 delegates from 20 countries.[44] Here, Rumsfeld reversed his own position stated at the same meeting the previous year, when he denounced China as a threat to regional peace because of its heavy military buildup. His conciliatory remarks at the 2006 Shangrila Dialogue coincided with the release of the Pentagon's annual Report on China's Military Power. While the 2006 Report used even stronger language than the 2005 Report in calling the People's Liberation Army (PLA) a "threat," the beginning paragraph of the Executive Summary, nevertheless, declares: "The United States welcomes the rise of a peaceful and prosperous China. U.S. policy encourages China to participate as a responsible stateholder by taking on a greater share of responsibility for the health and success of the global system from which China has derived great benefit."[45]

The softening of Rumsfeld's rhetoric was matched by substantially improved high-level military contacts between the U.S. and China. Rumsfeld himself visited China in late 2005, when he became the first foreign dignitary ever to visit the PLA's Second Artillery corps, the secretive strategic nuclear force of China. The visit was reciprocated by that of high-ranking Chinese military and security personnel, including PLA's Deputy Chief of the General Staff, General XIONG Guangkai, and General GUO Boxiong, a vice chairman of the Military Affairs Commission, an arm of the Central Committee of the Chinese Communist Party, in 2006. During the latter's visit, the two sides reached an agreement on improving cooperation in six areas, including maritime rescue, stepped-up exchanges of military personnel and cadets, and "non-traditional security" cooperation such as environmental control.[46]

The rapport was continued under Rumsfeld's successor, Robert Gates. Almost immediately after taking office, Secretary Gates made a two-day visit to China, in November 2007, to discuss the transparency of the Chinese military, the Taiwan issue, and the establishment of a hot line between the U.S. and Chinese militaries. What is most remarkable is that this was the first time that China, not Japan, was the first stop in the itinerary of a U.S. Defense Secretary's visit to East Asia.

To sum up, there is no question that the new intellectual thinking noted above has rubbed off on official U.S. attitude and policy. The ideas that intention, not power (capability), determines whether a rising powerful state will pose a threat, and that a rising power satisfied with the status quo is not likely to challenge and upset it—all seem to have been taken cognizance of and reflected in the changing U.S. policy on the rising China. Secretary Rice's point that the United States and other major powers have an "obligation" to make China feel and act as a "responsible" stakeholder fulfills the scholarly exhortation that the Rising China be made into a "satisfied" power with the prevailing world order. Likewise, the wording just cited in the Pentagon's 2006 Report seems to bend backwards to remind China that it should be "satisfied" with the status quo, as it is a country that, to reiterate, "has derived great benefit" from the existing "global system." This view seems to be both an expectation and a confirmation of the role that China plays in the new era.

WHAT LIES AHEAD IF THERE IS GOING TO BE A PAX SINICA?

The kind of changes, just noted, in both the intellectual and political climate in America's China debate came as no surprise when China's rise is assessed from the perspective of geoeconomics (as opposed to geopolitics), which as we argued is going to pervade through the 21st century as the key desideratum shaping the foreign policy of nations and directing the conduct of international relations. There is no lack of expectations that 2050 will usher in an Asian Era, in which three of the world's four largest economies will be Asian, and in this order: China, the U.S., India, and Japan.[47] This view was anticipated by the study of Ronald Tammen, et al.,[48] which foresaw China to eclipse the United

States economically by 2025 and militarily by 2050. Both these predictions seem to suggest there will be a *pax sinica* in the latter half of the 21st century. Let us pause to ponder for a moment over the veracity of the prevision of such an eventuality, before we venture to speculate on what is likely to prevail under a *pax sinica*.

Almost all forecasts regarding China's potential as an economic giant were based on its total GDP growth on the macro level; and the World Bank used a measure called Purchasing Power Parity (PPP), which tends to magnify by four times China's economic strength. Only in one study was *per capita* GDP used as a measure for comparison. I am referring to a collaborate study made by a group of top-notch economists, led by C. Fred Bergsten, and drawn from two think tanks in Washington, D.C.—the Center for Strategic and International Studies (CSIS), and the Peter G. Peterson Institute of International Economics. Using this micro-level measure as a gauge, the Bergsten group arrived at a very different conclusion. In 2005, they pointed out, China's per capita GDP was a paltry $1,700, compared to $42,000 in the United States, a gap of twenty-five to one (25:1). Even assuming China's economy would exceed the United States by 2035, they noted, based on U.N. medium variant population projections for both countries, per capita income in the United States could still be four times that of China.[49]

For its part, China has four times the population of the United States. Although there is no way to figure out how much more it would cost China to feed its huge population, taking care of the bare essentials for their well-being, it is self-evident that the total consumption in China will be much higher than in the United States, even factoring in the fact that the Chinese are generally more frugal and less given to a spendthrift way of life. While this cannot be quantified, it is safe to assume that the total savings after deduction from this colossal population-related consumption rate are at least four times less in China than in the United States. That would mean the resources available for defense, military buildup, R & D, etc. would fall short of keeping up with the United States. A logical inference from this very crude calculation is that it is questionable when, if ever, China, under the circumstances, will trounce the United States to become the next unipolar power.

Nevertheless, if we do not foresee the relations between the two countries in a zero-sum game, then it becomes clear that China and the United States will have a lot of mutual interests to be drawn together and much to share in common, including a joint responsibility—as the two largest economies in the second half of the 21st century—in leading the global economy. Since 2005, China is the third largest trading partner of the United States, and the second largest source of imports, supplying one eighth of U.S. total imports. Sino-dollars are recycled to purchase American debt, helping finance the sizeable U.S. consumer and government spending deficits. As Bergsten et al. notes, "Chinese authorities are the second largest foreign official creditor to the United States, holding hundreds of billions dollars of U.S. financial assets."[50] The United States is China's number one bilateral trade partner and export destination, and an important source of investment, technology, and expertise.

The revival of China and the significance it holds for the world economy may surpass even the stunning rise of Japan from the 1960s forward, and the ascendancies of the United States, Germany, and the Soviet Union in the twentieth century. By the sheer size and the possibility of its continued run of economic expansion, plus the uniqueness of its political and economic system for such a major economic sector, China therefore is seen by the Bergsten group as potentially posing "challenges that are literally unprecedented."[51]

This statement, casting aside the "intention" question and momentarily ignoring the huge population burden, focuses on the size and weight of the Chinese colossus as a natural economic force. It implicitly raises a question regarding whether there will be a *pax sinica,* even in the absence of a Chinese interest in seeking hegemony. And, more important, what does a *pax sinica* entail for the rest of the world?

Realists like to remind us that throughout the history of international relations, a rising major power will challenge the equilibrium of the existing system; and often a war, known as "hegemonic war," will ensue which will determine whether the current dominant power can keep its hegemonic leadership after defeating the challenger or else be replaced by a new hegemon (Gilpin 1981: 15 and 197).[52] The habitual examples given are:

- Britain after the Industrial Revolution (18th century);
- France after the French Revolution, hence the Napoleonic Wars;
- Japan after the Meiji Reform (1868-1912);
- Germany following the Germanic unification and acquisition of superior modern military technology; The Soviet Union under Stalin.

In view of this recurrent pattern, it is not surprising that realists both in academe and in government have an inexplicable fear about the rise of China. Even the revisionists who believed otherwise after noting the Chinese bandwagoning behavior and finding no solid evidence of an "intention" to challenge the existing power structure of the world, as noted above, have nothing but deductive reasoning to rely upon. I think it imperative to point out that all the examples above were first-time upstarts. But, a re-rising China is not a first-time upstart. In its previous incarnation, until its decline and trampling under by "imperialist" powers, China was the world's largest economy for a thousand years before 1800. As the vast "globalist" literature[53] reminds us, China had dominated the world economy for at least one thousand years before the West's rise after 1500. It was not until Columbus' discovery of America that Europeans used the silver extracted from their American colonies to buy their entry into an already flourishing and expanding Asian market.[54] During the 14th through the mid-17th centuries (the Ming Dynasty), China's GNP was 28-30 percent of the world's total output. By 1800, China did even better, accounting for 33 percent of world manufacturing output.[55] Even the lower figure during the Ming Dynasty (i.e., 28-30%) already exceeded the U.S.'s 22% share of the global GNP at the turn of the 21st century, when America is the reigning superpower.

How China behaved in the long historical period when its economy topped the world, as such, provides ample evidence of how a re-rising China is most likely to behave.

In other words, how China used or did not use its power in its earlier predominance would be most revealing. During 1405 through 1433, China, in a departure from its agrarian earth-bound tradition, began a series of seven seafaring expeditions. The first expedition, in 1405, preceded Columbus by 87 years. In the largest expedition, Zheng He (Cheng Ho), who led all the seven ventures, had 30,000 sailors and 400 ships under his command. The group sailed out from southern China, through southeast Asia, to reach as far as today's Persian Gulf and East Africa. A British submarine-captain turned naval historian, Gavin Menzies,[56] even found evidence that these Chinese explorers were the first ones to discover the Americas in 1421, or 71 years before Columbus arrived. But, in stark contrast to Western maritime expansion, Zheng He and his men did not claim title to the Americas or other lands they discovered, nor did they establish a single colony overseas. What does all this reveal about Chinese behavior when the country wielded superior power vis-a-vis other lands and peoples? The answer is: quite a lot.

First, it clearly demonstrates that the Chinese, to say the least, were not in a habit of grabbing other people's land or colonizing others for their own gains. It is important to keep in mind that all this happened NOT in a time when they were weak, but when they had the world's largest economy and the power that came with it.

Secondly, the reason why the Chinese behaved so modestly may have come from two sources, one economic and one cultural. The economic reason was that China's traditional agrarian economy, supported by a vast sub-continental landmass and an extensive web of navigable rivers and waterways, was more than self-sufficient. It had no need for overseas markets or material resources, hence no need to plunder other people's land. And, the cultural reason was that Confucius taught the Chinese to win people's hearts by suasion and exemplification (*wangdao*), not by coercion or violence (*badao*). When President HU Jintao of China today trumpets the building of a "harmonious society" as his goal, it has a distinct Confucian ring to it, regardless of whether the ancient sage is given credit for the ideal. It is not coincidental that Confucian Analects is now taught, beginning from the very first grade, in elementary schools in many parts of China; and even in national television programs taught by invited professors on CCTV-4.

Thirdly, the Chinese example provides a counterpoint against which Chinese culture—given its embodiment of a continental farmer's weltanschauung[57]—can be compared with other cultures descending from nomadic or "mercantile" origins. The nomadic tradition of searching for new oases anticipated the future mercantilist quest for colonies and overseas markets and supplies after the Industrial Revolution, which created the modern sinews of power to back up an ever expansive quest. Britain, the first beneficiary of the Industrial Revolution, thus used its newly found power to establish a colonial empire over all continents on which the sun would not set.

Fourthly, if the Chinese at the peak of their power, stretching over at least a thousand years before the arrival of the modern age, showed a record of not abusing their power at other people's expense, what would change their behavior in the event they regain their former pre-eminence? We don't have any example in world history of another nation on a Phoenix-like re-rise from a century and a half of decline to guide us in foretelling how China will likely act after its revival. But, the important thing is that even as a first-time upstart during its long previous incarnation, China did not have similar records of trespassing on other nations the way the Europeans did in reducing many foreign lands into colonies or satellites or, as in the German (and Japanese) case in the early twentieth century, in waging wars of aggression..

It is instructive to recognize that during its eclipse after the mid-19th century, China sustained humiliating defeats and encroachments at the hands of foreign predatory powers that were "momentarily" more powerful but less than scrupulous. It was thus made sorely aware of the evils of social Darwinism practiced in international relations (sometimes justified as "Whiteman's Burden"), at the expense of social justice. Hence, the only place the word "justice" is seen in the United Nations Charter, in Article 2 (3), it was an insertion made at the insistence of China into the original draft known as Dumbarton Oaks Proposals.[58] Unconvinced critics might question whether China, now under Communist rule, will make any difference. Elsewhere, I have addressed this question by contrasting how China under Mao and under the previous non-Communist regime behaved internationally in two similar cases; and no noticeable difference could be found.[59] Here I will not repeat myself, except to note that although China is no longer an agrarian society, the modesty associated with its agrarian past, as noted above, is not lost, thanks to the crucial changes in the international environment. The globalization of the market, plus the Chinese entry into the World Trade Organization, has made it unnecessary, for a re-rising China, to prey on others the way big powers did previously to gain access to vital resources from foreign lands.[60]

To sum up the discussion in this section, we can conclude that (a) China is not likely to disturb the existing equilibrium in the system because it is a beneficiary of the status quo; and (b) even if China is thrust forward by the sheer size and weight of its economy, and the momentum of its sustained growth, to be the next superpower, the *pax sinica* that comes with it will most likely usher in a world order built on an anti-social Darwin ethos, emphasizing social justice and, by extension, peace with equity, which will be a hot issue on the agenda of the 21st century as an era dominated by geoeconomics.[61]

Thus far, we have noted that power transition in the new geoeconomic era does not follow the earlier path of geopolitical conflicts and brutal wars. Below, we shall continue this discussion in ascertaining the future of the Taiwan question and the prospects of the island's integration with the mainland of China.

TAIWAN'S CHOICE IN THE DEEPENING GEOECONOMICS AGE

Although the majority of the 23 million people in Taiwan have consistently expressed their preference, in various opinion poll surveys, to preserve the status quo of the cross-strait division, the Democratic Progressive Party that ruled the island for eight turbulent years until losing the March 2008 Presidential election has a separatist platform, pledged to taking Taiwan out of the China orbit to legal independence. Most DPP leaders, including Chen Shui-bian, Taiwan's President until May 2008 believed that they could win over the status quo adherents to their cause, when given time. Thus, in their eight years in power, they mounted a ubiquitous campaign to build a Taiwanese nationalism ("Taiwan self-identity"), by trying to purge all traces of Chinese tradition from society, beginning with re-writing textbooks for schools. This was coupled with a concomitant campaign to vilify and demonize the late President Chiang Kai-shek, who brought the KMT Government to Taiwan after losing the civil war in 1949. Known as "De-Chiangization," the campaign stooped so low as to destroy his statues and busts, desecrate a memorial hall dedicated to him, and even change street names that had any remote connection to his legacy. Both campaign boomeranged, as DPP lost the crucial Legislative and Presidential elections within a span of three months, in January and March, respectively. Voters gave the KMT a landslide in both elections. Besides, in the run-up to the second election, 60% of the people polled indicated their opposition to De-Chiangization, and 65% named Chiang's son (Chiang Ching-kuo, who succeeded his father as the President) the best President ever in Taiwan.

While it is unclear whether the rumored revision of the DPP's separatist platform, following the party's devastating defeats, is going forward, one thing is clear. The majority of Taiwan's constituency remains divided on the reunification issue, with the majority supporting the maintenance of the status quo, which means continuing the cross-strait division that has lasted since 1949. Ma Ying-jeou, the KMT candidate, won a 59% landslide, largely because he ran on promises to revive Taiwan's sagging economy, which was in bad shape because cross-strait relations with the mainland had hit the bottom under Chen Shui-bian's Administration. While, Taiwan's economy is heavily dependent on its trade with mainland China, and its revival depends on prior improvement of the cross-strait relations, Ma was very careful in handling the delicate issue of cross-strait relations. Picking his words carefully, he zeroed in on technical moves such as opening up direct links with the mainland, beginning with direct flights between Taiwan and target mainland destinations. With this policy change, Taiwan's travelers to the mainland would not have to fly first to Hong Kong or any third-party stop before changing planes to proceed to their final destination, as required under the existing rules.

Ma avoided any reference to moving the two sides closer together beyond these technical contacts, relegating reunification to an "ultimate" goal. The reason is not hard to understand. Although at the macro level the Chinese mainland's GDP is eight times that of Taiwan, yet when divided by 1.3 billion population, its per capita income is only one seventh that of Taiwan today. However, by 2035, when the mainland's GDP is expected to catch up with the United States, its per capita income will also overtake Taiwan's. For most people in Taiwan, talks about unification with the mainland will be premature.

In earlier discussions above, on the question of how power is defined in the age of geoeconomics, we noted a number of components. Most relevant to the present discussion of Taiwan's choices are "percentage share of the global economy," and "influence over global economic decision-making. Furthermore, among the ingredients essential for a player in a geoeconomic balance-of-power game, most relevant for Taiwan's survival as a resource-deficient economy are whether it has (a) access to the needed basic natural resources, such as energy and steel; and (b) relative freedom from long-term dependency on far-away overseas markets. In addition, a player's viability in the age of geoeconomics depends very much on its economic competitiveness and participation in super trading blocs (including free trade areas, FTAs).

On the last two scores—competitiveness and membership in FTAs—Taiwan showed a slight improvement in 2008 over the previous year. According to assessments by the Swiss Lausanne Institute of Management (2008), Taiwan's competitiveness moved from No. 18 to No. 13 in ranking, while mainland China dropped two spaces from last year's No. 15 to No. 17.[62] On the institutional membership score, however, the island is excluded from most FTAs, and is shunned by the United States, its closest ally, on a proposed bilateral FTA relationship. All three major developments in the Pacific Asian region since the Asian Financial Crisis of the late 1990s are inhospitable to Taiwan: (a) Mainland China's replacement of Japan as the region's growth engine; (b) trends toward Asianism, such as the expansion of ASEAN to a 10-nation trading bloc, and the emergence of a CAFTA incorporating China and ASEAN-10 into the world's largest free trade area encompassing 1.7 billion consumers, a combined GDP of approximately $2 trillion, and total international trade of $1.23 trillion; and (c) the hatching of an Asia-wide FTA that encompasses the earlier ASEAN+3 (China, South Korea, and Japan), plus an additional outer three: Australia, New Zealand, and India. Possible future members include Russia, Timor-Leste, Pakistan, Bangladesh, and even Papua New Guinea. Both the United States and the European Union have expressed interest in playing an unspecified role in the future.[63] Taiwan has no claim to any part of this labyrinthian networking.

Nor is Taiwan participating in the deepening ASEM process that conjoins the EU and Asian members in a vast economic conglomeration. Taiwan has only limited access to EU markets. And, since mainland China has an early head start in energy investments in Africa, Asia, and Latin America, it leaves very little wiggle room for Taiwan. The oil and natural-gas pipelines under construction that will transport these energy resources from points of origin in Russia's Siberia and in the former Soviet Republics in Central Asia to parts of mainland China could, conceivably, offer some relief to resource-scarce Taiwan, provided the island abandons its seclusion policy pursued by the earlier pro-separatism regime and enters into a rapprochement with the mainland, as appears most likely under the new government that came to power after a landslide Presidential election in early 2008.

Concededly, opinion polls have consistently shown that over 60% of Taiwan's populace wants to maintain the status quo. But, "status quo" remains to be defined. The status quo of today is decidedly different from that of previous decades, the 1990s, 1970s, 1950s, etc. Already, Taiwan has 50,000 firms operating in mainland China, and in 2007 40 percent of Taiwan's products were sold to the mainland and Hong Kong. Two-way cross-strait trade has reached $120 billion, out of which Taiwan enjoys a $70 billion surplus. Despite the obstacles under the eight years of the DPP Administration, Taiwan investors sent an estimated 70% of their total external investment to mainland China. Such investment is concentrated in electronics. As many as one million Taiwanese, almost 5% of the population now lie and work on the mainland. If anyone is worried about Taiwan becoming too dependent on the mainland trade, a sobering look at the statistics will show that only 12.2% of the island's imports came from mainland China (as compared to South Korea's 15.7% and Japan's 20.4%). By contrast, 22.7% of Taiwan's exports were destined toward the mainland (as compared to Korea's 21.3% and Japan's 14.2%).[64]

As we have noted above, in the age of geoeconomics, relations between polities are not zero-sum games, for reasons explained by Richard Rosecrance in his concept of "vulnerable interdependence." In other words, the more closely integrated between Taiwan and the mainland in terms of trade and investment, the more mutual stakes they have, to the extent that it would be suicidal for either side to try to hurt the other side for any reason.

The vast open market on the mainland eased the heavy dependency of Taiwan's export-oriented economy on overseas markets, which may be far away and often unsteady. If bilateral agreements can be reached integrating the two sides across the Taiwan Strait into a Common Market that candidate Ma flaunted during the Spring 2008 Presidential campaign, it would at least in part make up for Taiwan's current isolation and exclusion from the array of FTAs and geoeconomic networks alluded to above.

After the DPP's devastating defeats in both the Legislative (January) and Presidential (March) elections in 2008, many of its prominent members have second thoughts about the separatist route as a solution to Taiwan's future. This change of view found strong endorsement of Lee Teng-hui, former President and god-father to the Taiwan Alliance Party (Tailian) that was formerly more pushy than the DPP on the separatist agenda until it reversed itself in recognition of the preferences of Taiwan's electorate.

It is clear that in the age of geoeconomics and globalization, Taiwan's rational choice for its own good, even survival, is greater integration with, not secession from, mainland China. This integration will begin in the economic domain first, pending the establishment of mutual trust following a transitional period of confidence building. The process will commence with a cross-strait free trade area, moving toward a customs union, a common market, and ultimately an economic confederation. If successful, a spillover into the political sphere will follow in a spontaneous progression.

Typical of the age of geoeconomics, to reiterate, this economic integration will not be a zero-sum game, because the close interdependence thus created is "mutually vulnerable," while it is mutually beneficial.

POSTSCRIPT: AN UPDATE

After the collapse of Wall Street, coming on the heels of the economic meltdown brought on by the sub-prime mortgage crisis in 2008, all economies in the world were scrambling for cover. To many former *laissez faire* economists in the West, the failed American-style capitalism was crying out for re-regulation. An increasing number of them were beginning to trumpet the virtues of the "China model" of state interventionism in a regulated market system. While many in Washington, as elsewhere, were looking for help from China, with the world's largest foreign reserves and a robust economy, the leaders from China, Japan, and South Korea met in a summit conference in Fukuoka, Japan. On December 13, 2008, they issued a joint statement in which they called for closer cooperation among the three countries, working in conjunction with ASEAN members, to reverse the downward trend of the world economy. The message was not lost on Taiwan. Calls were heard on the island that Taiwan should not miss the boat, as China was fast becoming the ultimate leader in a region that was mostly likely moving toward a Yuan Belt, named after the Chinese RMB currency. Some Taiwan economists are openly calling on their compatriots to cash in on the opportunity to join hands with the mainland in a closer economic union, turning away from its "fate" as Asia's lonely orphan, now that the long-awaited "Three Direct Links" (trade, transport, and mail) were opened up following a year-end agreement reached across the Taiwan strait.[65]

This growing awareness that Taiwan's future lies in its close union with mainland China received a anew fillip when Hu Jintao, General Secretary of the Communist Party, issued a Message to the Brethren in Taiwan, on December 31, 2008. In the message, Hu called for an end to the status of belligerency between the two sides straddling the Taiwan Strait, and offered a complement of measures for forging closer cross-strait economic, cultural, and political ties, culminating in a peace agreement. At a time of the great turmoil ravaging the global economy, resulting in a 40% cut in Taiwan's exports, these proposed measures will do more than adding a gigantic push toward closer integration between Taiwan and the mainland. This development is in keeping with the logic of cross-strait integration inherent in the workings of the age of geoeconomics and the rise of mainland China as an economic superpower that we have addressed in this chapter.

NOTES

* The author thanks the following journal for permission to reprint previously published article: "The Age of Geoeconomics, China's Global Role, and Prospects of Cross-Strait Integration," *Journal of Chinese Political Science*, vol. 14, no. 2, 2009.

[1] Robert Keohane and Joseph Nye, *Power and Interdependence* (Boston: Little Brown, 1977).
[2] James C. Hsiung, *Anarchy and Order: The Interplay of Politics and Law in International Relations* (Boulder, CO: Lynne Rienner, 1997), p. 203.
[3] James C. Hsiung, ed., *Twenty-First Century World Order and the Asia Pacific* (New York: Palgrave-Macmillan, 2001), p. 27.
[4] James C. Hsiung, ed., *Asia Pacific in the New World Politics* (Boulder, CO: Lynne Rienner, 1993), p.10.
[5] See "Japan to Mend China Ties While World Eyes the Gulf," *Japan Times Weekly*, September 24-30, 1990, p. 1.
[6] Chen Po-chih, "Analysis of the State of Japan-China Trade Relations," *Mainland China Studies* (Taipei), vol. 43, no. 2, 2000, pp.79-108.
[7] Max Singer and Aaron Wildavsky, *The Real World Order: Zones of Peace and Zones of Turmoil* (Chatham, NY: Chatham House Publishers, 1993), p. 29.
[8] Robert Strausz-Hupe, *Geopolitics, the Struggle for Peace and Power* (New York: Arno, 1972); Nicholas Spykman, *The Geography of the Peace* (New York: Harcourt Brace, 1944); Woodruff D. Smith, *The Ideological Origins of Nazi Imperialism* (New York: Oxford University Press, 1986).
[9] Robert S. Ross, "The Geography of Peace: East Asia in the Twenty-First Century," *International Security*, vol. 23, no. 4 (Spring, 1999), pp.81-118.
[10] Hans Binnendijk and Alan Hanikson, "Back to Bipolarity," *Strategic Forum*, No. 161 (May 1999). Washington, D.C.: Institute for National Strategic Studies (INSS), National Defense University.
[11] Ibid., p.1.
[12] Ibid., p. 3.
[13] On the U.S.-Europe rift, see Joseph S. Nye, Jr. 2000; Ivo H. Daalder 2001; Robert Kagan 2003.
[14] Robert Gilpin, *The Challenge of Capitalism: The World Economy in the 21ˢᵗ Century.* (Princeton, N.J.: Princeton University Press, 2000); Joan Spero and Gary Hart, *The Politics of International Economic Relations* (New York: St. Martin's Press, 1997).
[15] *Asian Wall Street Journal Weekly*, March 11, 1995, p. 5.
[16] *New York Times*, March 3, 1996, p. 3.
[17] The Asia-10 are: Brunei, China, Indonesia, Japan, South Korea, Malaysia, the Philippinjes, Singapore, Thailand, and Vietnam).
[18] With Cambodia, Laos, and Burma/Myanmar added, the original Asia-10 became Asia-13. On the European side were the EU-25 and the European Commission.
[19] The 45 included EU-25, the European Commission, Bulgaria and Romania, on the one side, and Asia-13, plus India, Mongolia, Pakistan, and the ASEAN Secretariat on the Asian side.
[20] The proposal to set up such a council was put forward at the U.S.-EU Summit, held in Washington, D. C., on April 30, 2007.
[21] Carsten A. Holz, "Why China's Rise Is Sustainable," *Far Eastern Economic Review*, vol. 169, no 3 (April 2006), pp.41-46.
[22] Ibid., p.41.
[23] Ibid., p.42

[24] Typical of these forecasts was found in Ronald L. Tammen (2000).
[25] John F. Mearsheimer, "The Future of the American Pacifier," *Foreign Affairs,* September-October issue, 2001, pp. 46-61.
[26] The discussion here is in part based on James C. Hsiung 2008.
[27] Kenneth N. Waltz, "Structural Realism after the Cold War," *International Security,* vol. 23, no. 1 (Summer 2000), pp.32, 41.
[28] Peter Van Ness, "Hegemony, Not Anarchy: Why China and Japan Are Not Balancing U.S. Unipolar Power," *International Relations of the Asia Pacific,* vol. 2, no. 2, 2002, pp.131-150.
[29] David Kang, "Hierarchy, Balancing, and Empirical Puzzles in Asian International Relations," *International Security,* vol. 28, no. 3 (Winter 2003-2004), pp.165-189,
[30] Kang can find support from Eric Labs 1992.
[31] Indicative of the return of scholarly interest in hierarchy is a study by Katja Weber 2000.
[32] Ibid.
[33] Jacek Kugler, "The Asian Ascent: Opportunity for Peace or Condition for War," *International Studies Perspective,* vol. 7, no. 1, 2006, pp.36-42.
[34] Ibid., p. 39.
[35] Ibid., p.36.
[36] Richard Rosecrance, "Power and International Relations: The Rise of China and Its Effects," *International Studies Perspective,* vol. 7, no. 1, 2006, pp.31-35.
[37] Ibid., p.34.
[38] Ibid.
[39] Ibid.
[40] President Bush repeated the theme that the U.S. welcomed an increasing powerful China, with which the U.S. could work together in facing the many challenges of the 21st century. See his interview with the Phoenix TV (Hong Kong) on November 10, 2005, NCNA On-line; *China Daily* report on his meeting with China's President, Hu Jintao, in Beijing <http://www.sina.com.cn>, Nov. 20, 2005.
[41] "Whither China? From Membership to Responsibility," reproduced in National Committee on U.S.-China Relations, *Notes,* vol. 34, no. 1 (Winter/Spring 2006), pp.6-9.
[42] Ibid.
[43] See <http://www.state.gov/secretary/rm/2006/59957.htm>.
[44] See <http://www.iiss.org/whats-new/iiss-in-the-press/june-2006/rumsfeld. says-ch>.
[45] Ibid.
[46] Report in *Qiao Bao* (The China Press) (New York), July 20, 2006, p. A2.
[47] Kishore Mahbubani, *The New Asian Hemisphere: The Irresistible Shift of Power to the East* (New York: Public Affairs, 2008), p.52.
[48] Ronald L. Tammen, et al., *Power Transitions: Strategies for the 21st Century* (New York: Seven Bridges Press, 2000).
[49] Ibid., p.19.
[50] Ibid.
[51] Ibid.
[52] Robert Gilpin, *War & Change in World Politics* (Cambridge: Cambridge University Press, 1981), pp. 15, 157.
[53] Andre Gunder Frank, *ReOrient: Global Economy in the Asian Age* (Berkeley, CA: University of California Press, 1998); Angus Maddison, *Monitoring the World Economy: 1820-1992* (Paris: OECD, 1995); Angus Maddison, *Chinese Economic Performance in an International Perspective* (Paris: OECD, 1998); Angus Maddison, *The World Economy: A Millennial Perspective* (Paris: OECD, 2001).
[54] Frank, pp. 52-230
[55] Gerald Segal, "Does China Matter?" *Foreign Affairs,* vol.78, no.5, 1999, pp.24-36.

[56] Gavin Menzies, *1421: The Year China Discovered America* (N. Y.: William Morrow, 2003).

[57] This theme that the Chinese cultural tradition reflects the preferences and weltanschauung of a continental farmer on the huge Chinese landmass surviving in an agrarian economy was developed by Feng Yu-lan 1968 (reprint).

[58] China Institute, *China and the United Nations* (New York: Manhattan Press, 1956), Chapter 1.

[59] Hsiung, 2002, pp. 109-111.

[60] Ibid., p. 108.

[61] I have dealt with this point about peace with equity in the 21st century in Hsiuing 2001:353.

[62] *Qiao Bao* [China Press] (New York), May 16, 2008, p. 16.

[63] See "East Asia Summit," sourced from Wikipedia, the free encyclopedia.

[64] "China's Rising Influence in Asia: Implications for U.S. Policy," *Strategic Forum*, No. 231 (April, 2008), p. 3: Tables 1 & 2.

[65] One example is Wei Ai, "Strategic Choice for Taiwan in the age of Economic Globalization," *Haixia pinglun* (Cross-Strait Monthly) (Taipei), No. 217 (January 2009), pp.8-12.

Chapter 3

Empire, Nation, State, and Marketplace: China's Complex Identity and Its Implication for Geopolitical Relationships in Asia

Xiaoyang Tang

A Chinese travel guide opens with "China isn't a country—it's a different world." Though China is more and more integrated in an increasingly globalized planet, this claim still rings true. China is not simply a geographic term, its millenniums-long history, unfathomable richness of cultural tradition, as well as its immense population and vast land make it a highly complicated entity.

Moreover China's drastic change in the modern times added complexity, especially with respect to its identity. Within a century it evolved from an ancient empire to a struggling nation, further to a modern communist state and finally to a huge open marketplace. The earlier stages were not simply replaced, but have remained as the underlayers of China's new appearance. The multiple identities affect China's communication and relationship with other countries, raise difficulties for each to predict the actions and reactions of the other, and may cause problems for the regional stability if the gap of understanding is not appropriately handled appropriately.

Four major types of identities can be recognized in the perceptions of China according to the major historical periods China experienced during last century, namely, empire, nation, state and marketplace. These identities are related, but each has its own significance and scope.

FOUR IDENTITIES AND THEIR FEATURES

Empire

First, China signifies an ancient empire, whose political center has always been based in the eastern part of today's People's Republic of China (PRC), which was called "Zhongyuan," meaning central region. However, the significance and extension of China under this definition were very ambiguous. In ancient classics like *Shangshu* and *Shiji*, China (in Chinese "Zhongguo," meaning Middle Kingdom) merely referred to the central areas of the Zhou and Han dynasties in contrast with neighboring barbarians. Following this tradition, the Qing empire began officially to call itself "Zhongguo" in its international treaties. After the Qing empire was overthrown and the republic was established in 1912, it officially adopted the name "Republic of China" and the abbreviation "China" ("Zhongguo"). Therefore, the territory of the Qing empire is sometimes regarded as the original scope of China, which includes Manchuria, Mongolia, Tibet and Xinjiang, among others, although these regions were not always included in the Chinese empires in the past thousand years.

Furthermore the empire had a unique sociopolitical hierarchy. The central government usually had a firm grip on "Zhongyuan," and provincial administrations were set up there. The remote areas like Tibet, Xinjiang, and Mongolia were managed through a specific department, "Li Fanyuan" (meaning court of suzerainty management). The socioeconomic connections with China's heartland were therefore limited and their relationship to Beijing was half administrative and half tributary.[1] Beyond these areas, there are a number of "countries not to be conquered" (Buzheng zhiguo), including Korea, Japan, Vietnam, Thailand, and so on. Their autonomy was granted, though nominally their rulerships were conferred by the Chinese emperors to whom they were required to pay tribute from time to time.[2]

Another important feature of the empire identity is its Sinocentric cultural order. For most of its history, the empires located in "Zhongyuan" viewed themselves as the only true civilization, which is also implied in the name "The Middle Kingdom" that it is the center of the world. The neighboring countries were all considered culturally backward and barbarian. The Middle Kingdom displayed its arrogance not merely against its neighbors but also against all other civilizations, until the Opium War smashed its illusion of highness. Together with the empire's defeat, its hierarchic order was no longer sustainable. The Western model of equal states and subordinate colonies replaced the old relationship. The empire system collapsed and a new identity was to be created in the context of modern regional politics.

Nation

Today China is a nation among others. Yet the consciousness of China as a nation did not arise until the end of the nineteenth century. In the ancient empires, merely dynastic identities mattered. The concept of nation originated in Europe in the eighteenth century. The founder of modern nationalism, German philosopher Johann Gottfried Herder, described the *Volk* (people, nation) as the bearer of a certain culture which sustains its members. Individuals can leave this cultural community only at the cost of great impoverishment.[3] In the Qing empire, not to mention the remote regions, even in the heartland of China, there was hardly any notion of being loyal to a cultural unity, but only the notion of being loyal to friends, lords and emperors. People valued their personal, familial, and regional interests much higher than the interest of an abstract cultural unity. For example, during the war against Japan in 1894, the Qing empire's Beiyang fleet was annihilated. There was actually another strong imperial naval force, the Nanyang fleet. Not only did the Nanyang fleet refuse to join the battle, but it even asked the Japanese navy to release two of their ships, which were detained "by mistake," because in the Nanyang fleet's opinion the war was only between Japan and the Beiyang fleet.[4]

Such mentality prevailed in the Chinese society until the 1930s. Local warlords often negotiated with foreign powers to secure their own interests at the cost of a weakened and fragmented China. The sense of belonging to a common united Chinese culture was gradually growing as foreign influences expanded and endangered the existence of this culture. As the dominant civilization in the neighboring region, nobody even thought of the possibility of losing this culture, because the barbarian invaders were always assimilated and absorbed into this culture. Yet it was the arrival of the modern Western culture that made the loss of culture a real question for the first time. Even the former tributary country Japan became an intimidating rival. People then began to think seriously about the value of cultural tradition and the importance of living in a cultural community. Japan's invasion in the 1930s finally united different forces under the same purpose of saving the nation.

Thus, the identity of modern China as a nation is a reaction to crisis and colonialism. It is engraved with the memory of humiliation. China's nationalism was of a different nature than those in the advanced countries of that time. It is more emotional, but contains less ideological systematization. Accordingly today, China's current national consciousness is still highly sensitive to foreign insults and interference, but has no interest in developing a "pure" or "uniform" nation.

In fact, the Chinese nation lacks a precise boundary and composition. Although it is mainly based on the Han culture, it also includes fifty-five other ethnic groups and diverse cultural forms within the scope of the Qing empire. The shape of the current Chinese nation was not formed by several clear principles, but rather through turbulent historic and political processes. The loose relationships between ethnic groups in the empire must be modified to fit the more intimate unity as a nation. This formation is still ongoing. Hence when we talk about China's national identity, we should fully consider its historic development, its lack of precise boundary and its relatively large plasticity.

State

During the cold war and even today, China is characterized as Red China, namely a communist state. This perception is only half true. Certainly the PRC has officially adopted Marxism-Leninism as its official state ideology, and the dominance of the Communist party in government is constitutionally guaranteed. However, at a closer look we can see significant deviation by China from the typical communist states in the Eastern Bloc. These entities represent two variations of the same ideology, but in China the functions of party and ideology are not ideological in general.

Although Marxism-Leninism served as the theoretic cornerstone of the Chinese Communist Party (CCP) in its early years, the party has been mostly independent of the international communist movement since Mao Zedong regained leadership in 1935.[5] For Mao, the Marxism-Leninism was no longer the standard principle, but merely provided tools and approaches. China's own practice was the true objective.[6] That is to say, theories and ideology in themselves are "dead": they have their value only when they serve the reality in China. This attitude toward ideology is a complete reversal from the Western— including the Soviet Union's—understanding of ideology, which is claimed, at least officially, as the highest principle and the goal of a political movement.

Consequently, the CCP focused on the national war against Japan, on expelling imperial power, and on saving China from social and economic crisis during the following years. The party was more famous for its nationalistic enthusiasm than ideological slogans.[7] It took land reform, a minor issue for Marxism-Leninism, as the priority, but did not abolish capitalism in the People's Republic until the late 1950s. All these so-called strategies concerning China's uniqueness demonstrated that the CCP was interested in national benefits rather than a fixed ideological agenda. It was true that the situation altered after 1957, when the Maoist ideology was elevated to that of lofty and divine truth.[8] Yet the party quickly returned to its old track of pragmatism after the Cultural Revolution. The central task is economic development. The Four Cardinal Principles of keeping the socialist system is just considered as one of the guarantees to realize the task.[9] Persevering in the reform and opening up is the other approach of equal importance.[10]

However, one might ask, why the CCP uses such an appearance of Marxist ideology to express nationalist contents. Why can a communist state machine guarantee the national interest? Aren't these talks about nation just pretexts for a political group to stay in power? First, Mao Zedong's understanding of Marxism-Leninism is already a Chinese version of communism, which has little in common with the original Marxist social critiques, but rather is an expression of Chinese traditional appeals in Marxist language. For example, regarding materialism, Mao asked, "What is the biggest problem in the world? The problem of eating is the biggest."[11] It is apparently a distortion of Marxist philosophy, but comes from a Chinese saying "People take eating as important as heaven" (Min yishi weitian). Consequently the political implication of this "materialism" is not to abolish idealist capitalism, but to satisfy the basic demands of people. Mao believed that the difference between classes is nothing but ignorant/intelligent, poor/rich and weak/strong. The revolution meant to "overthrow aristocracy and expel the rich."[12] This view of social division reflects commonplace resentment of the rich in the Chinese tradition rather than Marxist social theory. Hence it was no wonder that Mao's major policy in the rural areas looked very similar to the old Chinese egalitarian appeal, "sharing the land and equaling rich and poor" (Fentudi, junpinfu), than to orthodox communist programs.

Mao Zedong was inspired by the success of the Russian Revolution. He believed that only a violent revolution can finally achieve the goal of social equality, and that a strong political party is vital to such a mission.[13] Thus, Mao and his comrades were mostly interested in the Marxist-Leninist political organization and its impressive power. They wanted to adopt this form of modern political organization for a similar goal of their own. As Mao simplistically concluded, "Marxism has tens of thousands of threads, in the end, it's just one phrase: rebellion is justified."[14]

Such a pragmatic adaptation can also be found in the organizational structure of the People's Republic. The governmental control of the political and economic life certainly resembled the model of the Soviet Union, because the CCP believed that this model was the reason for the Soviet Union's emergence as a world class power in the 1930s.[15] Nonetheless, these two structures were based on different social dynamics. Unlike the Soviet Union's totalitarian regime, which sought to destroy the original social structure,[16] the CCP rule inherited much of the old Confucian order. The Chinese had always avoided public dispute on issues concerning the central government although they had various views on many subjects. There was always a state orthodoxy (not ideology) and experts who administer the country under this orthodoxy. It was the duty of the ruled to obey the rulers and within the defined framework to carry on their lives.[17] This deep-rooted practice in the Chinese society, which still has a very limited notion of Western-style individual rights and abstract social contract, helped the CCP state survive and prosper once it got rid of the ideological fever and the Stalinist factors.[18]

However, in order to avoid social turbulence and economic disasters like those in the former Soviet Union countries, the Chinese government has viewed political continuity as the norm since 1989.[19] From ideological appearance to political form to party organization, everything has been preserved for a practical purpose: stable political conditions for economic development. In fact, the content of this political system has changed so much that it does not make real sense to talk about a "communist" party, because with "the Three Represents,"[20] the party "represents" every Chinese, and everybody, including entrepreneurs, can become its members.[21] The CCP finds its identity now in the material and cultural wellbeing of the Chinese nation instead of in the Marxist theories. This echoes another old Chinese saying "Rulers take people as important as heaven" (Wangzhe yimin weitian).

To summarize, the PRC cannot be simply categorized as a communist state. Its primary interest is the nation's independence and prosperity. Marxist ideology and the one-party system used to be and are still helpful tools to build a modern nation thanks to their similarity to Chinese political tradition, but their implications have been essentially changed during the adaptation with Chinese characteristics. Likewise, the ongoing learning and adoption of the Western-style democratic system is selective and the criterion is whether it fits the nation and meets the nation's overall interest.

Marketplace

Since the party launched its economic reform and opening-up policy, China has obtained a new identity, which gradually overshadowed other identities. In the twenty-first century, China primarily doesn't mean an old empire, a large nation or a communist state, but a market with over 1.3 billion consumers and cheap labor, an economy that is rapidly climbing the global rank ladder towards the top, a place full of new success stories in business, and an investment destination promising exponential growth and a brilliant future.

This identity is significant because it is influencing almost everybody's daily life in the world. Consumers can feel the ubiquitous existence of products *"Made in China."* Workers around the world are concerned about the possibility of their jobs being outsourced to China. International companies are talking about their China strategies. It is worth noting that this identity is no longer defined by ethnical or spatial boundaries. By 2008, over 252,000 foreign companies set up their factories, branches, and joint ventures in China.[22] They have become an indispensable part of the Chinese economy. From 1980 to 2004 foreign investments contributed almost one-third of China's GDP growth. A quarter of the tax revenue came from foreign investment projects.[23] Meanwhile, since Beijing's "go global" policy was initiated at the beginning of this century, Chinese business has been expanding rapidly overseas. In 2008 China's FDI to other countries totaled U.S.$ 52.1 billion.[24] The investment, contracting and other kinds of economic engagements of Chinese enterprises in foreign countries have become extension of the Chinese economy. In the age of globalization, China is just one playing field interconnected with all other fields in the world for market competition. In a flattening world, China is becoming more and more homogenous with other countries and its identity is becoming coequal.[25]

However, even as an open marketplace, China still keeps its unique characteristics due to its history and politics. Compared with other big market economies, the Beijing government has an exceptionally strong influence on its national economic performance. First, scores of gigantic state-owned enterprises dominate strategic industries such as energy, telecommunications, metallurgy, machinery, automobile, transportation and chemicals. Second, the government can also use unconventional measures to control the market if needed: for example, the central bank can fix annual loan quotas for commercial banks in order to curb inflation and then remove the quotas in order to stimulate the economy. Third the government can swiftly organize and realize gargantuan infrastructure construction projects.

This feature of powerful central control is certainly a legacy of the socialist planned economy. Yet it is not just a remnant, but a pragmatic choice based on historical lessons. As for back to the early twentieth century, China used to be an open marketplace as well, but it was such a horrible experience that the communist party adopted totally opposite policies of collectivization. Despite the obvious shortcomings of a planned economy, people acknowledged its achievements in building an independent national industry, demolishing extreme income inequality, securing basic living standards, improving infrastructure and providing a relatively stable social environment. Through this zigzag path, China learned its proper approach to the market economy. As a latecomer, the "invisible hand" of its own market is not fully functioning and is vulnerable to foreign manipulation as well as accidental catastrophes. Thus individual persons and enterprises may not survive the fluctuating waves if they do not form a strong unity. As discussed above, when the empire was dissolved and the modern nation had not yet formed, individuals could not find a community to which they belonged. Officials and tycoons conveniently used power for their personal wealth, but left millions of workers, small businesses and ordinary people in despair.[26] Only after the national consciousness was forged through a powerful state with nationalist features, the boom of a national market, not several individuals, can be possible.

However, this market is still immature and needs further nurturing. The nurturing does not mean that it should be protected from external competition, but means to make the market function appropriately and benefit the nation. For example, commercial activities need more detailed legislation and the administrations ought to improve management skills. Maintaining a firm grip on the economy can facilitate smooth pragmatic progress. Moreover since the formation of the Chinese nation is still unfinished, the state has to guide the market to serve the integration. Otherwise, pursuit of sheer commercial interests may lead to local protectionism and harm the unity of the nation.

From the identity of marketplace, which incorporates national consciousness and national interests, we can see that the ongoing formation of the Chinese nation is not an isolating process, but an interaction with the external world. The foreign investments and engagements in China as well as Chinese engagements in other countries are essential components of the nation today. The increasing convergence with the external world does not contradict, but conforms to the national interests. Yet this doesn't diminish the importance of the national identity related to ancient culture and anticolonialism. Historical memory is essential for the nation to identify itself as a unity. Only with this consciousness of unity can all members talk about China's *own* interests and engage independently with other nations according to their *own* initiative.

The Synergism of Identities

These four identities of China came from different epochs, but they all can be found in the today's perception of China. The identity of empire is discussed from a historical perspective. The identity of nation is normally related to ethnicity and culture. The identity of state matters in politics and the identity of marketplace is an issue of economy. Each identity represents a certain aspect and may be highlighted in various contexts.

All these identities are interconnected. Nation, as the continuous cultural tradition, underlies all other identities. Yet the concrete content of nation is defined and altered by other identities. The empire shows the nation's origin, but also its limit. The concept of nation cannot be anachronistically applied to premodern politics. The state enhanced the national identity, but does not completely coincide with it. The problems of Taiwan and Tibet require coordination. Yet the state can modify or at least influence the boundary of nation through political measures. The market is the most dynamic sculptor. It expands and metamorphoses according to market forces, which are not constrained by preset ideas. Its changing shape is also transforming the notions of the state and the nation. Nevertheless, we should not overlook that a functioning market is only possible with the scaffold of the nation and the state.

It is essential to observe this multifaceted synergism as a whole. Isolated analysis of one point does not reveal the true meaning behind it. The rule of the communist party, the nationalism or the capitalist market economy—all these concepts have their special implications in China. Simply assuming their meaning according to the Western perspective without seeing their "Chinese characteristics" will necessarily distort the image and cause partial and inexact judgment.

This identity complex is not only China's own matter, but it impacts other countries as well, especially the neighboring countries. On the one side, these four identities are both China's self-image and others' images of China. Some neighbors have had close contacts with China since the imperial time and some have had more engagement since the socialist or market economy period. Their relationships with China are affected by their different views of China, which are complicated due to China's dramatic development. On the other side, China's neighbors themselves have been undergoing similar transformations since the nineteenth century. All of them encountered the problems of Eastern-Western cultural clash and adaptation as well; most of them also suffered from colonialism and struggled to form independent modern nations; some joined the socialist camp too and others chose the opposite; most of them support market economy now whereas several are still hesitating. Their own multifarious self-identity added to the complexity of their relationships with China. Is China a source of their own culture, a threat to their independence, an ally, a rival, or a business partner? Such perceptions do not merely depend on China's image, but also on these countries' self-images. In the following section, I provide a detailed analysis of the implication of China's identity complex to the geopolitical relationships in Asia from both angles.

IMPLICATIONS OF IDENTITY COMPLEX IN GEOPOLITICS

China-Japan

China and Japan both are heavyweights in the Asia-Pacific region. In 2008 they took the third and the second places in the ranking of global economies according to GDP. Their first intense exchange can be traced back to the Tang dynasty in the seventh century. At that time the Chinese empire was at its apex and Japan adopted numerous cultural and political practices from China. However, the bilateral relationship in the following centuries was not always pleasant. In the modern time, Japan quickly accepted the Western system, increased its military power and started to expand towards the continent. Japan's victory in the first Sino-Japanese War (1894-95) fundamentally shocked the Chinese empire. The often neglected former student became a serious rival for the first time. Then it became a model for China's modernization. The emperor launched a reform following the example of the Meiji Restoration in 1898, but failed. Many revolutionists, including Sun Yat-sen and Chiang Kai-shek, went to Japan to learn how to build a new China. After the 1930s, Japan was conceived as the biggest threat to China's existence as it was aggressively encroaching politically, economically and militarily. Japan's full-scale invasion and atrocities in the second Sino-Chinese War (1937-1945) provoked extremely fierce patriotism and a united front on the Chinese side. Chinese found the core of their existence and identity as a nation in its life-death struggle with a modern Japanese nation.

Therefore Japan was both the teacher and the contrasting reference for China in its early response to the modern world. Lu Xun, the famous essayist, recorded how he realized the need of a Chinese nation when he was studying in Japan. One day he saw a screening that documented the execution of an alleged Chinese spy during the Russo-Japanese War. The Japanese was to decapitate him as a "public example"; the other Chinese gathered around him and "enjoyed the spectacle." [27] Those Chinese onlookers might have considered such a decapitation just the same as other numerous examples in the wars between dynasties and regimes. Yet the Japanese classmates' cheers and his own experience in Japan enabled Lu Xun to recognize that it was of a completely different nature. Hence, he gave up his medical education and devoted himself to the spiritual building of Chinese people. In his and other thinkers' efforts, Japan's model can often be recognized as an example for the modern Chinese nation.

Similar dynamism can be found in the economy. In many aspects, China's development path is following that of Japan, the leader of the "flying geese" model in Asia.[28] Japan started from labor-intensive industries such as textiles, electronics and auto parts to catch up with the advanced countries, and later shifted to more technology-intensive industries. This experience was replicated in China after its reform in 1978.[29] At that time, China also largely depended on Japan for a large variety of imports of industrial goods, for advanced technology, for foreign investment, and for precious foreign exchange by selling oil and natural resources.[30]

However, China is not only one of the follower geese. Its sheer size and immense political power naturally pose a serious challenge to Japan's status. Its dazzling development has overshadowed Japan's economic dominance in the region. The gap of technical and social development between these two countries is rapidly closing. The relationship between both countries is becoming more and more competitive, above all in the race for energy and resources. The long battle over the direction of Russian oil pipelines from 2003 to 2005 and the heated dispute over the gas and oil fields in the East China Sea are just two examples of the escalating antagonism.

The economic fight easily can be linked to national struggles; therefore the fluctuation of economic relationships changes the temperature of nationalism in both countries as well. There used to be a Japanese sense of guilt over the war. "Helping China's development through trade was one way that Japan thought it could atone for the damage it caused."[31] This feeling can scarcely be found today. Instead, a few Japanese politicians insisted on visiting the Yasukuni Shrine, where Class-A war criminals are enshrined, to demonstrate certain nationalistic gestures. China was definitely always sensitive to such provocation. Yet the growing economic power and national pride created more aggressive anti-Japan sentiments. Several big Chinese cities held demonstrations to boycott Japanese products during last few years. Properties of Japanese companies were damaged during the parades. Japanese sport teams were treated in a very unfriendly manner on a few occasions.

Paradoxically, China and Japan did not grow apart completely with intensifying competition; on the contrary their economic cooperation became more and more integrated. Bi-lateral trade could be totally cut off for four years as a result of the Nagasaki flag incident in 1958.[32] Now such actions would be absolutely impossible, because the annual trade volume increased over 2000 times from $105.0 million in 1958 to $236.6 billion in 2007. Moreover the dependence used to be relatively one-sided. Japan's importance for China was much larger than China's importance for Japan. For example in 1989 Japan counted 18.8% of China's total exports and 16.7% of its imports; whereas China only counted 3.1% of Japan's exports and 5.3% of its imports.[33] In 2007, China became Japan's largest trading partner and counted 17.7% of Japan's total trade.[34] Japan was also the second largest trading country for China, counting 10.8% of China's total trade.[35] China is no longer merely a supplier of oil and natural resources, but exports mainly electric equipment and imports semiconductors, high-end electronics and automobiles. Their relationship is now a two-way mutual interdependence.

Economic intertwinement is the stabilizing basis to avoid escalating conflicts. However, this economic cooperation can be affected or impeded by nationalistic hostility and mistrust. Japanese companies used to be the market leaders in China in the 1980s. However, they simply positioned China as an overseas production base. The feeling of their superiority to China hindered them from objectively analyzing China's huge potential and realizing its growth.[36] Later, in order to evade the fate of losing its manufacturing competitiveness to China, Japanese companies moved their production bases back home, but only saw companies from other countries filling the space they left.[37] Further, the emphasis on China's threat, the political tension and the cultural prejudice caused a series of misjudgments and inconsistent behaviors in their Chinese operations, ranging from investment strategies, market evaluation, enterprise management and public relations.[38] As a consequence, Japanese business in China lost market to competitors from the U.S., Europe and South Korea. Conversely, the Chinese investment in Japan is making similar mistakes.

The accumulated net overseas investment from China to Japan totaled merely $558 million by the end of 2007, even less than those to Indonesia and Mongolia.[39]

A comparison between Japanese and American business in China shows more clearly that the issue of nation has a much larger impact on Sino-Japanese economic relations than the cultural and political aspects. Japan and China have similar cultures and languages, while the U.S. is from a very different background. After the Tiananmen incident in 1989, the U.S. government imposed economic sanctions against China, whereas Japan did not strictly follow the U.S.'s measures and continued aid to China. Yet the U.S. enterprises were actively carrying out their China strategies in spite of the governmental restriction, but the Japanese companies were reluctant and inconsistent due to their complicated views on China. Hence the Japanese companies now lag significantly behind the U.S. companies in the Chinese market.[40]

Nonetheless, the economic reality and needs are also reshaping the views on national competition. Over the last five years, the Japanese community widely acknowledged that China's rise greatly helped Japan to get out of economic stagnation and to regain momentum. The "China pull theory" is taking the place of "China economic threat theory."[41] China is no longer a follower or a rival, but a rescuer. This new view encouraged Japanese enterprises to launch a new round of investment in China from 2005 on.[42]

In sum, national consciousness continues to be a crucial point in the Sino-Japanese relationship. Since the memory of struggling with Japan is imbedded in the core of the Chinese nation, any slight provocation recalling the past pain would irritate the nation massively and affect a broad spectrum from politics to business. Meanwhile, the geographic proximity and the market demands bring both countries into close economic collaboration. Therefore, their relationship is both the most emotional and the most realistic one. Within each of these two aspects, there are again contrasts. Historically, they were not only rivals in the battlefield, but China was the ancient teacher of Japan and Japan was the model of the modern Chinese nation. Economically they are not merely competitors, but also highly interdependent and mutually beneficial.

Such subtle divisions raise the unpredictability of the bilateral relationship. Small incidents may stir up the antagonistic resentment, which leads to a downturn of business activity. Deteriorating economic ties may cause more misunderstanding and less dialogue. Yet this vicious circle can be turned around if the positive aspects are emphasized. This will reduce political confrontation and nationalistic prejudice. A friendly atmosphere will promote more investments and trade, which further stimulates cultural and social exchange. These two scenarios are both possible. Political leaders and specific incidents may play important roles in determining the direction and fluctuation of trends.[43] Hence, cautions and a balancing attitude are requisites for dealing with sensitive issues.

Another unforeseeable factor is the inevitable reversal of relative strength. Japan's economy was eight times that of China in 1990, but only slightly larger than that of China in 2007, and is expected to be surpassed within five years. By

2030 China's economy will be several times larger than Japan's. This will finally mark the end of China's inferior status since the end of the nineteenth century. Then what will happen to China's national consciousness, which is so intrinsically related to humiliation, crisis, and striving for survival and dignity in the modern times? What will happen to Japan, which has been used to feeling its superiority vis-à-vis China? [44] Will the premodern relationship between a continental hegemony and an island secondary power be restored? Is a replication of the old relationship possible between modern nations and in a globalized market? These questions and their implications are still wide open.

China-Koreas

China and the two Koreas were victims of colonialism. Thus Chinese feel some sort of sympathy with Koreans' resentment against Japan and America. The Koreans, however, have a different view. The Chinese empire is seen as one of the biggest, if not the biggest, threats that Korea has ever faced. Historically, the Korean kings paid tribute to China, but ruled their own country independently. Many Chinese cultural traditions were adopted by Koreans, including writing and Confucianism, because the Chinese culture was regarded as the high culture. This perception was abandoned after Korea established its modern national identity. To further its definite and unique cultural identity, Koreans tried to wash out Chinese influence. For example, the Chinese writing characters (called Hanja in Korea) were mainly replaced in the mid-twentieth century by Hangul, the Korean alphabet. Reviewing its history from the modern perspective of equal nations, Koreans also consider their former tributary status as an indignity. The Chinese imperial superiority, together with the Japanese occupation and the American hegemony, is central to Korea's national consciousness. [45]

With China's reemergence as a superpower, Koreans' anxiety is visible. In 2005 South Korea announced that the Chinese translation of Seoul would be changed from "Han Cheng" to "Shou er." Though the official explanation for this change is to standardize the translation of geographic names, people wonder why South Korea abandoned a translation that has been used for over 600 years. The unspoken reason may be that "Han Cheng" sounds like the city of Han (the major ethic group in China) in Chinese, and Koreans want to avoid such association. [46] At the end of 2007, South Korean media criticized China's "impolite diplomacy," because the Chinese ambassador asked the newly elected president, Lee Myung-Bak, to send a special envoy to Beijing to discuss a bilateral relationship. This request was viewed unfavorably and was compared to the old tributary custom of Korean kings' sending envoys to ask for Beijing's formal approval of their thrones. [47]

China was puzzled by this criticism. To invite a special envoy is to stress the importance of a bi-lateral relationship. Several former South Korean presidents like Roh Moo-hyun did that as well. [48] Why is anti-China nationalism growing in South Korea? Most Chinese accuse Koreans of narrow-mindedness and exaggerating fear, but the Chinese scholar Wang Yigui pointed out that

China's boast of renaissance may be responsible too. Chinese often enjoy remembering their previous glory and they mistakenly believe that national renaissance means rebuilding the country as powerful as it was in ancient times. To some, this seems to be a natural and justified goal because China would merely regain what it lost. However, today's political concept of nations with equal rank as well as current international relationships are completely different from those in the eighteenth century. Any emphasis on restoring the historical Chinese empire can become very disturbing to other nations.[49]

This insight actually raises a critical question for the Chinese national identity: how should China consider its history in a changed world? China's national identity was formed as a reaction to foreign humiliation and invasion, thus the memory of past prosperity and the restoration of the old power is essential to the nation's consciousness and pursuit. Yet the regional and global reality does not allow a fully restoration of ancient China, and neighboring nations like South Korea are highly sensitive to any resemblance of the old empire. China is performing a difficult balancing act between its own internal passion and its neighbors' wariness. Thus far, there has been no simple resolution to this question. Perhaps more in-depth regional communication can promote mutual understanding. The neighbors should see that China's fondness of the past does not imply aggressive imperialism, but is just nostalgic memory after painful suffering and tragedy. Chinese should also take into account other nations' feelings and restrain themselves from touting historic glory and power. It is necessary for both sides to make a clear distinction between China as an ancient empire and China as a modern nation. The Chinese nation is simply a member in the international community with the same status as South Korea, North Korea, Japan, Vietnam and others. The nation and the empire may look similar in geographical area, population and power, but their roles in the international community have nothing in common. Even when China's economy eventually becomes so large that its proportion in the region can be compared to that of ancient Chinese empires, the modern political consciousness and relationships with other nations will not permit a "restoration of empire."

In spite of a few cases of misunderstanding, bilateral exchanges have been wide-ranging, interdependent, and mutually beneficial in the areas of economy, culture, and politics since the establishment of a diplomatic relationship between China and South Korea in 1992. The trade volume amounted to $159.9 billion in 2007 and is expected to reach $200 billion by 2010. Investment in China accounted 41% of South Korea's total overseas investment in 2005. For China, the investment from South Korea exceeded that from Japan and USA in 2007,[50] and it plays a vital role in China's key industries such as electronics, IT, automobiles, and chemistry. The "Korean Wave" (Hanliu) has become a buzzword in China's pop culture, leading trends in TV and cinema, pop music, fashion, and online games.[51] Correspondingly, the "Chinese Wind" (Hanfeng) is growing popular in South Korea. Over 300,000 Koreans are right now learning Chinese. Korean participants in the Chinese Proficiency Test (equivalent to Chinese TOEFL) made up 67% of all the participants worldwide in 2007.[52] Any increase in business and cultural friction is understandable given the intensity of the interactions. Actually some cultural disputes and competitions reflect exactly the commonness of both traditions.[53] A proper division between history and reality, between the old imperial system and the new national relationship is crucial to preventing benign contests from turning into irrational conflicts. Both Chauvinistic arrogance and oversensitive nationalism may spoil the bilateral relationship.

In politics, China and South Korea have to cooperate to solve the conundrum of Pyongyang. North Korea, due to its own riddle-like situation, has its own very complicated views of its big neighbor. North Korea is an ethnically purist country. Recently a North Korean general even chastised South Korea for allowing intermarriage.[54] Such extreme nationalism cannot tolerate being subordinate to another nation: therefore North Koreans have an inherent resentment against China, exactly because China is its factual protector. There is neither display in the museums nor introduction in the textbooks about China's role in the Korean War. Instead, Kim Il-sung is described as the sole leader of the victory.[55] Related to the ethnic purism is a radical ideological orthodoxy. North Korea views itself as the true leader of Marxism and no longer sees China as a communist country.[56] However, Kim Jong-il's regime would quickly collapse without China's political support. Its economy relies on China for food and energy, for as much as 80% of its imports of consumer goods and for roughly 40% of its trade—double that of South Korea.[57] North Korea's economic reform, which started in 2002, uses China's successful experience as its example.[58] North Korea's economy is so dependent on and integrated with China that it is often referred to as China's fourth northeastern province.[59]

In contrast, South Korea and North Korea are from the same nation and their interaction is free of problems related to national dignity. Yet South Korea is a political and military rival, threatening the existence of the North Korean regime. These two aspects are precisely complementary to China's roles as both a powerful foreign nation, but a political ally to some extent. Hence combined efforts by China and South Korea are vital to a smooth transformation of North Korea and future stability in the Korean Peninsula.

China-Southeast Asia

Historically, most Southeast Asian countries have had little conflict with China, and they do not feel any direct concrete threat to their existence by China. Only Vietnam, like Korea, has been at war with Chinese troops several times; but it has adopted many Chinese cultural traditions as well and has a unique relationship with China.

The Chinese emperors believed that military actions in Southeast Asia would be too costly and the value of conquest would be too little due to its remoteness from China's heartland.[60] The emperors' disinterest in overseas expansion can be seen from their policy of banning all maritime activities (Haijin) since the fourteenth century. The only exception was Zhen He's expeditions between 1403 and 1433. Yet with an immense fleet of up to three hundred ships and 28,000 crewmen,[61] Zhen He neither took an inch of land nor promoted trade. His purpose was merely to look for a missing emperor and to display the might of the newly established Ming dynasty.[62] Most Southeast Asian countries paid tribute to China, but they were always rewarded with more presents thanks to the emperors' diplomatic slogan of "Giving more and getting less"(Houwang Bolai). Thus, many countries very actively and happily joined China's tributary system for the benefits it provided.[63] Because of distance and historic peace, the notion of a Chinese empire is much less intimidating and sensational in the national consciousness of Southeast Asia compared with Korean and Japanese perceptions. Their relationships with China are less affected by nationalistic feelings, but more by realistic interests and needs.

Southeast Asian countries' more recent concerns about China are related to their own social and political realities. A major issue is the role of the Chinese ethnic community: nearly 28 million Chinese diaspora reside in Southeast Asia today.[64] Most of them are descendants of nineteenth-century migrants from southern China. Called "Jews of the East," they dominate the region's business activity, controlling a large portion of these countries wealth. (see table 3.1)

Table 3.1 Percentage of Corporate Wealth of Chinese Owned Companies in the Stock Market and the Percentage of Ethnic Chinese in the Population

	Thailand	Singapore	Malaysia	Philippines	Indonesia
% of the total corporate wealth	80%	80%	62%	50%	>70%*
% of the total population	10%	80%	26%	2%	3%

Note: *This figure is disputed.
Source: Mangai Balasegaram, "Analysis: South-East Asia's Chinese," BBC News, August 29, 2001, at http://news.bbc.co.uk/2/hi/asia-pacific/1514916.stm (accessed on March 18, 2009).

Ethnic Chinese businessmen greatly facilitated investment and trade between China and Southeast Asia. Their dominance in local economies is even more obvious with China's rise and enhanced bilateral economic ties. China is now among the top two or three trading partners for all the Southeast Asian countries. Sino-ASEAN trade has grown from $8 billion in 1981 to over $130 billion in 2005.[65] However this tendency contributes to unease among the local societies. The increasing wealth gap upsets other ethnic groups, especially when they lose their jobs to the cheaper labor in China. The governments worry about political and economic sovereignty.[66] They are suspicious that ethnic Chinese communities move capital from local economies to invest in mainland China.[67] The impact of China in these countries is translated into domestic problems through the Chinese diaspora. The domestic ethnic conflict may adversely influence diplomatic relations. This dynamics is perpetuated by the implication of China for this region's ethnical composition.

Contemporary Southeast Asian history has witnessed several times how concern about China's power and the tension of domestic ethnic relations affect each other. For example, when China was exporting communism to Southeast Asia in the early 1960s, many Chinese Indonesians joined the Indonesian communist party. After the failed coup by the communist party, the anti-communist purge not only targeted ethnic Chinese for ideological reasons, but also because of enmity against wealthy Chinese. Consequently, China cut its diplomatic relationship with Indonesia.[68] Other countries like Vietnam, the Philippines, and Cambodia have similar anti-Chinese histories.

However, as the meaning of China itself is transforming as globalization increases, the identity of Chinese diaspora is adjusting to the new environment as well. While the old generation still had strong attachment to mainland China because of its Sinocentric vision and tradition of returning to its roots, the younger generation does not see China as motherland. An ethnic Chinese may even be offended by being addressed as "overseas Chinese," since the country of residence has become the real home.[69] Often, the purpose of investing or running a business in China is to take profit back to the new home. The Chinese diaspora keep their ethnic networks, Chinese language education and Confucian values for social capital and as business tools.[70] Learning a lesson from Indonesia of the 1960s, the Chinese government also cautiously avoids making any impression of manipulating the ethnic Chinese community to interfere in local politics.[71] In the case of inter-ethnic conflicts, like the attacks against Chinese in Indonesia in May 1998, it was no longer an issue between two countries, but the international community came to assistance in accordance with international common practice.[72]

In the territorial dispute over Spratly Islands, China and Southeast Asian countries are willing to negotiate multilaterally with each other and work towards common development of the South China Sea. China assiduously participated in ASEAN-led institutions and became the first external signatory to the Treaty of Amity and Cooperation in 2003, a symbolic gesture towards its acceptance of ASEAN norms.[73] The establishment of the China-ASEAN Free Trade Area is progressing and expected to be completed in 2010 as scheduled.

From these latest developments, we can see that China and Southeast Asian countries in general have little difficulty in settling controversies peacefully through dialogue and agreements between governments. Thanks to a less conflictive history of bilateral interaction, the pragmatic diplomacy does not receive much pressure from domestic public sentiment. A powerful China is acceptable and even welcomed by Southeast Asia, because when China has been strong and stable, regional order has been preserved. The region suffered from chaos when China was weak.[74] As long as the anxiety over their independence can be soothed by unambiguous distinction between historic ethnicity and the modern nation-state, as long as their sovereignty and demands can be guaranteed and respected through multilateral negotiation and international institutions, the Southeast Asian countries are ready to integrate with China to form the world's largest free trade marketplace of 1.8 billion people with a total trade volume exceeding $1.2 trillion.

Taiwan and Tibet Issues

Officially Taiwan and Tibet are unequivocally recognized by the international community as belonging to the People's Republic of China. However, there are numerous sub-positions and sub-trends with very different interpretations and consequences under the formal consensus. These sophisticated disputes make the status of Taiwan and Tibet extremely controversial. Due to the complexity and importance of these two areas, they constitute the primary issues of China's relationship with other countries. Primary here means both basic and fundamental. The issues are basic because the first condition for developing bilateral relations is to recognize One China and China's territorial integrity. The issues are fundamental because deviations from these principles may result in severe consequences in political and economic cooperation. Moreover, several great powers are involved in these two considerations, including the U.S., Japan, India, Europe and others. Thus appropriate understanding of the disputes and cautious actions can contribute to the stability and prosperity of the entire region.

Various viewpoints can basically be divided into two contradictory understandings. On the one hand, China stated that Taiwan and Tibet have been parts of China for many centuries, and any moves towards independence are separatist behaviors. On the other hand, China is accused of using overwhelming political power and military force to annex neighbors and suppress their autonomy. Those who hold this view observe Tibet and Taiwan as nations originally outside of China, while China considers dealing with them merely as domestic affairs. These arguments produce two opposing images of China, as an aggressive expansionist or as a self-defender posing no threat to foreign countries. Which one is true?

Both sides seem to find support from history and international analogies. As to Tibet, it was not only a tributary state like Vietnam or Korea. Since the thirteenth century, Beijing has set up central and local level administrations to manage Tibet as a region within the empire. [75] However, this kind of administration was not the same as the provincial system in China's heartland. Tibet had a good deal of autonomy in religious, cultural, economic and administrative affairs. Hence, this historic relationship is a double-edged sword for a modern interpretation. It is possible for some people to define Tibet as a nation in respect of its unique culture and relative independence; but it is also plausible to say that Tibet has been in the multiethnic Chinese nation, which basically inherited the border of the empire. For the former view, Mongolia is an example; for the latter, Manchuria and Xinjiang are examples. Here the question is to which extent the premodern empire structure can be translated into the definition of a modern nation.

In contrast, Taiwan's ethnicity, culture, and language are almost homogenous with those of the mainland, but the sixty-years-long division of political power created an apparent gap of understanding. The different ideological outlooks, the factual autonomy, and the stress on local culture have recently encouraged the consciousness on Taiwan that Taiwan is an independent nation.[76] Here, the original separation of state power within a nation gradually led to the transformation of national identity on Taiwan.[77] However, this identity is not widely acknowledged internationally. Even within Taiwan, many people still believe that Taiwanese culture is just a part of Chinese culture.

Hence, the puzzle of these two questions does not merely stem from the clashes between imperial system and national system or between national boundary and the border of state, but principally from the ambiguity of the concept of nation. What defines a nation? Politics, culture, ethnicity, religion, language, history, and so forth? All of these factors are related, but none of them alone are decisive. There are nations like Japan with a relatively clear identity, but also nations like India having extreme diversity. Originating from Europe in the eighteenth century, the meaning of nation lost its clarity when it was applied in an Asian context. A detailed discussion of how to define a nation is beyond the scope of this chapter. The point is just to show that China's dramatic changes last century and an imported ambiguous concept make the identities of Tibet and Taiwan very problematic.

Therefore, it is understandable that there are disagreements on these issues. However, it is remarkable that the choices of various viewpoints are further complicated by the mixed perceptions of China. First, from the political perspective, the countries which want to counter China certainly tend to accept the pro-independence interpretation, and the countries which have befriended China choose the opposite view. This criterion was most visible during the Cold War, but still remains influential in the real politics of today. Second, from the social perspective, different collective memories create different thinking patterns. China's memory focuses on Western colonialism and imperialist intervention. Thus Britain's invasion and manipulation was stressed in Tibet's departure from China in the early twentieth century. Likewise the U.S.'s naval fleet and its self-interest were regarded as the main obstacle to Taiwan's reunification. In contrast, Westerners have images of a totalitarian communist regime crushing small countries and building an immense state machine. Accordingly their observation emphasizes ideology and political system. Finally, from the emotional perspective bystanders tend to give sympathy to the small and weak parties vis-à-vis the gigantic China. However, China feels an unfair affront by such sympathy to Tibet and Taiwan, because these problems were caused by colonialism and foreign intervention. China is itself a victim.

With all this structural, conceptual and perceptional bifurcation, it's no wonder that Tibet and Taiwan are becoming conundrums in the regional politics. With nationalistic feelings and state interests combined, these questions are both emotional and realistic. Inappropriate actions may trigger serious international crises and threaten regional stability. Hence the first step toward a peaceful solution is to have a comprehensive view of different angles and to discard single-minded self-righteousness. Simplistic rejection of the opposite side contributes to nothing but provoking confrontation, hurting feelings, and disrupting normal life of related people. People can have multiple identities, to be a Chinese citizen as well as an ethnical Tibetan, to belong to the Chinese nation as well as to the Taiwanese community. Only when tension escalates, the coexistence of these identities becomes a painful dilemma.

Accordingly, to respect the status quo and avoid tensions can guarantee the essential well-being of these two regions and lead to a coordinated solution. Overstress of a certain identity is always partial and arbitrary. Radical change of political status and structure will certainly bring a series of radical reactions and counter-reactions. Only stable political systems can provide the framework for peaceful coordination, transformation and convergence by eliminating violent conflicts. Besides, stable politics can also promote the cultural and economic interactions between different regions, construct infrastructures to facilitate communication and eventually realize a mutual respect and mutually beneficial integration.

Nonetheless economic development is not an omnipotent recipe. At times market competition can cause new grievances among people. For instance, many Tibetans feel disadvantaged in the market economy because their language and education hinder them from sharing equally with the Han-Chinese the benefits of development. Their economic dissatisfaction and fear for their cultural existence can enlarge their distance from the main body of the China. The unemployed Taiwanese may as well blame mainland China for taking away their jobs and hope to reduce ties with the mainland.

To summarize, no one-dimensional, one-party, or one-time program can really solve the Taiwan and Tibet problems. The complexity left by their history requires comprehensive and long-term response too. That's to say, caution and patience are the two keys. Cautions are needed to understand different positions and the whole situation, to make any political and institutional move, and to examine the impact of every concrete practice so as to ensure mutual benefits. Patience is invaluable because the Chinese nation is still in formation. There are inevitable fluctuations and disagreements in this process. People should not hasten to reach a conclusion or an ultimate solution, but instead focus on mutually beneficial interactions in economic, cultural, and social fields. Common development and prosperity in the long run will naturally eliminate all the unreasonable barriers and forge essential ties.

CONCLUSION

To understand China and its role in the geopolitics of the Asia-Pacific region, the unique complexity of China's identity should never be neglected. The uniqueness is rooted in the relatively isolated history and culture of this region in ancient times. The complexity is molded through the collision of the original tradition with Western civilization in the modern era, and through the ensuing drastic metamorphosis of this region.

The most crucial point is that China as a substantial entity basically survived the turbulence. Hence it has incorporated various aspects into a unity. Contemporary China has inherited so many antique features that it can be observed as the continuity of the old empire, but it has also absorbed so many modern elements that it appears in completely new outlooks. This makes China comparable to the huge crystal New Year's Eve Ball in New York's Times Square, which has tens of thousands of facets and can demonstrate kaleidoscopic patterns. On various occasions, from various angles, and for various people, this ball displays various views. It also mirrors the change of the observers themselves.

Roughly speaking, today's China has four main sides: empire as the primary source of identity, nation as the substantial unity, state as the definite political entity, and market as the versatile transformer. These sides are not separated, but depend on one another and affect one another. However there is no one universal rule to decide the display patterns of these identities because they are formed through an unusually complicated history and they are constantly evolving in a changing world. The highlight of one aspect or the co-appearance of several aspects as well as the concrete form of appearance is contingent on specific countries, specific contexts, specific issues and specific reactions

The relationship between China and Japan centers on nation and economy because of history and business reality. The intense emotion and interest involved drives the synergy of nation and economy up and down. The Koreas and China also have nationalistic friction, but to a much milder degree. Their cultural, political and economic collaborations are rarely distracted by nationalism. Without a complicated history, China and Southeast Asia can solve their disputes and enhance their ties principally through calculation of economic interest. In contrast, Taiwan and Tibet issues are highly controversial and sensitive because they are outcomes of the East-West confrontation at multiple levels and question the core identity of the Chinese nation.

This complexity is both a challenge and an opportunity. Inappropriate exaggeration of a certain aspect, such as nationalism or ideology, may harm other aspects and severely affect the overall bilateral relationship or the regional stability. Yet multiple facets also provide plenty of flexibility and leeway for solutions from other paths. The key is to comprehend the whole picture, grasp the fundamental origin and reasoning of conflicts, analyze the issues concretely and implement the strategies cautiously and pragmatically.

Finally, the identities and their dynamism are created by historic process, but can also be further modified by future events. Conflicts may agitate new waves and forms of nationalism, cultural and economic exchange may promote the image of an open and nonexclusive nation. The process of formation and adaptation is still ongoing. It's up to us to guide it appropriately with a thorough understanding of the historic roots and fundamental concepts.

NOTES

[1] See Zhao Yuntian, "Primary Investigation of the court of suzerainty management in Qing Dynasty" [Qingdai lifanyuan chutan], *Journal of the Central University for*

Nationalities (Philosophy and Social Sciences Edition) [Zhongyang minzu daxue xuebao], No. 1, 1982.

[2] Hong Huanchun, "the friendly external relationship in the early Ming Dynast and Zhenhe's voyage" [Mingchu duiwai youhao guanxi yu zhenhe xiaxiyang], in *Anthology of Papers on Zhenhe's Expeditions* [Zhenhe xiaxiyang lunwenji], China, Beijing: People's Transportation Publishing House [Renmin jiaotong chubanshe], 1985, pp. 148-71.

[3] Charles Taylor, *Hegel and Modern Society*, UK, Cambridge: Cambridge University Press, 1979, p. 2.

[4] Zheng Xiyuan, *The Memory of an Empire* [Diguo de huiyi], China, Beijing: Joint Publishing [Sanlian shudian], 2001, p. 361.

[5] The central research office of the history of the Communist Party of China [Zhonggong zhongyang dangshi yanjiushi], *A Brief History of the Communist Party of China*, Chapter [Zhongguo gongchandang jianshi], chapter II, at http://cpc.people.com.cn/GB/64184/64190/65724/4444690.html (accessed on March 17, 2009).

[6] Mao Zedong, "Chang Our Study" in *Selected Works of Mao Zedong* [Mao Zedong xuanji], China, Beijing: People's Publishing House [Renmin chubanshe], Vol. 3, 1991, p. 801.

[7] CCP organized several national campaigns in the 1930s and 1940s to address anti-imperialism issues like "U.S. army out of China" [Meijun tuichu zhongguo] (1946) and acute social crisis like "Save education crisis" [Qiangjiu jiaoyu weiji], "Anti-hunger" [Fan ji'e] (1947), but mentioned little about proletariat revolution.

[8] The ideological campaigns from 1957 to 1976 deserve a detailed analysis, which I cannot do here. It is to point out that this unusual period was related to the ideological fever and political tension in the Cold War. This period left deep scars in the nation's memory, impacted the structure of state and marketplace, and produced lots of prejudice against the state.

[9] "The Four Cardinal Principles" are 1. to keep to the socialist road, 2. to uphold the people's democratic dictatorship, 3. to uphold leadership by the Communist Party of China, and 4. to uphold Marxism-Leninism and Mao Zedong Thought.

[10] Constitution of the Communist Party of China, General Program, amended and adopted on November. 14, 2002.

[11] Mao Zedong, "Opening announcement" *Xiang River Comments* [Xiangjiang pinglun], Vol. 1, July 14, 1919.

[12] Mao Zedong, "The Grand Union of People" [Minzhong de dalianhe] *Xiang River Comments* [Xiangjiang pinglun], Vol. 2-4, July-August, 1919.

[13] Li Rui, The Early Years and Late Years of Mao Zedong [Mao Zedong de zaonian yu wannian], China, Guiyang: *Guizhou People's Publishing House* [Guizhou Renmin chubanshe], p. 119-34.

[14] Mao Zedong, "Speech in the Convention of Celebrating Stalin's 60th Anniversary in Yan'an" [Zai yanan gejie qingzhu sidalin liushi souchen dahuishang de jianghua," December 21, 1939.

[15] Doug Gutherie, *China and Globalization*, New York: Routledge, 2006, p. 30.

[16] Richard Pipes, *Russia Under the Bolshevik Regime*, New York: Vintage Books, Random House Inc., 1995, pp. 272-82.

[17] W. Scott Morton and Charlton M. Lewis, *China: its History and Culture*, New York: McGraw-Hill Inc., 2005, p. 205.

[18] Tang Xiaoyang, "Beyond the Red Tiananmen" conference paper presented in symposium *1989 and Beyond: The Future of Democracy*, New York, April 19, 2008.

[19] Morton and Lewis, *China: its History and Culture*, p. 242.

[20] Three Represents mean: the CCP represents the development trend of China's advanced productive forces, the orientation of China's advanced culture and the fundamental interests of the overwhelming majority of the Chinese people.

[21] Morton and Lewis, *China: its History and Culture*, p. 244.

[22] Emage Company, *Directory of Enterprises with foreign investment in China 2009*, at http://industry.emagecompany.com/foreign/investment.html (accessed on March 17, 2009).

[23] Yu Mi, "Does Foreign Investment affect China's economic safety?" [Waizi yinxiang zhongguo jingji anquan?] at http://www.southcn.com/FINANCE/hot/200411240473.htm (accessed on March 17, 2009); Chen Mo, "How to understand Foreign Investment's impact on China's economy" [Ruhe kandai waizi dui zhongguo jingji de yinxiang], *China Economic Times* [Zhongguo jingji shibao], October 20, 2004.

[24] Ministry of Commerce of the People's Republic of China, February, 2009.

[25] See Thomas L. Friedman, *The World is Flat: A brief history of the twenty-first century.* New York: Farrar Straus Giroux, 2006, Chapter 2.

[26] See Morton and Lewis, *China: its History and Culture*, pp. 198-99.

[27] Lu Xun, "Preface to *Nahan*" [Nahan zixu] in *Collected Classics of Lu Xun* [Luxun jingdian quanji], China, Beijing: Beijing Publishing House, 2007.

[28] On the "flying geese model," see Kiyoshi Kojima, "The 'flying geese' model of Asian economic development: origin, theoretical extensions, and regional policy implications," *Journal of Asian Economics*, Vol. 11, No. 4, Winter 2000, pp. 375-401.

[29] Tri Widodo, "Dynamic changes in comparative advantage: Japan "flying geese" model and its implications for China." *Journal of Chinese Economic and Foreign Trade Studies*, Vol. 1, No. 3, 2008, p. 200.

[30] Tomozo Morino, "China Japan trade and investment relations" *Proceedings of the Academy of Political Science* Vol. 38, No. 2, 1991, pp. 89-90; Deborah Brautigam, *China's African Aid, Transatlantic Challenges*, The German Marshall Fund of the United States, 2008, p. 10.

[31] Tomozo Morino, "China Japan trade and investment relations," p. 89.

[32] See Jerome Alan Cohen, *The Dynamics of China's Foreign Relations*, Association for Asian Studies Edition: 2, Harvard University Asia Center, 1973, pp. 46-7.

[33] Tomozo Morino, "China Japan trade and investment relations," p. 89.

[34] Japan External Trade Organization, "China Overtakes the U.S. as Japan's Largest Trading Partner," at http://www.jetro.go.jp/en/news/releases/20080229066-news (accessed on March 17, 2009).

[35] Ministry of Commerce of the People's Republic of China, Import and Export Statistics 2007.

[36] Park SeungHo, "A Korean Analyzing the Puzzle of the Decline of Japanese Enterprises in China" [Hanguoren fenxi riben qiye zaizhongguo shuaibai zhimi], at http://news.21cn.com/luntan/retie/2007/11/08/3855454.shtml (accessed on March 17, 2009).

[37] Asia-Pacific Economic Times [Yatai jingji shibao] "Underestimation Cost Japanese Enterprises in China" [Riqi qingshi zhongguo fuchu daijia], at http://www.ce.cn/new_hgjj/hgplun/more/200411/26/t20041126_2398824.shtml (accessed on March 17, 2009).

[38] Park SeungHo, "A Korean Analyzing the Puzzle of the Decline of Japanese Enterprises in China"; Lin huasheng, "Why Japanese Enterprises' Development in China Lag Behind?" [Riben qiye xiang zhongguo fazhan weihe luohou], at http://www.zaobao.com/special/china/sino_jp/pages/sino_jp221101.html (accessed on March 17, 2009).

[39] Ministry of Commerce of the People's Republic of China, Statistical Bulletin of China's Outward Foreign Direct Investment 2007.

[40] Lin huasheng, "Why Japanese Enterprises' Development in China Lag Behind?"

[41] Hitoshi Tanaka, "A Japanese perspective on the China Question," *East Asia Insights* Vol. 3 No. 2, May 2008, p. 2.

[42] Zhang Liming, "New Round of Storm: Japanese Enterprises Enter Automobile and Home Appliance Industries" [Xinyilun fengbao: Riqi jinjun jiadian he qicheye], at http://finance.qq.com/a/20050422/000169.htm (accessed on March 17, 2009).

[43] For example, Zhou Enlai played a major role in repairing Sino-China relationship. See Tomozo Morino, "China Japan trade and investment relations," p. 91.

[44] Hitoshi Tanaka, "A Japanese perspective on the China Question," pp. 1-2.

[45] Philip Bowring, "A potent, troubling nationalism" at http://www.iht.com/articles/2008/06/16/opinion/edbowring.php (accessed on March 17, 2009).

[46] Zhou Yongsheng, "Deep Cultural Root behind the Name Change of Seoul," at http://www.gmw.cn/CONTENT/2005-01/22/content_169645.htm (accessed on March 17, 2009).

[47] Huanqiu Times [Huanqiu Shibao], "South Korean Media Criticizing Chinese Diplomatic Manner and Provoking Anti-Chinese Sentiments" [Hanmei wuduan zhize zhongguo waijiao lijie, jiqi wangmin fanhua qingxu], at http://www.krdrama.com/bbs/viewthread.php?tid=261751&extra=&page=1 (accessed on March 17, 2009).

[48] Ibid.

[49] Wang Yigui, "Facing the concerns of South Korean nationalism about China's renaissance" [Ying zhengshi hanguo minzu zhuyi dui zhongguo fuxing de danyou], at http://hi.baidu.com/zhangjunjun101/blog/item/5f559803362de58cd53f7c71.html (accessed on March 17, 2009).

[50] Ministry of Commerce of the People's Republic of China, Import and Export Statistics 2007.

[51] http://news.sohu.com/20071226/n254299730.shtml

[52] Chuan Wang, "Korean Wave vs. Chinese Wind" [Hanliu vs Hanfeng], at http://www.fmprc.gov.cn/chn/wjb/wjly/t476110.htm (accessed on March 18, 2009.

[53] Lianhe Morning News [Lianhe zaobao], "Chinese Wind against KoreanWave, South Korea concerned" [Hafeng fanhanliu, hanguo biaoyiulu], at http://www2.irib.ir/worldservice/chinese/news/05-10-06/05100603.htm (accessed on March 18, 2009.

[54] Peter Maass, "Ratioactive Nationalism," *The New York Times Magazine*, Oct 22, 2006, p. 36.

[55] Jinsi Wang, "How North and South Korea Describe China in Korean War" [Chaoxian hanguo ruhe xuanchuan zhongguo kangmei yuanchao], at http://world.huanqiu.com/roll/2009-03/393306.html (accessed on March 18, 2009).

[56] International Crisis Group. *China and North Korea: Comrades Forever?* Crisis Group Asia Report No. 112, February 1, 2006, p. 15.

[57] International Crisis Group. *China and North Korea: Comrades Forever?* pp. 3, 26.

[58] Ma, Jin and Zhang Le, "North Korean Economic Reform Launched with Experiments, Reform Borrowing Chinese Experience?" [Chaoxian jingji gaige tansuozhong qidong, gaige jiejian zhongguo jingyan?], at http://www.china.com.cn/chinese/HIAW/1184645.htm (accessed on March 18, 2009.

[59] International Crisis Group. *China and North Korea: Comrades Forever?* p. 4.

[60] Hong Huanchun, "the friendly external relationship in the early Ming Dynasty and Zhenhe's voyage."

[61] Richard Gunde, Zheng He's voyages of discovery, at http://www.international.ucla.edu/asia/news/article.asp?parentid=10387 (accessed on March 18 2009).

[62] Hou Yangfang, "The Truth of Why Ming Dynasty Banned Maritime Activities" [Mingchao weihe shixing haijin de zhenxiang], at http://culture.163.com/06/0206/10/2996MI9100281M4P.html (accessed on March 18, 2009).

[63] Dong Wei, "Four Anecdotes of 'Gettting less and Giving more' in Zhenghe's expeditions" [Zhenghe zhilu houwang bolai de siduan yiwen], at http://www.chinanews.com.cn/news/2005/2005-07-12/26/597914.shtml (accessed on March 18, 2009).

[64] Overseas Compatriot Affairs Commission, *Statistical Yearbook of the Overseas Compatriot Affair Commission,* China, Taiwan, 2007.

[65] Evelyn Goh, "China and Southeast Asia," Foreign Policy in Focus Commentary, at http://www.fpif.org/fpiftxt/3780 (accessed on March 18, 2009).

[66] Mangai Balasegaram, "Analysis: South-East Asia's Chinese," BBC News, August 29, 2001, at http://news.bbc.co.uk/2/hi/asia-pacific/1514916.stm (accessed on March 18, 2009).

[67] Steven Jackson, "Book Review of *China and Southeast Asia's Ethnic Chinese,*" *Journal of Third World Studies,* spring 2005, p. 235.

[68] Adrian Vickers, *A History of Modern Indonesia,* UK, Cambridge: Cambridge University Press, 2005, p. 158.

[69] Michael Jacobsen, "Re-Conceptualising Notions of Chinese-ness in a Southeast Asian Context," *East Asia* Vol. 24, 2007, p. 226.

[70] Gordon Cheung, "Chinese Diaspora as a Virtual Nation: Interactive Roles between Economic and Social Capital," *Political Studies,* Vol 52, p. 675-78.

[71] Li, Meng, "Ethnic Chinese Remembering 98 Anti-Chinese Riot in Indonesia" [Huaqiao huiyi 98 yinni paihua saoluan], at http://news.qq.com/a/20080619/001351.htm (accessed on March 18, 2009).

[72] Michael Jacobsen, "Re-Conceptualising Notions of Chinese-ness in a Southeast Asian Context," p. 227.

[73] Evelyn Goh, "China and Southeast Asia."

[74] David Kang, "Getting Asia Wrong", *International Security* Vol. 27, No. 4, Spring 2003, p. 66; Evelyn Goh, "China and Southeast Asia."

[75] Zhang Chuanxi, *A brief history of ancient China,* [jianming zhongguo gudaishi], China, Beijing: Beijing University Publishing House [Beijing daxue chubanshe], 1991, Chapter VII, section 3.

[76] Chen Shuibian, Speech in the 29th Annual Convention of Global Taiwanese Association, Japan, Tokyo, August 2, 2002.

[77] See Wang Horng-luen, *In Want of a Nation: State, Institutions and Globalization in Taiwan,* Ph. D. diss., The University of Chicago, 1999.

Chapter 4

Globalization and Cross-Strait Relations

Jing Men

INTRODUCTION

To define globalization is not an easy task. As has been pointed out by Scholte, there are a variety of ways to understand what globalization is.[1] "The problem with globalization" is that "it is not a single process, but a complex of processes,... it is therefore difficult to reduce globalization to a single theme."[2] The impact of globalization has been studied by many scholars in the social, political and security fields, but "these are derived from economic change where the basis of production and of finance are said to have shifted from the confines of national boundaries to encompass the world as a whole."[3] The economic interaction between states to facilitate global economic activities has repercussions in many fields and at different levels, and recasts interstate relations. Generally speaking, the three dimensions of globalization, the material, ideational and institutional—constitute "the context of habits, pressures, expectations and constraints within which actions take place."[4] The examination of these three dimensions will illustrate the impacts of globalization on the participants in this process.

Globalization has introduced a new factor to the traditional understanding of international relations in the post-Cold War era. Economic development has joined political and security concerns to become a high political issue. China, as a beneficiary of globalization, has not only successfully turned its economy into the fastest developing and one of the most influential, but has also become a widely recognized political power in contemporary world affairs. China has just overtaken Germany this year to become the world's third largest economy. Globalization has integrated China more closely to regional and international organizations. China became a member of the World Bank and International Monetary Fund in 1980 and was accepted by the World Trade Organization in 2001 after fifteen years of negotiations. What is worth noting in such a series of developments is that China has been changing its approaches in the field of diplomatic relations. Rather than focusing solely on bilateral relations, China has been paying more attention to multilateral cooperation and coordination. China has changed from being an isolated country into an open and active actor in world affairs.[5] China's rising influence worldwide goes together with increased confidence, flexibility and pragmatism in its international relations.

Globalization has also brought new dimensions to the analysis of cross-Strait relations. Unification of Taiwan is the ultimate goal of Mainland China. Beijing takes the opportunity of economic globalization to realize its peaceful rise. Apart from diplomatic and political efforts, Beijing has been active in promoting economic interdependence across the Taiwan Strait. The developments in cross-Strait relations in the era of globalization indicate that the deepened economic connections between the two sides will lay an important foundation for ultimate unification. But what is the impact of globalization on cross-Strait relations? To find the answer to this question, the chapter will first examine the impact of globalization on the developments of both Mainland China and Taiwan in economic growth, institutional buildup and changes of foreign policy, and ideational adjustments. It will then study investment, trade and economic cooperation across the Strait, review the evolution of "1992 consensus" and the recent interactions between the two sides on identity formation, and analyze the implications of these developments. The conclusion of the chapter will summarize the research results and tentatively outline the possible future development of the Taiwan issue.

GLOBALIZATION AND ITS IMPACT ON MAINLAND CHINA AND TAIWAN

Economic Impact

Mainland China and Taiwan have different experiences of economic development. They started with different initial conditions and adopted different development strategies in the three decades starting from 1950.[6] However, at the beginning of the 21st century, marked by China's accession to the WTO (Taiwan gained the membership on the same occasion as a customs union), the two sides of the Taiwan Strait demonstrated their positive attitude to globalization and their expectations of greater gains by supporting this trend.

In his report to the 17th National Party Congress, Chinese General Party Secretary Hu Jintao stated that "reform and opening up constitute the most salient feature of the new period." Thanks to reform and opening up, "China is standing rock-firm in the East, oriented toward modernization, the world and the future.... Facts have incontrovertibly proved that the decision to begin reform and opening up is vital to the destiny of contemporary China, that reform and opening up is the only way of ...rejuvenating the Chinese nation."[7] Hu's report indicated that Beijing strongly believes that openness is the right choice. Thanks to the decision of reform and openness at the end of 1970s, the country has been able to benefit from the process of globalization.

When the People's Republic of China was founded in 1949, the first generation leadership led by Mao Zedong chose to follow an economic policy of self-sufficiency against the hostile Cold War background. Under the planned economy system, the Ministry of Foreign Trade was set up in 1952. The Chinese government kept tight state control over imports and exports and only a limited number of state trade corporations were allowed to do business with foreign companies. With the major purpose of import-substitution, foreign trade played only a subordinated role in the national economy. As explained by the Chinese Minister of Foreign Trade in 1955, trade policy was: "Export is for import and import is for socialist industrialization."[8] Foreign trade was operated within national plan and administrative orders up until the decision on economic reform was taken by Chinese leader Deng Xiaoping.

Notwithstanding hesitation and problems, the Chinese leadership has been adhering to the open-door policy and has adapted many practices to meet the challenges of globalization. Gradually, the country's development strategy shifted to an active interaction with the world economy in which foreign trade becomes the major engine of growth. During the past three decades, Mainland China has grown to be a world economic power. Its membership of the World Trade Organization (WTO) is particularly important in stimulating trade relations with other countries. Its foreign trade grew 22.4 percent in 2002, 34.6 percent in 2003 and 35.4 percent in 2004.[9] Currently, it has become the world's third-largest trading nation, after the United States and Germany—it is the largest trading partner of Japan, Australia and South Korea, the second largest trading partner of the United States and the European Union, and the third largest trading partner of Africa. It overtook Japan in 2006 and has become the world's largest holder of foreign currency reserves. Due to China's undeniable influence in the international economy, the G8 has noticeably strengthened its cooperation and coordination with China in recent years concerning important international economic and financial affairs.[10]

Compared to Mainland China, the development of Taiwan has followed a different but comparable trajectory. After the Nationalist Party fled to Taiwan in 1949, Taiwan's economic success had for several decades been widely reported by the world. Having benefited from the security protection offered by the United States, the Nationalist Party could focus on stimulating economic development and participating in the post-war revitalization of the Western economy. Between 1952 and 1980, Taiwan kept an annual economic growth rate of 9.21 percent, the highest in the world during that period.[11] With its noticeable economic achievements, Taiwan had become one of the four Asian Tigers with a strong economy and a respectable level of economic prosperity. From 1980 till the end of 1990s, due to the changes in the international economic and political environment, the economic growth rate in Taiwan was affected negatively and lowered to an average of 7.15 percent.[12] The growth rate further declined in the first years of the 21st century to around 4 percent. Although such a performance is not as satisfactory as it was, compared to the other developed economies, it indicates a normal and stable mode of development.[13] It is worth noting that despite all the problems, Taiwan remains an important economic power. In 2007, it was the world's 16th largest economy, the 10th largest trading power, and the third largest holder of foreign exchange reserves after China and Japan.[14] Dynamic foreign trade leads Mainland China and Taiwan to be more interdependent in the 21st century. Nevertheless, Taiwan is outperformed in its economic growth by Mainland China. Steve Tsang, a Taiwan scholar at St. Antony's College, Oxford, said, "We are in the midst of a China fever. Taiwan is no doubt losing out in its efforts to attract attention from the rest of the world when the latter is infatuated with China."[15]

Institutional Development

Mainland China gained membership of the United Nations and its Security Council in 1971, but only showed real willingness to be engaged in this global organization in the 1980s. The changes were due to the fact that under the leadership of Deng Xiaoping, China decided to open itself to the outside world. The goal to revitalize China and to bring power and prosperity to the country mobilized Deng Xiaoping and his supporters to embrace international institutions and to benefit from cooperation with the other members in these institutions. China's membership of intergovernmental organizations (IGOs) grew from 21 to 37 between 1977 and 1989, and further rose to 52 till 1997.[16]

In the era of economic reform, China understood that those capitalist multilateral regimes not only serve as an important source of capital but also offer technical assistance, technical training, and information on how to develop and modernize China.[17] China's membership in global and regional economic organizations extends together with its economic growth. The modernization drive motivates more than ever the contacts with the global and regional economic institutions, the help from which strengthens China's economic achievements and stimulates China to increasingly participate in the international economic activities. As a matter of fact, Beijing discontinued its disparaging political attacks on the World Bank only in 1978. In April 1980, China entered the International Monetary Fund (IMF). One month later, China became a member of the World Bank Group including the International Bank for Reconstruction and Development (IBRD) and the International Development Association (IDA).[18] China obtained a permanent observer status in the General Agreement on Tariff and Trade (GATT) and was affiliated to the Multifibre Arrangement (MFA) in 1984. China became a member of the Asian Development Bank (ADB) in 1986 and has been active since 1991 in the Asia-Pacific Economic Cooperation (APEC). Negotiations for China's access of the GATT started from 1986, and China finally joined the WTO in 2001. China's participation in a broad range of international economic agencies has highlighted the fact that it has become a member of the world economic community. As pointed out by Zhiguang Tong, the former Vice-Minister of Commerce of China, as one of the fastest growing economies, China has benefited from the economic globalization process. Economic globalization has not only helped China to get more foreign capital and get on the right track towards a market economy, but also to deepen its internal reforms and to ameliorate the world trade environment, following its accession to the WTO.[19]

The process whereby China is integrated into world economy is a process that China learns to make necessary adjustments so as to fit itself into the existing arrangements of the international economic system. It is a process that has great significance to the further development of the country. First, it is a process whereby China modifies itself "from a society mobilized by revolution to one motivated by modernization."[20] China's international economic policies have clearly indicated, and increasingly do so, a preference of evolutionary rather than revolutionary changes in the existing international economic system.[21] Second, regular participation in international economic institutions brings in a constant and steady flow of information about the world economy, which has helped to modify China's view of the existing international economic order and to adjust its economic decision-making process. The accession to the WTO obliged China to undertake huge institutional and policy changes with regard to its trade practices. The efforts effectively narrowed down the gap between the practices of Chinese trading institutions and the requirements of these institutions, which facilitate the transformation of the Chinese economy into a market-oriented one.[22] Third, the international economic organizations, the same as the political ones, are dominated by Western idea and practices. China's participation in these regimes demonstrates its willingness to adhere to commonly accepted requirements and regulations. According to Jeffry Frieden and Ronald Rogowski, globalization has increased incentives for greater economic openness by raising substantially the opportunity costs of economic closure.[23] Once China opened itself to the international economic norms and practices, there were powerful incentives for it to stick to the reform and opening-up policy. Controls on the domestic market were eased in face of the impetus in favor of deeper reform. The process of integration has a major influence on the country's domestic policies and its political institutions. Chinese policies have been made increasingly consistent with the requirements of the international regime.[24]

In contrast to the opening-up experience of Mainland China, Taiwan's diplomatic space has been squeezed due to the fact that it lost the seat in the United Nations when Beijing became the sole representative of China in 1971. Before the 1970s, Taipei was an active member of the Security Council of the UN on behalf of the Republic of China. In 1966, Taipei was a member of 39 IGOs, whereas Beijing was a member of only one that year. Eleven years later, Taipei had membership in only 10 IGOs, whereas Beijing's membership of IGOs grew to 21. One year after the U.S. established diplomatic relations with Mainland China, Taiwan had to leave the IMF, the IBRD, and the IDA.[25] Due to Taiwan's special status, it has great difficulties to join IGOs.[26] Taiwan is member of the World Trade Organization (WTO), Asia-Pacific Economic Cooperation (APEC) forum, and Asian Development Bank, among which, Taiwan accessed the WTO in name of "Separate Customs Territory of Taiwan, Penghu, Kinmen and Matsu" and joined the APEC and the ADB as "Chinese Taipei."[27]

Taiwan has shown its interest in joining the World Health Organization (WHO) since 1997. However, the problematic political relationship with Mainland China prevents Taiwan from joining the WHO. Its application for full WHO membership in 2007 was rejected by the WHO Director-General due to the "One China" policy of the organization and its members. In the same year, Taiwan again applied for membership of the UN in the name of Taiwan, but the UN Secretary-General Ban Ki-moon stressed that its bid is legally impossible because the People's Republic of China is recognized as the only legitimate representative of China in the United Nations. [28]

Ideational Change

With three decades of the implementation of the reform and open-door policy, Mainland China has been noticeably improving its national power and influence. China is no longer a poor country isolated from world development. Economically, the reform has fundamentally transformed China from the one which challenged the international system and wanted to establish a new international economic order to a full participant in the capitalist economic system which is open, integrated, and rule-based.[29] China's global emergence is a natural consequence of its economic growth and development. [30] The membership of the UN Security Council, the participation of all the important IGOs, the increasing involvement in maintaining international peace and stability[31] has turned China from a revisionist outsider into a stakeholder. In the meantime, China's integration into the international system and its increasing global influence leads to the rising confidence of the Chinese government in international affairs.

The ideological content has been in a process of constant revision ever since Marxism and Leninism was introduced to China in the early twentieth century. The Chinese leader of the first generation, Mao Zedong, was deeply inspired by the revolutionary spirit of Marxism and Leninism. Applying Marxist and Leninist ideas to the realities of the Chinese situation, Mao Zedong and his colleagues developed Mao Zedong Thought. Regarded as Chinese Marxism, Mao Zedong Thought had helped the Chinese Communists defeat the Nationalist Party.

However, in the years of reform, the role of Marxism has been declining. More capitalist elements have been allowed to be put into practice in China. The liberation of mind has an unexpected side-effect on the ideological basis. In words of Brugger and Kelly, Chinese ideology has been developed into "Marxism without Marx." [32] Deng Xiaoping avoided the debate in the ideological field and sought to convince the Chinese people with noticeable economic achievements. Jiang Zemin promoted the "Three Represents" to broaden the social base of the CPC from workers and peasants to the overwhelming majority of the people in China, including capitalists. While recognizing the irreversible trend of reform, Hu Jintao focuses on correcting the problems brought by reform and emphasizes the construction of a harmonious society closing the gap between the rich and the poor.[33]

Starting from the 1980s, following the changes in international politics and the domestic situation, the Chinese government attaches great importance to patriotism in order to unite the Chinese together. Patriotism replaced communism as "the common spiritual pillar" of the Chinese people and "the powerful spiritual force that supports the Chinese people."[34] Hu's leadership emphasizes that patriotism is the core of the national spirit which "encourage(s) our people of generations to come to make concerted efforts for a prosperous and strong China."[35] Education in patriotism has been specified in the form of the "Eight Glories and Eight Shames" proposed by Hu Jintao in March 2006. Among the eight aphorisms, the first is to urge the people to "love the motherland, do not harm it."[36]

In contrast, since the 1970s, due to the fact that Taipei could not represent China any more in any IGOs, and all the countries which established diplomatic relations with China follow the "One China" principle, Taipei's political influence in international politics has been largely reduced. Although between the Island and many other important countries in the world, economic and cultural exchanges and cooperation have been going on without being much affected, Taipei's efforts to resume its international space seems to be very difficult. In fact, the loss of the UN membership was a "symbol of Beijing's decisive victory in the cross-Strait competition for international legitimacy and of Taiwan's international isolation."[37] At the end of the 1960s, Taipei had diplomatic relations with 56 countries, while the number for China was only 41. However, up to 1988, when Lee Teng-hui became the leader of Taiwan, only 22 countries officially recognized Taipei including Saudi Arabia, South Africa, and South Korea. Twenty years later, there are 23 countries now which recognize Taipei, but almost all of them are small and less developed countries in Africa, Latin America and the Asia-Pacific region.

The frustration of Taiwan in international politics has a direct impact on its identity formation. As Lowell Dittmer pointed out, Taiwan's emergent identity has a direct link with the PRC, "despite their distinct developmental trajectories, both 'sides' of the Strait, competing for the same sovereignty, have been shaped by some of the same watershed events."[38] Although separated by different political ideologies and political systems, the common history in the past binds the destiny of the two together. Like it or not, the actions and interactions of one side with other political actors in international relations have a strong impact on the other side. In the post-Cold War era, the fact that China is getting stronger and influential exerts pressure on Taiwan's diplomatic space, which obliges the Taiwanese to search for a new identity.

What is also noticeable in recent years in Taiwan is that since the Martial Law was lifted in 1987, Taiwan has been developing rapidly from an authoritarian system to a democratic system and has successfully realized a smooth evolution from a system of one-party domination to that of multi-party competition. Since the first direct presidential election was organized in 1996, there has been four such elections. The democratic developments in Taiwan attract world attention and win sympathy for Taiwan widely in the West. Starting from the end of the Cold War, the Western world seems to be convinced of the final victory of democracy. Mainland China, as the biggest authoritarian country in the world, has been constantly criticized for its non-democratic regime and its unsatisfying human rights record.

Without much left for the Taiwanese government to play against Mainland China, Taipei plays its democratic card. Lee Teng-hui in his article on *Foreign Affairs* claimed that China does not enjoy sovereignty over Taiwan: "The attacks that Beijing makes on the legitimacy of the democratic government affront the people of Taiwan and the prevailing values of the international community. Such attacks also threaten world peace and stability."[39] Taiwan's democracy is recognized and supported by the West. In this way, Taiwan wishes to make a breakthrough in its international relations.

CROSS-STRAIT RELATIONS

Economic Interdependence

As mentioned earlier, although Mainland China and Taiwan have different experiences of economic development, both of them are now active participants in the process of economic globalization. In such a process, due to geographical proximity, ethnic, cultural and language homogeneity, and different development levels, the two have established close economic cooperation. This relationship is exemplified by a large inflow of Taiwanese investment to Mainland China and a growing trade volume year by year between the two.

To a certain degree, the economies of Mainland China and Taiwan are complementary. The former has implemented economic reform policy and opened itself to the world in order to develop its economy. The latter eagerly explored the opportunity to go to the vast Chinese market and to take advantage of the low cost of labor there. The rapid growth of economic cooperation across the Strait started in late 1987 when the Taiwanese government decided to allow its citizens to visit their relatives on Mainland China. Since then, "natural integration of these two economies creates economic benefits for both sides of the Taiwan Strait."[40]

Between 1987 and 1995, Taipei further relaxed its controls on investment abroad which offered an opportunity for indirect trade with and investment in Mainland China. As Mainland China enjoys the comparative advantage of cheap labor and offers tax privileges for joint ventures, many Taiwanese enterprises were attracted to invest there. Taiwan's exports to China more than tripled from U.S.$1.2 billion to U.S.$4.4 billion between 1987 and 1990, more than doubled to U.S.$10.6 billion by 1992, and approximately doubled again to U.S.$19.4 billion by 1995 before stabilizing at about U.S.$20 billion during the second half of the decade and then starting to rise again in the early 21st century.[41] The rapid development of bilateral trade across the Strait made Taiwan the second largest supplier to Mainland China by 1995.[42] Together with the rapidly growing trade relations, Taiwan's total cumulative investment to Mainland China jumped to about U.S.$30 bn by the end of 1995 by nearly 30,000 companies.[43] China accounted for about half of the Island's annual investment abroad. By then, Chinese exports produced by Taiwan-invested enterprises were estimated to be between 14 percent and 18 percent of China's total exports. 36 to 38 percent of Taiwan's entrepreneurs had partnerships with Chinese local enterprises, and local governments.[44]

During the years of growing economic cooperation and trade relations across the Strait, the Taiwanese government has not been without fear that the increasing degree of interdependence between the two sides will exert an influence on their political relations. Before 1987, the Taiwanese government had followed the "Three No's" policy made by Chiang Kai-shek: no contact, no negotiation, and no compromise. Even after its abolition, the Taiwanese government has been alert to the possible negative impact of close economic contact with Mainland China. In the wake of the missile crisis between 1995 and 1996 across the Strait, Lee Teng-hui brought forth the "No Haste, Be Patient" policy to limit Taiwanese entrepreneurs in their trade with and economic activities in China. The Taiwanese government was afraid that the business development with Mainland China would give Beijing leverage in Taiwan's economy and allow it to push Taiwan for political concessions.[45] However, it seems that the mutually beneficial economic exchange and cooperation are enthusiastically embraced by Taiwanese entrepreneurs. The Taiwanese government's limitation of economic contact with Mainland China, among many other reasons, cost Lee Teng-hui popular support in the Island. Between 1996 and 1998, Lee's public approval rating dropped rapidly from over 80 percent to less than 40 percent.[46]

On the other hand, the Chinese leadership, since the early 1990s, has promoted economic relations and contact between people across the Strait, with the idea that such contacts between the two sides may create a favorable environment for the ultimate reunification. Jiang Zemin put forward eight propositions on the development of cross-Strait relations in 1995, in which he mentioned that both sides "shall spare no effect to develop economic exchange and cooperation... so that both sides enjoy a flourishing economy and the whole Chinese nation benefits." The Chinese government shall continue "to implement a policy of encouraging Taiwanese investment on the mainland." He stated that "The historical course of reunifying the motherland is irreversible, and the continuously developing relations between the two sides of the Taiwan Straits are in accordance with the general trend and the will of the people."[47]

When the Democratic Progressive Party (DPP) came to power in 2000, it faced the same problem of how to handle economic relations with Mainland China. Similar to Mainland China, Taiwan's economic development mainly relies on the growth of export, which occupies 49 percent of its GDP.[48] From the 1950s to 2000, the major export destination of Taiwan was the United States. However, from 2001 on, the situation has changed. Export from Taiwan to Mainland China for the first time surpassed those to the U.S. Since then, the gap between export to China and exports to the U.S. has been growing steadily year by year. Mainland China has become Taiwan's largest trading partner since 2003, passing Japan and the U.S. Mainland China is also the number one destination for investment by Taiwan residents. By 2005, the investment from Taiwan on the mainland had reached $47.32 billion and accounted for 53.28% of Taiwan's total outward investment over the period since 1991. There is a large number of Taiwanese living on the mainland. It is estimated that approximately one out of 23 Taiwanese work full-time in China. Taking the year 2007 as an example, 24.9 percent of its exports went to Mainland China, making the latter number one of its export destination. Hong Kong Special Administrative Region, as number two on the list, took 14.6 percent of Taiwan's total export. If Taiwan's exports to both Mainland China and Hong Kong were calculated together, then, the two digested nearly 40 percent of Taiwan's exports. In other words, Taiwan's foreign trade and economic development depend strongly on China. Whereas the U.S. was only number three, after Hong Kong, absorbing 13.2 percent of its total exports.[49]

This growing dependence only made the DPP leaders more worried. Annette Lu strongly opposed the development of cross-Strait relations, fearing that "Taiwanese investments in China have had a 'grotesque' impact on Taiwan's economic development over the past ten years."[50] This was echoed by another important DPP leader Peng Ming-min, who argued that "Taiwan should not invest on the mainland until the Chinese agreed to 'treat Taiwan as an equal' and guaranteed...protection of Taiwan's investment."[51] The DPP's China policy, together with the unsatisfactory economic performance of the Island during its eight-year-rule, led to its defeat in the Presidential elections in March 2008. The Taiwanese, particularly businessmen, have long complained that "antipathy between Taiwan and China under Mr. Chen has constrained Taiwan's stock market and economy."[52] The newly elected Taiwanese government, represented by Ma Ying-jeou, is in favor of establishing closer economic links with the Mainland. Different from the DPP's China policy, Ma pointed out during his election campaign that closer economic relations with the Mainland would help lift the Taiwanese economy. To a certain degree, the economy card helped him win the election in March 2008. Just several months later, as a result of close cooperation and coordination between Beijing and Taipei, two agreements have been signed in June 2008. Since July 20, residents in the four municipalities of Beijing, Tianjin, Shanghai, Chongqing and the provinces of Liaoning, Jiangsu, Zhejiang, Fujian, Shandong, Hubei, Guangdong, Yunnan and Shaanxi have been allowed to visit Taiwan in groups.[53]

From Confrontation to Peaceful Cooperation: Institutional Change

Since the founding of the PRC, while the leadership in Beijing has been following the "One China" policy consistently, the intended approach of unification and the ideas for the future across the Strait have been changing. A looking back on the PRC's history indicates that there has been an increasing emphasis on peaceful unification, although the use of force has never been renounced. After the Korean War, China attempted to improve the relationship with the United States and to defuse the tension across the Strait. On 13 May 1955, Zhou Enlai pointed out at the 2nd plenary session of the 1st National People's Congress, "Under possible conditions, the Chinese people would like to liberate Taiwan in a peaceful way."[54] This was the first time that the PRC ever expressed the willingness to peacefully reintegrate Taiwan. In the 1970s, the improved bilateral relations between Beijing and Washington motivated China to adjust its Taiwan policy by taking a more cautious attitude: "To liberate Taiwan is our set policy, but it depends on the development of the international situation as a whole and our own preparation. If it cannot be solved by force, peaceful liberation is the best. For the present it is better to sustain the status quo."[55]

After China carried out the reform and open-door policy, the Chinese leadership has been adjusting its attitude on the Taiwan issue. The opening-up process allowed the leaders to broaden their outlook and to adopt a more pragmatic and flexible approach. On the other hand, economic globalization created a good opportunity for development and brought wealth to the country. The rising economic power gave the leadership more confidence to deal with the historical legacy. Chinese leader Deng Xiaoping put forward the "one country, two systems" model which was successfully applied in the return of Hong Kong and Macau to Mainland China. The successful practice of this model encourages Beijing toward peaceful unification.

Dialogues established across the Strait in the early 1990s led to the "1992 consensus" between the two sides. In comparison to the official standpoint in the past, the "One China, each with its own definitions" formula was a big step taken by the Chinese leadership. The consensus implied that while adhering to the "One China" policy, the Beijing government became more flexible in seeking common ground with Taipei. Rather than emphasizing Taiwan as a province of China, Beijing allowed Taipei to enjoy more freedom in defining its status. Beijing took a softer strategy: unification is the long-term goal which can be realized upon the completion of economic and cultural integration.

The emphasis on a peaceful approach by the Chinese leadership is mainly a result of the following considerations. First, since the economic reform policy was carried out at the end of the 1970s, the economic achievements have not only noticeably improved the living standards of the Chinese people, but also helped legitimize the leading position of the Communist party (CCP) in China. Maintaining economic growth is deemed an important task, which serves both the interest of the country and the CCP. Domestic economic development requires a peaceful external environment. For three decades after the PRC was founded, Mao Zedong believed that war would break out soon. Lots of national resources were consumed by the preparation for war. The focus was diverted to economic development only after Deng Xiaoping made the judgment in the 1980s that peace could possibly be maintained. Benefiting from the favorable external environment, China has been growing rapidly in its economic capacity. The experience of both war and peace motivates the Chinese to highly appreciate peace and stability. Second, along with the improvement of external relations with the outside world, China attaches great importance to its international image-building. China tries hard to dispel the suspicions of other countries on the negative consequences of China's rise and promotes a peace-loving image globally. To counter against the "China threat" discourse, China has reached all kinds of partnerships with many other countries, solved most of the territorial disputes with its neighbors, and promoted loudly its strategy of peaceful development.

While it is clear that Beijing strives for a peaceful approach concerning the Taiwan issue, the deployment of short-range missiles targeting Taiwan indicates that military approach has not been completely given up. The anti-secession law passed by China's National People's Congress in March 2005 stated that Beijing is obliged to resort to military means if Taiwan declares independence. [56] National unification and territorial integrity are the top concerns of the Chinese leadership. Particularly after Hong Kong and Macau were taken over in the late 1990s, the unification of Taiwan has become the principal unresolved issue. Taiwan's return symbolizes the end of China's humiliating history and its rise as a great power. Both the military and the peaceful approaches serve Beijing's "One China" policy, with the peaceful approach as the preference. Beijing intends to keep the status quo at present and promotes the ultimate unification in the long run.

Vis-à-vis the consistent "One China" policy followed by Beijing, Taipei has experienced salient changes in its China policy. In the diplomatic battles between the PRC and the ROC, the ROC has been a big loser. When the PRC replaced the ROC to become a member of the UN Security Council in 1971, the diplomatic space for the ROC was largely reduced. The different paths of economic and political development prompted the Taiwanese to change their policy by emphasizing a distinct identity and seeking the possibility of independence.

As mentioned earlier, Taiwan lifted Martial Lawand allowed people-to-people contact across the Strait in 1987. Between 1990 and 1992, some institutional developments in Taiwan further promoted bilateral contact. They included the Act Governing Relations Between Peoples of the Taiwan Area and the Mainland Area which set the legal framework on cross-Strait activities; the establishment of the Cabinet-level Mainland Affairs Council (MAC) and the Straits Exchange Foundation (SEF) to administer relations between Taiwan and China; and the more noticeably, the establishment of National Unification Council (NUC) and the draft of Guidelines for National Unification. [57] It was against this background that the "1992 consensus" was reached.

Nevertheless, Taiwan and Mainland China have different interpretations on the content of "One China" policy. As a native Taiwanese who was educated both in Japan and the U.S., Lee held a different understanding of the status of Taiwan compared to the other Nationalists who came from the Mainland. Lee Teng-hui promoted those who were born in Taiwan to important leading positions in the government in order to diminish the political influence of the Nationalist mainlanders. Lee made his separatist policy more pronounced in July

1999 by declaring that the relations between the PRC and Taiwan should be conducted as "state-to-state" or at least "special state-to-state" relations.

When the DPP came to power in 2000, Chen Shui-bian pushed Taiwan further towards independence. Despite the fact that Chen announced his cross-Strait policy as "Four Noes and One Not"[58] in his inaugural speech, a series of revisionist actions had been taken by Chen's government. First of all, Chen rejected the "1992 consensus." In 2002, Chen defined the cross-Strait relations as "one country on each side of the Taiwan Strait," implying that Taiwan is an independent country. Since late 2003, in order to cut the historical link between Taiwan and China, the Taipei government has added "Taiwan" to the cover of local passports. In March 2004, Chen called for a referendum and was in favor of a new ROC constitution. In July 2005, Chen said that the ROC and the PRC "are two separate countries with divided rule and do not exercise sovereignty over each other." In February 2006, Chen announced that the National Unification Council and its guidelines, which had committed Taiwan to unification if China adopts democracy, had ceased to function. During the Chinese New Year of 2007, Chen took another step by asserting Taiwan's separatist policy and reverting the "Four Noes and One Not" into "Four Wants and One Without." [59] In early 2007, the Taiwan government revised the high school history textbook with the object of 'de-sinicization,' highlighting the differences between Taiwan and China, identifying Taiwan as "self" and China as "the other." The state-owned enterprises of the ROC were also asked to change their names by removing the word "China" from them.

Chen's efforts toward independence were stopped with the failure of the DPP in the presidential election of 2008. In his inaugural speech, Ma Ying-jeou pledged to renew cross-Strait relations based on the principles of "no independence, no unification and no use of force" under the "1992 Consensus."[60] His vision was further clarified in his interview with *The New York Times/The International Herald Tribune* that, "After the eight years of very bitter experience with Taiwan, I'm sure they (the Taiwan people) welcome a leader in this country who does not favor *de jure* independence."[61] Concerning the relations with Mainland China, he wishes that "a modus vivendi between Taiwan and the mainland" can be based on pragmatism. As a matter of fact, Ma's China policy can be regarded as a response to Hu Jintao's "16-word maxim," issued during Hu's meeting with former Nationalist Party Chairman Lien Chan on April 29, 2008 that China and Taiwan should "seek to build mutual trust, shelve disputes, seek common ground while reserving differences, and create 'win-win' development."[62]

The contact between the Chinese Communist Party of the Mainland and the Nationalist Party of Taiwan started from 2005 when Hu Jintao invited both Lien Chan, the Chairman of the Nationalist Party and James Soong, the Chairman of the People's First Party from Taiwan to visit Beijing. This historical meeting of the two sides was realized after more than five decades of mutual political animosity. The ice-breaking meeting turned the Chinese Communist Party and the Nationalist Party from enemies to potential partners. The recent interaction between the two sides seems to promise a rapprochement in the coming years.

Based on pragmatism and flexibility, cross-Strait relations may develop towards closer and peaceful economic and political cooperation.

Identity Changes across the Strait

Needless to say, the solution of the Taiwan issue rests in the hands of the leaderships across the Strait. How each side views itself and the other, how each side interprets the sovereignty issue, how much each side appreciates peace in the region, will to a large degree decide the future development of the situation across the Strait. In the past two decades, together with economic cooperation and political interaction, the identities of both sides have been evolving in a noticeable way.

In general, Chinese national identity has a close link with Chinese history. National pride consists of part of the Chinese identity. In view of the Chinese, a country's cultural greatness determines its power in the world. Therefore, a state with superior cultural achievements is entitled to esteem and influence.[63] The bitter experience subsequent to the Opium War shattered China's self-confidence and added a kind of inferiority complex to China's national identity. The unification of China in 1949 not only marked the end of foreign devastation and domestic chaos but also revitalized China's efforts to resume its past glory.

During the Cold War era, China stressed its shared experience with the Asian, African, and Latin American countries: "Both the Chinese people and the people of these countries have for a long time been subjected to the oppression and exploitation of imperialism and have suffered long enough."[64] Standing together with these countries, China intended to promote world revolution and to transform the international order. In the era of reform, despite the fact that China is getting richer and stronger, there still exist lots of problems in its economic development. With a relatively low per capita GDP,[65] the gap in development between the east and the west of the country, and the alarming difference of income between the rich and poor, Chinese government stresses on many occasions that China is still a developing country.[66]

On the other hand, the rising influence of Beijing in international affairs and its ambition to construct a multipolar world in the post-Cold War era reveals China's changing attitude from being the victim of Western expansion to a rising great power which actively participates in the formation of a new international political order.[67] While managing to keep friendly relationship with all the countries in the world in general, China makes special efforts in its relationship with the United States, the European Union, Russia and Japan. The partnership established with these countries in the late 1990s demonstrates China's changing identity and its aspiration to great power status.[68]

Economic globalization has a direct impact on China's opening-up process and has changed China's identity from a victim of colonial powers to a rising power with increasing confidence in international affairs. Yet, the historical legacy, particularly the Taiwan issue, works on the nerves of the Chinese and reminds them of the humiliation in the last centuries. As a country which is getting stronger and more influential in the 21st century, China is eager to find a solution to the Taiwan issue so that it can say goodbye definitively to its past.

Influenced by Chinese patriotic education, most Chinese believe that Taiwan is part of China and Taiwan should come back to China sooner or later.

According to a survey undertaken by Social Survey Institute of China (SSIC) in 2000, when the DPP won the election, 95.4 percent out of the total 1689 respondents held the opinion that the Taiwan issue would only be solved by force. 92 percent of those who participated in the survey held the view that it would be better to fight militarily sooner than later. All the participants of the survey thought that whether the cross-Strait tension could be relaxed and whether cross-Strait relations could be improved and develop would depend on whether the Taiwanese government would accept and adhere to the "One China" principle.[69]

Four years later, the SSIC did another survey and interviewed 1000 people from all parts of Mainland China. Among those people, 87 percent were angry at the new developments of Chen's separatist policy; 53 percent believed that the change of Chen's policy toward independence was a result of careful consideration rather than a hasty decision and felt fed up at Chen's government; 68 percent thought that before the next election in Taiwan in 2008, the Taiwan question should be solved.[70]

When the Chair of the Nationalist Party Lien Chan visited the Mainland in 2005, the Social Investigation Centre of China Youth Daily selected randomly 737 people from the thirty-one provinces, municipalities, autonomous regions and Hong Kong and Macau Special Administrative Regions for a survey. 95.8 percent of the respondents expressed interest to the visit of Lien Chan to the Mainland. 65.1 percent of the respondents believed that Lien and Soong's visit to the Mainland would promote the process of peaceful unification. 52.4 percent of the respondents believed that they would be able to witness the final unification in their life times. 33.5 percent of the respondents thought that they would probably be able to see that day come.[71]

On the other side of the Strait, the situation has been changing noticeably. During the fifty-one-year domination of the Nationalist Party on the Island before 2000, the people there encountered the problem of national identity. Particular since the 1970s, "Taiwan has no clear national identity but rather an unresolved national identity dilemma."[72] When the Nationalists withdrew to Taiwan in 1949, they took pains to cast the view on the Island that "both Taiwan and the Chinese mainland were parts of China and China was their motherland."[73] During the years of the Nationalist domination, there has been a division between the Mainlanders and local residents on the Island. The prejudice against the local people backfired against Nationalist control and finally ended the one-party system. Lee Teng-hui's policy to dilute the heritage from the Mainland and to re-establish a local identity played an important role in enlarging the gap of mutual perceptions across the Strait.

The founding of the DPP and its success in the Presidential election in 2000 marked another step to foster Taiwanese consciousness on the Island. While the changing identity of the Taiwanese in the 21st century has been used by the political parties to attract votes, researchers and scholars in Taiwan point out in their publications that the identity of Taiwan is not that clear-cut. As Huang, Liu, and Chang stated in their research, "For most of recorded history, Taiwanese identity has been subordinate to Chinese identity, but with recent political developments, the two now stand side by side in Taiwan."[74]

A review of the changes of identity in Taiwan, six surveys conducted by Chang and Wang, indicated that from 1994 to 2002 the proportions of Chinese identifiers dropped substantially among all the generations in Taiwan. Despite the efforts of the Nationalist government to "re-Sinicize" local residents for several decades, an increasing number of the Island dwellers have been indigenized. However, rather than taking a Taiwanese identity, many people consider themselves as both Chinese and Taiwanese and such changes are visible among all generations. In the meantime, there is a declining support for unification and a rising tendency for pursing independence or taking a "wait and see" attitude. Among the younger citizens, keeping the status-quo without making a commitment to future action is the dominant idea throughout the period between 1994 and 2002.[75]

While the majority of Taiwanese people tend to have a double identity and maintain an indecisive attitude on the future of cross-Strait relations, an increasing number of people in the Island think that economic cooperation with Mainland China is important to stimulate Taiwan's economy and it is necessary to have direct transport between the two sides. According several surveys from 2004 to 2008, the proportion supporting direct flights has been increasing rapidly. Whereas in 2004 only 48.6 percent of the respondents agreed to this policy, in 2006 60 percent of the respondents supported it.[76] In 2008, more than 90 percent of the respondents are in favor of direct flights. 68.7 percent of them think that cross-Strait relations would be improved in the coming year.[77] The recent changes in the survey indicated that the contacts across the Strait since the spring of 2008 have already exerted an impact on the attitude of the Taiwanese on their relations with the Mainland. How Taiwan identity will further evolve and how cross-Strait relations will develop in the future will depend on the wisdom of the leadership of the two sides.

CONCLUSION

This chapter has an examination of the changes in Mainland China and Taiwan and the evolution of cross-Strait relations against the background of globalization. Taking the opportunity of globalization, China has successfully carried out economic reform and turned itself from a revolutionary state to a reformist power, and from an isolated nation into a globally influential actor. China's rise in the era of globalization is not only economic but also political and strategic. In comparison, the impact of globalization on Taiwan is rather mixed. Although it helps maintain Taiwan to be an impressive trade power, it has also largely increased Taiwan's dependence on Mainland China. Without the Chinese market, it would be difficult for Taiwan to solve its economic problems.

Despite the sovereignty dispute, the leaderships on both sides seek to bring power and prosperity to their people. The convergence of national construction objectives and the aversion to war may serve as important factors to guide the two sides to find a solution acceptable to both. The success of Ma Ying-jeou in the election seems to be a good starting point for cross-Strait relations. The independence of Taiwan seems not to be the goal of Ma's government. Beijing will be more patient on the goal of ultimate cross-Strait integration and unification, on the condition that the status quo is safeguarded. The day after Ma Ying-jeou became the new leader of Taiwan, Chen Yunlin, Chairman of the Mainland-based Association for Relations across the Taiwan Straits, stated on behalf of Beijing that "We understand, trust and care about Taiwan compatriots and respect the desire of Taiwan compatriots to be masters of their own destiny." Concerning cross-Strait relations, Chen Yunlin emphasized that China and Taiwan should "establish mutual trust, set aside disputes and differences and create a win-win (situation)," China hopes to "gradually establish a new cross-Strait framework for peace and development."[78]

As a result of increasing interdependence across the Strait, commercial ties "may have greater potential to transform relations between Taiwan and China."[79] Noting that economic interaction has been little affected by the political problems across the Strait, Steve Chan suggested that it might be a matter of promoting "peace by pieces."[80] What happened recently across the Strait is a positive development for regional peace. The "big three links," a landmark development in cross-Strait relations, have been realized since December 2008. The direct transport and communication links will benefit both Mainland China and Taiwan and create a "win-win" situation.

While economic cooperation has been intensified and economic integration seems to be the unavoidable tendency across the Strait, the Taiwan people still put a question mark on the "One China" policy. Discussing the future of cross-Strait relations, Denny Roy argues that it would depend on "whether leaders in Beijing would continue to see intimidations as their best or only option, or shift to the alternative strategy of attempting to attract and win over Taiwan."[81] In order to further improve ties with Taiwan, Chinese President Hu Jintao in his address to mark the 30th anniversary of the announcement of Message to Compatriots in Taiwan on the last day of 2008 offered six proposals for peaceful development of cross-Strait relationship. He specifically stated that "If the DPP could change its 'Taiwan independence' stance, we would make a positive response to them."[82]

In the long run, as a consequence of economic and political reform, China will possibly be more open and economically more developed. The degree of economic and cultural integration between the two sides will be further strengthened. When both economic and political conditions are mature, it is not unimaginable that the PRC and the ROC will form a "Greater China." This term has already been widely used although mainly for economic and geographical convenience. Integration across the Strait would give political content to this term.

NOTES

[1] See Jan Aart Scholte, *Globalization: A Critical Introduction* (London: Macmillan, 2000), 44-6.

[2] Andrew Heywood, *Politics* 2nd Edition (New York: Palgrave Macmillan, 2002), 137.

[3] Michael Yahuda, "China's Win-Win Globalization," *Yale Global Online*, 19 February 2003, <yaleglobal.yale.edu/display.article?id=1017>

[4] See Robert W. Cox, "Social Forces, States and World Orders: Beyond International Relations Theory," in Robert W. Cox and Timothy J. Sinclair (eds.), *Approaches to World Order* (Cambridge: Cambridge University Press, 1996), 85-123.

[5] See Jing Men, "The EU-China Strategic Partnership: Achievements and Challenges" *Policy Paper Series* 12 (2007), European Union Centre of Excellence, University of Pittsburgh, 7-10.

[6] Gregory Chow and An-loh Lin, "Accounting for Economic Growth in Taiwan and Mainland China: A Comparative Analysis," *Journal of Comparative Economics* 30: 3 (2002), 508.

[7] HU Jintao, "Hold High the Great Banner of Socialism with Chinese Characteristics and Strive for New Victories in Building a Moderately Prosperous Society in all," Report to the Seventeenth National Congress of the Communist Party of China on 15 October 2007, part 3, <www.china.org.cn/english/congress/229611.htm#3>

[8] Quoted in Nicholas R. Lardy, *Foreign Trade and Economic Reform in China: 1978-1990* (London: Cambridge University Press, 1993), 16.

[9] Zhiguang Tong, "The Development of China and World Trade," *Journal of World Trade* 40: 1 (2006), 132.

[10] Representatives from China participated in the meetings with the group of seven financial ministers for the first time in 2004. Since then, there have been more contacts between the two, however, China has no immediate plan to join G7.

[11] Taiwan Information Office, "The Story of Taiwan," <www.gio.gov.tw/info/taiwan-story/economy/edown/3-5.htm>

[12] Ibid.

[13] See Department of Investment Services in Taiwan, "Taiwan Institute of Economic Research Revises GDP Growth Rate up to 4.09%," 29 May 2007, <investintaiwan.nat.gov.tw/en/news/200705/2007052901.html>

[14] John J. Tkacik, Jr. and Daniella Markheim, "Free Trade with Taiwan Is Long Overdue," 15 August 2007, <www.heritage.org/Research/TradeandForeignAid/bg2061.cfm>

[15] Steven Crook, "Taiwan Studies Goes Global," *Taiwan Review*, 10 January 2007, <taiwanreview.nat.gov.tw/ct.asp?xItem=24694&CtNode=128>

[16] Lowell Dittmer, "Leadership Change and Chinese Political Development," *The China Quarterly* 176 (December 2003), 919.

[17] See John R. Faust and Judith F. Kornberg, *China in World Politics* (Boulder, Colorado and London: Lynne Rienner Publishers, Inc., 1995), 221.

[18] Robert Kleinberg, *China's "Opening" to the Outside World: The Experiment with Foreign Capitalism* (Boulder, Colorado: Westview Press, Inc., 1990), 168-169.

[19] Zhiguang Tong, "The Development of China and World Trade," 129-130.

[20] Yongjin Zhang, *China in International Society Since 1949: Alienation and Beyond* (London: Macmillan Press Ltd., 1998), 195.

[21] Ibid., 226.

[22] Ibid., 196.

[23] Jeffry Frieden and Ronald Rogowski, "The Impact of the International Economy on National Policies: An Analytic Overview," in Robert Keohane and Helen Milner (eds.), *Internationalisation and Domestic Politics* (New York: Cambridge University Press, 1996), 33.

[24] Margaret M. Pearson, "China's Integration into the International Trade and Investment Regime," in Elizabeth Economy and Michel Oksenberg (eds.), *China Joins the World: Progress and Prospects* (New York: Brookings Institution Press, 1999), 188.

[25] Chien-pin Li, "Taiwan's Participation in Inter-Governmental Organizations," *Asian Survey* 46: 4 (2006), 598.

[26] For most of the IGOs, one of the most important prerequisites is that the applicants should be sovereign states. As Taiwan's sovereignty is in dispute, and Mainland China becomes an ever more influential actor in the international stage, Taiwan's application to the many important IGOs will need Beijing's consent.

[27] Government Information Office, Republic of China, "World Bodies," <http://www.gio.gov.tw/ct.asp?xItem=35619&ctNode=2588>

[28] "UN chief says Taiwan's Bid to Join UN Legally Impossible," *People's Daily Online*, 19 September 2007, <http://english.people.com.cn/90001/90777/6265660.html>

[29] G. John Ikenberry, "The Rise of China and the Future of the West," *Foreign Affairs* 87: 1 (January/February 2008), 24.

[30] Thomas J. Christensen, "China's Role in the World: Is China a Responsible Stakeholder?" remarks before the U.S.-China Economic and Security Review Commission, 3 August 2006, <http://www.state.gov/p/eap/rls/rm/69899.htm>

[31] This can be exemplified by China's increasing participation of the UN peacekeeping missions, China's involvement in the hot issues such as Iran, North Korea, Sudan and Myanmar.

[32] Bill Brugger and David Kelly, *Chinese Marxism in the Post-Mao Era* (Stanford, California: Stanford University Press, 1990), 171.

[33] See Jing Men, "Changing Ideology in China and Its Impact on Chinese Foreign Policy," in Sujian Guo and Shiping Hua (eds.), *New Dimensions of Chinese Foreign Policy* (New York/Lexington: Rowman & Littlefield Publishers, 2007), 7-39.

[34] Suisheng Zhao, "A State-led Nationalism: The Patriotic Education Campaign in Post-Tiananmen China," *Communist and Post-Communist Studies* 31: 3 (1998), 296.

[35] "Hu Jintao Calls for Unity of Chinese Nation," *People's Daily Online*, 3 September 2005, <http://english.people.com.cn/200509/03/eng20050903_206345.html>

[36] Edward Cody, "Eight-Step Program for What Ails China," *Washington Post*, 23 March 2006, <http://www.washingtonpost.com/wp-dyn/content/article/2006/03/22/AR200603 2202042.html?nav=rss_world>

[37] G. Andy Chang and T. Y. Wang, "Taiwanese or Chinese? Independence or Unification? An Analysis of Generational Differences in Taiwan," *Journal of Asian and African Studies*, 40: 1-2 (2005), 32.

[38] Lowell Dittmer, "Taiwan's Aim-Inhibited Quest for Identity and the China Factor," *Journal of Asian and African Studies* 40: 1-2 (2005), 72.

[39] Lee Teng-hui, "Understanding Taiwan: Bridging the Perception Gap," *Foreign Affairs* 78: 6 (1999), 10.

[40] Tse Kang Leng, "Securing Economic Relations across the Taiwan Straits: New Challenges and Opportunities," 261.

[41] Cal Clark, "Economic Interdependence and Growing Taiwanese Identity in cross-Strait Relations," paper presented at the Annual Meeting of the International Studies Association, Honolulu, March 1-5 (2005), 6.

[42] Seanon S. Wong, "Economic Statecraft across the Strait: Business Influence in Taiwan's Mainland Policy," *Asian Perspective* 29: 2 (2005), 42.

[43] Cal Clark, "Economic Interdependence and Growing Taiwanese Identity in cross-Strait Relations," 6.

[44] Chen-yuan Tung, "China's Economic Leverage and Taiwan's Security Concerns with Respect to Cross-Strait Economic Relations," paper presented to the Taiwan Studies Workshop Fairbank Center, Harvard University, 1 May 2003, <http://www.fas.harvard.edu/~fairbank/tsw/text/Tung.htm#_ftnref9>

[45] Tse Kang Leng, "Securing Economic Relations across the Taiwan Straits: New Challenges and Opportunities," *Journal of Contemporary China* 11: 31 (2002), 262.

[46] Seanon S. Wong, "Economic Statecraft across the Strait: Business Influence in Taiwan's Mainland Policy," 66.

[47] Taiwan Affairs Office of the State Council, "Jiang Zemin's Eight-point Proposal," 30 January 1995, <http://www.gwytb.gov.cn:8088/detail.asp?table=JiangEP&title=Jiang+Zemin's+Eight-point+Proposal&m_id=3>

[48] Zhuang Kunnan, *The Impact of China's Macroeconomic Policy on the Development of Taiwan's Industries* (Zhongguo hongguan tiankong jingji zhengce dui Taiwan chanye fawhan zhi yingxiang), 2006, Master's degree thesis of National Sun Yat-sen University, Taiwan, <thesis.lib.cycu.edu.tw>

[49] Taiwan Facts Sheet, <www.dfat.gov.au/geo/fs/taiw.pdf>

[50] Quoted in Paul J. Bolt, "Economic Ties across the Taiwan Strait: Buying Time for Compromise," *Issues & Studies* 37: 2 (2001), 88.

[51] Quoted in Denny Roy, *Taiwan: A Political History* (Ithaca, N.Y.: Cornell University Press, 2003), 197-198.

[52] Quoted in John Chan, "Taiwan's ruling party suffers major defeat in parliamentary election," 23 January 2008, <http://www.wsws.org/articles/2008/jan2008/taiw-j23.shtml>

[53] "ARATS, SEF chiefs hold historic talks in Taipei," 4 November 2008, <http://news.xinhuanet.com/english/2008-11/04/content_10304423.htm>

[54] Quoted in Gong Li, *Mao Zedong Mao Zedong's Diplomacy (WaijiaoFengyunlu)* (Zhengzhou, Henan Province: Zhongyuan nongmin Publishing House, 1996), 120.

[55] Quoted in Joseph Camilleri, *Chinese Foreign Policy: The Maoist Era and its Aftermath* (Oxford: Martin Robertson, 1980), 180.

[56] *Anti-cessation Law (Fan fenlie guojia fa)*, National People's Congress, Beijing, 14 March 2005, <news.sina.com.cn/c/2005-03-14/09396077697.shtml>

[57] See Jim Hwang, "No Bridging the Divide," *Taiwan Review*, 8 January 2006, <taiwanreview.nat.gov.tw/ct.asp?xItem=22910&CtNode=128>

[58] The "Four Noes" referred to no declaration of independence, no formal change of Taiwan's name from the Republic of China, no writing the "state-to-state" model of cross-Strait relations into the Constitution, and no referendum on formal independence. "One Not" meant that neither the NUC nor the Guidelines for National Unification would be abolished.

[59] "Four Wants and One Without" referred to that Taiwan wants independence, Taiwan wants to change its official title, Taiwan wants a new constitution, Taiwan wants development. Taiwan does not have left or right wing politics, only the issue of reunification and independence.

[60] "Full text of President Ma's Inaugural Address," *The China Post*, 21 May 2008, <www.chinapost.com.tw/taiwan/national/national%20news/2008/05/21/157332/Full-text.htm>

[61] "An Interview With President Ma Ying-jeou," *The International Herald Tribune*, 20 June 2008, <www.iht.com/articles/2008/06/20/asia/19taiwaninterview.php>

[62] Quoted in Russell Hsiao, "Ma's Inaugural Address as President of Taiwan," *China Brief* 8: 11 (May 21, 2008), 1, <www.jamestown.org/terrorism/news/ uploads/cb_ 008_011c.pdf>

[63] See Akira Iriye, "Culture and Power: International Relations as Intercultural Relations," *Diplomatic History* 3: 2 (1979), 118-119.

[64] Quoted in Joseph Camilleri, *Chinese Foreign Policy: The Maoist Era and Its Aftermath* (Oxford: Martin Robertson, 1980), 82.

[65] China still lags behind more than 100 other countries in terms of economic output per capita.

[66] See, for example, Xinhua net, "China Remains World Largest Developing Country," 20 December 2005, <http://news.xinhuanet.com/english/2005-12/20/content_ 3947262. htm>

[67] Gilbert Rozman, "China's Quest for Great Power Identity," *Orbis* 43: 3 (1999), 384.

[68] See Jing Men, "China's Rise and its Relations with the Other Major Powers— Competitors or Partners?" in Sujian Guo and Jean-Marc F. Blanchard (eds.), *Harmonious World and China's New Foreign Policy* (Lanham: Rowman & Littlefield-Lexington, 2008), 83-103.

[69] "A Survey Showed that 95% of Mainlanders support that the Taiwan issue should be solved militarily" (Diaocha biaoming 95% de dalu minzhong zhichi wuli jiejue Taiwan wenti), 19 May 2000, <news.sina.com.cn/china/2000-05-19/90899.html>

[70] "The Latest Survey in China: 70 percent of the Chinese Held that the Taiwan Question Should Be Solved before 2008" (Zhongguo zuixin mindiao qicheng minyi: 08nianqian jiejue Taiwan wenti), 11 November 2004, <military.china.com/zh_cn/news/ 568/200 41111/11958568.html>

[71] "An Investigation Indicated that 95.8 percent of the Mainlanders are Concerned about Lian Chan's visit" (Minyi diaocha xianshi 95.8% de gongzhong guanzhu Lien Chan daluxing), 2 May 2005, <www.southcn.com/NEWS/hktwma/zhuanti/lzfw/dlzs/ 2005050 20290.htm>

[72] Lowell Dittmer, "Taiwan's Aim-Inhibited Quest for Identity and the China Factor," 72.

[73] G. Andy Chang and T. Y. Wang, "Taiwanese or Chinese? Independence or Unification? An Analysis of Generational Differences in Taiwan," 32.

[74] Li-Li Hang, James H. Liu and Maanling Chang, "'The Double Identity' of Taiwanese Chinese: A Dilemma of Politics and Culture Rooted in History," *Asian Journal of Social Psychology* 7: 2 (2004), 150.

[75] G. Andy Chang and T. Y. Wang, "Taiwanese or Chinese? Independence or Unification? An Analysis of Generational Differences in Taiwan," 38-40.

[76] "Surveys in Taiwan showed that Direct Flight across the Strait Is Supported" (Taiwan minyi diaocha xianshi kaifang liangan zhihang shi duoshu minyi), 19 October 2006, <news.xinhuanet.com/tai_gang_ao/2006-10/19/content_5225635.htm>

[77] "The Latest Survey in Taiwan shows that 96.1% of Its People Are in Favor of Direct Flight across the Strait" (Taiwan zuixin minyi diaocha xianshi 96.1% minzhong zancheng liangan zhihang), 31 March 2008, <news.sohu.com/20080331/n256014918.shtml>

[78] Quoted in Benjamin Kang Lim, "China pledges reconciliation with Taiwan," 22 May 2008, <http://www.iht.com/articles/reuters/2008/05/22/asia/OUKWD-UK-CHINA-TAI WAN.php>

[79] Greg Mastel, "China, Taiwan, and the World Trade Organization," *Washington Quarterly* 24: 3 (2001), 46.

[80] See Steve Chan, "Peace by Pieces? The Economic and Social Bases for 'Greater China,'" *American Asian Review* 14: 2 (1996), 35-50.

[81] Denny Roy, *Taiwan: A Political History*, 202.

[82] "President Hu offers six proposals for peaceful development of cross-Strait relationship," 31 December 2008, <http://news.xinhuanet.com/english/2008-12/31/ cont ent_10585635.htm>

Chapter 5

Democratic Peace across the Taiwan Strait

Antonio C. Hsiang & Jerome S. Hsiang

INTRODUCTION

The establishment of democracy is a paramount issue facing both China and Taiwan. But while Taiwan has shown increasing resilience as a newly democratic state, China's central government remains largely authoritarian. For democracy advocates who see the democratic process as an instrument for peace, "Successful democratization in China will not only usher in freedom for 1.3 billion Chinese citizens, but also strike a blow against the stubbornness of authoritarianism worldwide."[1]

To the chagrin of those espousing traditional democratic-peace theory, democratizing Taiwan did not appear at first to reduce the threat of war. In fact, the first two decades of Taiwan's democratic experiment brought heightened tensions between China and Taiwan. Unlike some predictions, "as Taiwan has democratized, its relations with the Mainland has become more unpredictable and dangerous."[2] Cross-strait relations were arguably worse in the first decade of the new millennium than in the late 1990s.[3]

The culprits of this development were two-fold. The first is that the immaturity of Taiwanese democracy prompted imprudent politicians to combine nascent nationalism with populist rhetoric in order to secure electoral victory. This is consistent with the research of Edward D. Mansfield and Jack Snyder, who argued that "statistical evidence covering the past two centuries shows that in this transitional phase of democratization, countries become more aggressive and war-prone, not less . . ."[4]

The second half of the blame lies with China. The Chinese government has long cultivated an uneasy nationalism. Beijing often encouraged the trend by "assiduously publiciz[ing] its claim to control Taiwan, a claim that seems to enjoy wide popularity on the mainland."[5] As Chinese power grows, more and more Chinese will assert their national pride in ways that may alienate foreign powers—including Taiwan.

With these two burgeoning forces of nationalism heading for an eventual collision, the Kuomintang's ("KMT") March 2008 Taiwanese presidential victory is a truly positive development. Ma Ying-jeou, the KMT candidate sworn in on May 20, 2008, had promised to alleviate tensions with the mainland. Taiwanese voters overwhelmingly approved of his message after two straight terms of Democratic Progressive Party ("DPP") rule. As Taiwan's democracy matures, peaceful relations between Taiwan and China seem more possible now than they have in a very long time.[6]

LITERATURE REVIEW

Traditional democratic-peace theory posits that democratic nations tend to be peaceful and are unlikely to wage war against each other.[7] Secondary conclusions are that: 1) democratic states tend to prevail in armed conflict against non-democratic states[8]; 2) when initiating armed conflict, democratic states suffer fewer casualties and fight for a shorter amount of time than non-democratic counterparts[9]; 3) democratic states locked in disputes with each other tend to favor more peaceful means of resolution than pairings of non-democratic states[10]; 4) democratic great powers do not initiate preventive wars.[11] Some scholars therefore relied on traditional democratic-peace theory to argue that, "empirically supported regularities can be used to ease the transition from autocratic to democratic regimes, increasing the well-being of the population and reducing the probability of international conflict and global war."[12]

But the Cold War showed that traditional democratic-peace theory was not airtight. States in the process of democratizing were often more war-prone than their politically mature counterparts. Moreover, democratic states were hardly immune from fierce security competitions and armed conflicts. When deploying force to fight these conflicts, democratic states often resort to proxy or covert actions. Faced with the development of bellicose democratic states, dissenters argued that traditional democratic-peace theory is the result of correlative phenomena mistaken for causal relationship—a sure sign of a theory's questionable veracity and utility.

By modifying traditional analysis and accounting for volatile states, democratic-peace theory can be salvaged. In his book, *Political Order in Changing Societies*, Samuel P. Huntington argues that rising political participation leads to conflict and instability in states with weak political institutions.[13] Mansfield and Snyder's research confirms Huntington's four-decades-old theory, "show[ing] that incomplete democratic transitions—those that get stalled before reaching the stage of full democracy—increase the chance of involvement in international war in countries where governmental institutions are weak at the outset of the transition."[14] By reconciling traditional democratic-peace theory with institutionally weak transitional democratic states, Mansfield and Snyder are able to conclude that,

> "In the short run, however, the beginning stages of transitions to democracy often give rise to war rather than peace . . . In democratizing states, nationalism is an ideology with tremendous appeal for elites

whose privileges are threatened . . . Nationalist rhetoric demands government for the people, but not necessarily by the people. States risk nationalist violence when they attempt to transition to democracy without institutions of public accountability . . . our research shows that this insight is important not only for understanding the stability of democracy within countries, but also for understanding international conflict between them. In an era in which troubled, incomplete democratic transitions may engulf such geopolitically salient locations as the Middle East and China, this dynamic could be one of the fundamental determinants of the course of world politics . . . [For the divided countries], where institutional groundwork was in place, transitions were peaceful even in geopolitically challenging cases where unresolved national partitions raised the risk of war, as in South Korea and Taiwan."[15]

TAIWAN'S DEMOCRATIZATION: INTO THE FIRE

Taiwan's democratization has been generally viewed as a positive development by the United States. The opening chapter of the 2002 *National Security Strategy of the United States of America* reads, "When we see democratic processes take hold among our friends in Taiwan ... we see example of how authoritarian systems can evolve, marrying local history and traditions with the principles we all cherish." [16] The next year, President George W. Bush expressed his support for improving U.S.-Taiwan relations through the Foreign Relations Authorization Act, Fiscal Year 2003.

Washington was hopeful that Taiwanese democracy would provide a bulwark of stability against an irrational and unilaterally-induced conflict between China and Taiwan. According to Edward Chen, professor of the Graduate Institute of American Studies at Tamkang University, "this move was undoubtedly as a big step forward for relations with the U.S. as when Washington adjusted its Taiwan policy in 1994."

But Washington's hopes were quickly dashed. At the same time Washington was heaping praise upon Taiwan, Taipei was busy drumming up support for a confrontation with China. The ruling party, the DPP, crafted a platform of extolling Taiwanese nationalism with populist rhetoric. President Chen Shui-bian stoked the fire to inferno proportions on August 3, 2002 by calling for a referendum on Taiwan's formal independence from China. Beijing shot back, warning that "Taiwan choosing independence is tantamount to choosing war."[17]

Chen had gone too far. He and his political agents had created a "ticking bomb" and escalated the tensions in the Taiwan Strait without any consideration for geopolitical stability. Taiwan's unilateral actions were also seriously hampering Washington's major goal of enticing China to become a responsible international stakeholder. Faced with intense criticism, Chen sent Tsai Ing-wen, former chairwoman of Taiwan's Mainland Affairs Council and DPP chairwoman to Washington several times to assuage American concerns.

The Rise of Taiwanese Nationalism

The simultaneous rise of the DPP and Taiwanese nationalism was no coincidence. Like many other institutionally immature democracies throughout history, the ruling clique recognized the electoral possibilities of harnessing nationalist fervor. As a popular trend, nationalism is practically tailor-made for the democratic process, as it "helps define the people who are exercising self-determination. It thus clarifies the line between 'the people' and their external foes, who become scapegoats in a self-fulfilling strategy that rallies support for defense against external threat."[18]

As Taiwan steadily crystallized the line between "the people" and "the other," even America seemed to be seduced by this new nation-building exercise. Chen's wife, Wu Shu-jen, visited the United States in September of 2002 and made a speech to the American Enterprise Institute in which she referred to Taiwan as a "country." Later, while on his way to celebrate the 100th anniversary of Panama's independence, Chen was allowed to receive the International League for Human Rights Award in New York City. During his three-hour visit to Panama, then Secretary of State Colin Powell even met briefly with Chen. The DPP naturally saw this as a clear sign of Washington's support for Taiwan's democracy and Chen's policies.

Washington soon realized how dangerous Chen had become. Chen's second term was largely defined by his initiative to bid for a seat in the United Nations. It would become a formidable symbol of Taiwanese nationalism and Chen was determined to milk the benefits. The summer of 2007 may well be remembered for the fiercest wave of nationalist fervor to hit Taiwan as its United Nations campaign shifted into overdrive. However, "this time, Taiwan directly defied Washington's warning not to do so . . . For the first time, Chen's UN bid was made—twice in July (July 19 and July 27) and then officially in September during the annual UN session—under the name Taiwan, not 'Republic of China.'"[19]

The United Nations predictably rejected all three bids. The DPP's referendum on UN membership also failed to pass in March 2008, suggesting that the nationalist fervor in Taiwan may be spent for the time being. Washington and the international community collectively breathed a loud and clear sigh of relief.

The Triumph of Populism

The first decade of Taiwanese democracy is best remembered for the rise of nationalism and the triumph of populist manipulation. Security and development were sacrificed on the altar of expedient political victories as politicians made deliberately inflammatory statements to rile up the voter base. Ballot initiatives became political tools to secure victory for the DPP. In short, Taiwan's first two democratically elected presidents, Lee Tung-hui and Chen, flagrantly defied good judgment to transform the Taiwan Strait into one of the world's most dangerous flashpoints. David M. Lampton and Richard Daniel Ewing, the former director and assistant director of Chinese Studies at the Washington-based Nixon Center, accurately predicted in 2002 that, "Domestic political calculations in Taipei may drive U.S.-Taiwan relations, not to mention U.S.-China ties, into unwelcome and dangerous territory."[20]

It began with Lee, a nationalist leader with notoriously populist tendencies; he set the stage for the eventual explosion of populist/nationalist politics in Taiwan. In 1999, he called for "special state-to-state relations" between Taiwan and China. After he stepped down as president, Lee continued to stir up controversy by vocally supporting Taiwan's cultural separation from China. In early September 2002 he asserted that "Taiwan should unhook itself from China culturally" because Chinese culture is "regressive." In late September and mid-October of the same year, Lee tried to throw all of East Asia into turmoil by proclaiming Japan's claim over the Diaoyutai (also known as the Tiaoyutai or the Senkaku) Islands superior to the Republic of China or the People's Republic of China's claim. Lee took the next step and argued that "The Republic of China in fact no longer exists . . . Taiwan must begin by correcting its name, making the nation and its official name consistent with reality."[21]

Chen was eager to jump on a bandwagon that promised such tantalizing electoral prospects after his policies failed to produce results. He first looked to internationalize the "Taiwan problem" by remarking on August 3, 2002, that, "simply put, with Taiwan and China on each side of the Strait, each side is a country." By the time his reelection efforts got under way in 2004, Chen realized that his domestic policies were failing. Chen responded by forcibly diverting the electorate's attention to the "pressing" issue of independence.

World opinion was unequivocal: Chen's tack was foolish and abuses democratic mechanisms. Former French president Jacques Chirac succinctly explained that "it would be a grave mistake. It would be taking a heavy responsibility for stability in the region." [22] James Lilly, former U.S. Ambassador to China, warned that "Taiwan should give careful consideration to the referendum issue and ask itself what concrete results will come from it . . . referendums are not a good way to do business."

Across the Pacific, the United States became increasingly worried about the fledgling democracy's excesses. Bush told Chinese Communist Party ("CCP") General Secretary Hu Jintao that the United States would not support Taiwanese independence. During the Evian meeting, Bush reiterated Washington's commitment to the One China Policy as articulated in the 1971, 1978, 1982 communiqués and the Taiwan Relations Act of 1979. Without mincing any words, Bush delivered a clear message to Taiwan's pro-independence faction: don't expect American support, proceed at your own risk.

But Chen could not (and did not want to) retract his populist message once he had set the forces of nationalism in motion. This became even more evident when his reelection prospects dimmed in 2004. Chen introduced the 2004 referendums on arms purchase and independence as a last ditch effort to save his incumbency. Beijing had no choice but to issue the usual threats against Taiwanese independence. While his machinations would win him the election, Chen lost a tremendous amount of credibility. He had blatantly played a dangerous game of brinkmanship, even going so far as to demonize Washington, saying that he would play the hero and not bow to U.S. meddling in Taiwanese politics. Worse still, both referendums failed to pass, strongly suggesting to Taiwanese observers that the DPP engaged in strategy of populist manipulation.

Four years later, Taiwan experienced a laughably predictable case of déjà vu. On February 2, 2008, Taiwan's Central Electoral Commission declared that a referendum on United Nations membership in the name of Taiwan would be held along with the presidential election on March 22. This time Chen and the DPP proceeded with slightly more subtlety. According to him, the referendum "is aimed at rejecting unification with China rather than moving toward de facto Taiwan unification."[23]

Nevertheless, no one would be deceived a second time. The new referendum squarely put Taiwan back on the fast-track to geopolitical instability. America was not amused. In the measured words of U.S. Secretary of State Condoleezza Rice, "Taiwan's referendum . . . is a provocative policy. It unnecessarily raises tensions in the Taiwan Strait and it promises no real benefits for the people of Taiwan on the international stage. That is why we oppose this referendum."[24]

By now Chen had completely worn out his welcome in Washington and was overstepping his role in the greater scheme of security in the Far East. Although Chen declared that "the reason Taiwan enjoys its democracy today is because of the encouragement and support of the U.S. government and American people," he threatened that U.S. opposition to his policies could trigger an emotional backlash from the Taiwanese people and lead to unfavorable relations between the two parties.[25] Implicit blackmail aside, Chen was unilaterally attempting to dismantle Washington's strategy of insuring that all parties in the Taiwan Strait act as "responsible stake-holders."[26]

On March 22, 2008, the Taiwanese people demonstrated their commitment to a free and open political system and overwhelmingly elected Ma as president. With 76% of eligible voters turning out, Ma beat the DPP candidate, Frank Hsieh, with 58% of the votes. Faced with the options of reunification, independence or continuation of the status quo, the substantial majority of Taiwanese chose the status quo, at least for the foreseeable future.[27]

DEMOCRATIZATION IN CHINA: THE RIDDLE

Although it may not seem obvious to the outsider, political and social change is brewing in China. Before 2006, "Beijing ha[d] limited legal reform only to politically safe area, such as commercial and administrative law, and ha[d] barred legal reform from politically sensitive areas such as political dissent, labor unrest, and religious freedom."[28] However, in April of 2006, Hu himself proclaimed that without democracy there could be no modernization. One year later, in a much-publicized speech, Hu acknowledged the growing public demand for a say in politics. China had indeed been on a road toward democratization, although as Hu notes, "over the three decades since China began its 'reform and opening up,' changes to China's political structure had proceeded in an 'active and prudent way.'"[29]

On October 23, 2006, the *Beijing Daily News* published an essay entitled "Democracy is a Good Thing." It was republished later by the *Study Times*, one of the CCP's leading theoretical journals. The essay's author, Yu Keping, is the deputy director of China's Central Translation Bureau and a leading member of the think tank under the Hu Jintao-Wen Jiabao administration. Yu's stature and the essay's placement sparked wide discussions inside and outside of China. In an illuminating passage, Yu writes,

"Democracy is a good thing, and this is not just for specific persons or certain officials; this is for the entire nation and its broad masses of people . . . Democracy is a good thing, but that does not mean that everything about democracy is good . . . among all the political systems that have been invented and implemented, democracy is the one with the least amount of flaws . . . Democracy is a good thing, but that does not mean that democracy can do everything and solve every problem, but democracy guarantees basic human rights . . . Democracy is a good thing, but that does not mean that democracy does not come without a painful price . . . the price of democracy is sometimes high to the point of unacceptability . . . Democracy is a good thing, but that is not to say that democracy comes unconditionally. Implementing democracy requires the corresponding economic, cultural and political conditions . . . Democracy is a good thing, but that does not mean that democracy can force the people to do things. When one country uses mostly violent methods to force the people in other countries to accept their so-called democratic system, then this is international autocracy and this is international tyranny . . . For us, democracy is all the more so good thing, and it is all the more so essential."[30]

The essay represented a significant step towards political liberalization in China. It is all the more remarkable when viewed under the light that "economic growth, at least in the short term, stabilizes and legitimizes authoritarian regimes more than it undermines them."[31] The CCP's decision to liberalize China's political system shows its determination to act as a "responsible stake-holder" in world politics. It also deserves to be noted that "economic development increased the chance of peaceful evolution toward democracy."[32]

But much like all the reform initiatives undertaken by China in the past thirty years, the results have been mixed and sometimes contradictory. While Hu did use the word "democracy" 269 times in his reports at the 17th Party

Congress of the CCP in October 2007, there are no plans for national elections. On November 14 of the same year, despite the non-existence of any other political party, a white paper on the country's political system stated that China has a system of "multiparty cooperation and political consultation under the leadership of the Communist Party of China."

China's democratization process, therefore, would fit what Mansfield and Snyder call "incomplete democratic transitions." Countries with weak governmental institutions in this stage are especially prone to involvement in international war. [33] According to Susan L. Shirk, "It is China's internal fragility, not its growing strength, that presents the greatest danger. The weak legitimacy of the Communist Party and its leaders' sense of vulnerability could cause China to behave rashly in a crisis involving Japan and Taiwan, and bring it into a military conflict with the United States."[34]

Firebrand Nationalism

China has a multifaceted relationship with its own nationalism. It is a relationship fraught with dangers, sometimes threatening to overthrow Beijing's own authority. Nevertheless, Beijing has long been tapping Chinese nationalism to legitimize its policies: "China's demand to incorporate Taiwan into the People's Republic of China, its animosity toward Japan, and its public displays of resentment at U.S. slights are themes that resonate with the Chinese public and can easily be played upon to rally national solidarity behind the regime."[35] Some scholars argue that, "the Communist Party . . . seems more concerned with rallying domestic opinion by using and responding to the deep strains of nationalism in Chinese Society."[36]

As any student of history can testify, rampant nationalism often leads to disaster for a government increasingly basing its legitimacy on economic development and defense of the "motherland." Joshua Kurlantzick, author of *Charm Offensive: China's Soft Power is Transforming the World*, writes, "in the long run, this explosive nationalism calls into question what kind of democracy China could be. Many Chinese academics, for example, believe that at least in the early going, a freer China might be a more dangerous China. Able to truly express their opinions, young Chinese would be able to put intense pressure on a freer government to adopt a hard line against the West—even, perhaps, to invade Taiwan."[37]

Indeed, the more China encourages virulent nationalism the more likely the international community will shun the country. David Shambaugh, author of *China's Communist Party: Atrophy and Adaptation*, argues that "if Chinese nationalism continues to show its insecure rather than its self-assured side, other nations will adapt their China policies accordingly, and instead of winning the world's respect, China may bring upon itself exactly the kind of 'containment' policies it regularly denounces."[38] Such international ostracism will only serve to alienate the Chinese more and start a vicious circle of recriminations.

Combined with China's rising military power and declining ability to control its own public, the prospects of war rise ever increasingly.[39]

IMPLICATIONS

With two radically different approaches to democratization, Taipei and Beijing should work to avoid "the clash between Taiwan's new nationalism and China's old nationalism."[40]

Taiwanese Democracy: A Period of Consolidation

Taiwan has just passed Huntington's "two turn-over test" and is now entering an era more conducive to regional stability. Not only did the KMT victory in the 2008 presidential election confirm Taiwan's status as a consolidated democracy, it ushered in a possibility of reversing a decade of dangerous and needlessly incendiary policies. According to Minxin Pei, a senior associate at the Carnegie Endowment for International Peace, the resounding KMT victory "has raised hopes for a new era of stability across the Taiwan Strait." The *Chicago Tribune* similarly writes that Ma's victory "is a refreshing break from the position of outgoing President Chen, who antagonized the mainland by rejecting the 'one-China' principle."[41]

President Ma's primary goal should be reversing the trend of deteriorating Taipei/Beijing relations. A complimentary goal would be to strengthen Taiwan's base from which the island can stand its own against China while becoming a credible player in the greater East Asia sphere. By reinforcing the domestic strengths of Taiwan, President Ma has a better chance of projecting Taiwan as a confident and equal actor in both cross-strait and international relations. Continuing a program of what amounts to begging international organizations to admit Taiwan has been shown to be mostly counterproductive.

Taiwan can redefine its role in the East Asia region by pursing a reassessment of the island's priorities. First, the government must redirect attention to the economy as the foundation of Taiwanese policy. Taiwan's stature on the international stage is a direct result of sustained economic growth. Its export driven economy is highly dependent on smart policies and receptive markets—none more important than China. With China absorbing the lion's share of Taiwanese exports, now estimated to have topped more than 33%, any responsible discussion will have to include China's role in Taiwan's economic future.

President Ma's strategy has been to call for a proactive effort to achieve economic normalization between China and Taiwan. His guiding philosophy is that economic growth promotes peaceful relations.[42] To further his agenda, President Ma has called a relaxation of restrictions for Chinese investors in Taiwan, direct sea and air cargo links, and an unprecedented expansion of number of Chinese tourists allowed to visit Taiwan.[43]

Second, President Ma must define the concept Taiwanese sovereignty to reincorporate the "One-China" principle. Beijing has repeatedly reiterated that "as long as they [Taiwan] agree to the one-China principle, everything can be discussed." [44] This includes Taiwanese participation in international organizations such as the World Health Organization. Official white papers coming out of CCP's bureaus have long ago dropped any pretenses of invading Taiwan save in the event of Taiwan's declaration of formal independence. China's Anti-Secession Law of 2005 codified the Chinese government's (though not necessarily the military's) complacency with the status quo arrangement regarding Taiwan's sovereignty.

Under such circumstances, Taiwan's interests would be best served by maintaining the status quo sovereignty arrangement. That is to say, exercise full sovereignty in internal and international affairs while never deviating from the letter of the "One-China" policy. A Taiwan that comfortably acts without stepping on China's toes will elicit greater cooperation from foreign partners. When the June 10, 2008 fishing boat incident near the Tiaoyutai Islands erupted into a crisis between Taiwan and Japan, President Ma issued a strong rebuke against Japanese behavior and recalled Taiwan's chief representative to Tokyo. [45] Through a strong and assured response, Taiwan defanged Japan's bully tactics, forcing Tokyo to come to the negotiating table as an equal. Indeed, in January of 2009, Japan and Taiwan agreed to restart stalled talks over the Tiaoyutai Islands. [46]

Moreover, a self-confident Taiwanese foreign policy will not need to engage in a costly war of recognition. President Chen's policy of engaging in an escalating war of dollar diplomacy yielded few tangible results. Moreover, as China's economy grows, Taiwan grows less and less able to keep up with Beijing's expenditures.

Nevertheless, Taiwan should strive to maintain relationships with those countries that do recognize the island. As President Ma puts it, "the 23 countries are very important to us as a source of dignity." [47] To ensure Taiwan's continued recognition by these countries, President Ma must work to declare a diplomatic truce with Beijing. He has already made overtures in this direction by declaring his intention to proceed under the "1992 consensus" and calling for "dignity, autonomy, pragmatism and flexibility" to serve as the guiding principles for the future of Taiwan. [48]

Chinese Diplomacy: Carrot, not Whip

Beijing's best option is to accommodate and cooperate with Taiwan, rather than aggressively pursue reunification. To that end, "Beijing has stressed the use of 'extra-military' strategies in dealing with Taiwan . . . [and] has expanded its tools to influence Taiwan including economic, cultural, social as well as other extra-military means." [49] Hu even offered to negotiate a "peace treaty" with Taiwan. These are hardly the signs of an aggressive behemoth, bent on domination.

However, China can do more. To alleviate the still-present tension, "Beijing needs to think creatively about how to gradually allow Taiwan international space. This is a crucial subject and necessary to win the hearts and minds of Taiwanese people."[50] On the economic front, China can give Singapore the green light to sign a free trade agreement with Taiwan. Militarily, China should reassure the world that it's increasing military budget does not rise to the level of actual threat to peace—that the "infusion of funds into military modernization . . . does not match the all-out military buildups that occurred in early twentieth-century Germany and Japan and led them to war."[51] Moreover, China should withdraw missiles pointed at Taipei on the condition that Taiwan scale back arms purchases. Such a deal would be highly symbolic and win public-relations points for China and Taiwan.[52]

Domestically, China can make a major effort to rein in virulent nationalism and competitive populism. In the past, the government had often riled up nationalistic fervor to support questionable policies against foreign entities, e.g. anti-Japanese, anti-Soviet, anti-American campaigns. But now, with the proliferation of mass media outlets, nationalism in China runs the danger of spinning out of the control of the central government. If such sentiments come to incorporate an aggressive claim to Taiwan (and all indicators seem to suggest this to be the case), peace prospects will grow ever dimmer.

CONCLUSION

The future of Taiwan/China relations must be determined by the rational and practical policies of the two sides. Ideology and poorly conceived saber-rattling have not produced any satisfactory results: those favoring unification believe the past decade to be lost; those hoping to keep the status quo saw an exponential rise in danger in the late 1990s and early 2000s that has only just begun to subside; even for proponents of formal independence, the past decade's policies have led nowhere—Taiwan remains excluded from international organizations, economic ties with China are increasing, not decreasing, and Taiwan's biggest ally, America, grows less tolerant of Taipei's rhetoric with each passing day. Consolidation and a return to the fundamental policies of economic growth and stabilization will give the island a better chance at becoming an institutionally mature democracy. This, in turn, will allow the island ever greater *de facto* autonomy in dealings with China and the world.

As democracy becomes ever more entrenched in Taiwan, the island can indeed become the bastion of reason the United States envisioned. Successful and full maturity of Taiwan's democracy could be the world's best hope for defusing a "nearly six-decade conflict with China and put to rest one of the last vestiges of the cold war in Asia."[53]

NOTES

[1] Ying Ma, "China's Stubborn Anti-Democracy." *Policy Review*, Feb/March, 2007.
[2] Susan L. Shirk, *China: Fragile Superpower*. New York: Oxford University Press, 2007, p.182.
[3] "High official of KMT: Cross-Strait confrontation worse than the time of 'two-state theory' and 17th Party Congress must strongly oppose Taiwanese independence." *Mingbao*, Oct. 1, 2007.
[4] Edward D. Mansfield and Jack Snyder, "Democratization and War." *Foreign Affairs*, Vol. 74, No. 3 (1995), pp. 79-97.
[5] Michael Mandelbaum, "Democracy Without America." *Foreign Affairs*, Vol. 86, No. 5 (Sept/Oct 2007), pp. 129-130.
[6] "Taiwan's new comfort zone," *Chicago Tribune* (editorial), March 31, 2008.
[7] David A. Lake, "Powerful Pacifists: Democratic States and War," *American Political Science Review*, Vol. 86, No. 1 (1992), pp. 24-37.
[8] David A. Lake, Dan Reiter and Allan C. Stam III, "Democracy, War Initiation, and Victory," *American Political Science Review*, Vol. 92, No. 2 (1998), pp. 377-390.
[9] D. Scott and Bennett and Allan C. Stam, "The Duration of Interstate Wars, 1816-1985," *American Political Science Review*, Vol. 90, No. 2 (1996), pp. 239-257. Randolph M. Silverson, "Democracies and War Participation: In Defense of the Institutional Constraints Argument," *European Journal of International Relations*, No. 1 (1995), pp. 481-490.
[10] William J. Dixon, "Democracy and the Peaceful Settlement of International Conflict," *American Political Science Review*, Vol. 88, No. 1 (1994), pp. 14-32. Michael Mousseau, "Democracy and Compromise in Militarized Interstate Conflict, 1816-1992," *Journal of Conflict Resolution*, Vol. 42, No. 2 (1998), pp. 210-230.
[11] Randall Schweller, "Democratic Structure and Preventive War: Are Democracies More Pacific?" *World Politics*, Vol. 44, No.2 (1992), pp. 235-269.
[12] Jacek Kugler and Yi Feng, "Explaining and Modeling Democratic Transitions," *Journal of Conflict Resolution*, Vol. 43, No. 2 (April 1999), p. 139.
[13] Samuel P. Huntington, *Political Order in Changing Societies*, New Haven: Yale University Press, 1968.
[14] Edward D. Manfield and Jack Snyder, *Electing to Fight: Why Emerging Democracies Go to War*, Cambridge: MIT Press, 2005, p. 4.
[15] Edward D. Mansfield and Jack Snyder, *Electing to Fight: Why Emerging Democracies Go to War*, Cambridge: MIT Press, 2005, pp. 2, 8, 13.
[16] "National Security Strategy of the United States of America." United States State Department. 2002. <www.state.gov/documents/organization/63562.pdf>
[17] Xing Xhigang, "Army Blasts Pro-Independence Comment," *The China Daily*, Aug. 7, 2002.
[18] Edward D. Mansfield and Jack Snyder, *Electing to Fight: Why Emerging Democracies Go to War*, Cambridge: MIT Press, 2005, p. 10.
[19] Yu Bin, "America's Rogue Ally," *Foreign Policy in Focus*, November 1, 2007.
[20] *The China Post*, Sept. 14, 2002, p. 19.
[21] Lee Tung-hui, "Rectifying Taiwan's Name," *Far East Economic Review*, Oct. 16, 2003, p. 29.
[22] "Taiwan Regrets Chirac's Referendum Comments," *The China Post*, Jan. 28, 2004, p.1.
[23] "U.N. Referendum 'Rejection of Unification,'" *The China Post*, Jan. 3, 2008, p. 19.
[24] "U.S. Opposes 'Provocative' Taiwan Referendum Bid: Rice," *Reuters*, December 21, 2007. <www.reuters.com/article/politicsNews/idUSN2160129120071221>

25 Denny V. Hickey, "Reading China's 'Peace' as 'Sugar-coated Poison,'" *Chicago Tribune*, Jan. 6, 2008.
26 "U.S. Opposition may Create Backlash: Chen," *The China Post*, Dec. 7, 2007, p. 15.
27 John R. Bolton, "What's Good for Taiwan," *Los Angeles Times*, March 29, 2008.
28 Matthew Stephenson, "A Trojan Horse in China?" in Thomas Carothers, ed., *Promoting the Rule of Law Abroad: In Search of Knowledge*, Carnegie Endowment for International Peace, 2006, p. 203.
29 "Democracy? Hu Needs It," *The Economist*, June 30, 2007, p. 31.
30 Translation from "Democracy is a Good Thing."
31 Bruno Bueno de Mesquita and George W. Downs, "Development and Democracy," *Foreign Affairs*, Vol. 84, No. 5 (Sept/Oct 2005), pp. 77-86.
32 Jacek Kugler and Yi Feng, "Explaining and Modeling Democratic Transitions," *Journal of Conflict Resolution*, Vol. 43, No. 2 (April 1999), p. 143.
33 Edward D. Mansfield and Jack Snyder, *Electing to Fight: Why Emerging Democracies Go to War*, Cambridge: MIT Press, 2005, p. 4.
34 Susan L. Shirk, *China: Fragile Super Power*, New York: Oxford University Press, 2007, p. 255.
35 Edward D. Mansfield and Jack Snyder, *Electing to Fight: Why Emerging Democracies Go to War*, Cambridge: MIT Press, 2005, p. 15.
36 Jim Yardley, "Nationalist at Core of China's Reaction to Tibet Unrest," *International Herald Tribune*, March 30, 2008.
37 Joshua Kurlantzick, "China's Next-generation Nationalists," *Los Angeles Times*, May 6, 2008.
38 David Shambaugh, "China's Competing Nationalism," *International Herald Tribune*, May 5, 2008.
39 Susan L. Shirk, *China: Fragile Superpower*, New York: Oxford University Press, 2007, p. 183.
40 Ian Buruma, "Taiwan's New Nationalists," *Foreign Affairs*, Vol. 75, No. 4 (1996), pp.77-91.
41 "Taiwan's New Comfort Zone," *Chicago Tribune* (editorial), March 31, 2008.
42 Keith Bradsher and Edward Wong, "Taiwan's Leader Outlines His Policy Toward China," *New York Times*, June 19, 2008.
43 Jonathan Adams, "The Key to Cross-Strait Détente," *The Far East Economic Review*, July 6, 2008.
44 David R. Sands and Bill Gertz, "Taiwan Talks Rest on Sovereignty Conditions," *Washington Times*, June 6, 2008.
45 "Taipei Reaffirms Sovereignty Over Tiaoyutai Islands," The *China Post*, June 13, 2008. <http://www.chinapost.com.tw/taiwan/foreign%20affairs/2008/06/13/160750/Taipei-reaffirms.htm>
46 "Senkaku Fishery Talks to Restart," *The Japan Times Online*, Jan. 7, 2009. <http://search.japantimes.co.jp/cgi-bin/nn20090107a8.html>
47 Keith Bradsher and Edward Wong, "Taiwan Leader Outlines His Policy Toward China," *New York Times*, June 19, 2008.
48 "President Ma's Inaugural Address (Translated)," Office of the President, Republic of China (Taiwan), May 20, 2008. <http://www.president.gov.tw/en/prog/news_release/document_content.php?id=1105499687&pre_id=1105499691&g_category_number=145&category_number_2=145&layer=&sub_category=>
49 Chong-Pin Lin, "More Carrot Than Stick: Beijing's Emerging Taiwan Policy," *China Security*, Vol. 4, No. 1 (Winter 2008), p. 5.
50 Chong-Pin Lin, "More Carrot Than Stick: Beijing's Emerging Taiwan Policy," *China Security*, Vol. 4, No. 1 (Winter 2008), pp. 15-16.

[51] Susan L. Shirk, *China: Fragile Superpower*, New York: Oxford University Press, 2007, p. 72.
[52] Jonathan Adams, "Cross-Strait Missile Games," *Far East Economic Review*, April 2008.
[53] Michael Schuman, "Ma Ying-jeou," *Time*, April 28, 2008.

Chapter 6

China's Policy on Regional Cooperation in East Asia

Marion Chyun-Yang Wang

INTRODUCTION

In the era of globalization, the power constellation in East Asia is shifting. Because of China's opening-up policy, market scale, and huge capital and human resources, the Greater China (China, Hong Kong, Macao and Taiwan), Association of Southeast Asian Nations (ASEAN)-China (ASEAN+1) and ASEAN-China, Japan and Republic of Korea (ASEAN+3) have operated materially under the framework of China's *hongguan tiaokong zhengce* (macro economic control policy). Based on its opening-up policy, China has received foreign investment *via* Special Economic Zones (SEZs) and the opening of coastal cities and delta areas to get geo-economic and socialcultural advantages both in Asia and globally. China has appealed to Greater China to invest in China's market. The vertical division of labor among China, Hong Kong, Macao, and Taiwan has been formed gradually; this in turn has shaped Greater China as a subregional economic zone in East Asia. The new wave of regional cooperation in East Asia, which is based on open regionalism and led by the nations from within, is shaping a new arrangement of power in this region. As a regional internal power, China *per se* pushes a multilateral strategy of regional cooperation in East Asia, i.e., China drives Greater China *via* the Closer Economic Partnership Arrangement (CEPA) for Hong Kong and Macao and the Pan Pearl River Delta Regional Cooperation and Development Forum (PPRD, 9+2) as well as the newly proposed Comprehensive Economic Cooperation Agreement (CECA) and *haixia jingjiqu* (Cross-Strait Economic Zone) for Taiwan as core of this strategy.[1] Then, *via* ASEAN+1, ASEAN+3 and Boao Forum for Asia (BFA) China will set the agenda for the regional cooperation in East Asia aiming to *zouxiang shijie* (go globally).

In this chapter the way in which China puts this strategy into play will be analyzed in four parts, from the perspectives of economic interdependence, security cooperation and power sharing. The first part is an overview of the power constellation in East Asia. In the second part the progress of interdependence within Greater China is examined. In the third part China's strategy on regional cooperation in East Asia is comprehensively analyzed. The relevant study in prospect is set out in the final part.

THE POWER CONSTELLATION IN EAST ASIA

The key players shaping power constellation in East Asia are the U.S., China and Japan. With the end of Cold War the bi-polar world system collapsed; the ongoing global financial crisis, which began in the U.S. in 2008, accelerated a new process of power shift in the world system. This in turn has weakened the influence of U.S. as the leading *status quo* power in East Asia. After 1945 the U.S. government opted for a hub-and-spokes system of bilateral alliances in Asia with the U.S. at the center.[2] America's national interests in Asia are as follows: to prevent domination of the continent by a single power, especially an adversarial one; to enlist the contribution of Asian nations to mitigate intra-Asian conflicts, to prevent or at least to limit the further spread of nuclear weapons, and to support the nations of Asia in that effort. The geopolitical interest of every major Asian nation, including China, is how to prevent their neighbors from combining against it. Japan's nightmare is the consolidation of the Chinese giant. American relations with China will have an important affect on Japanese-American relations. Sino-Japanese relations are dominated by ambivalence on both sides.[3]

After its defeat in the Second World War, Japan has concentrated on its economic recovery, leaving security policy largely to the U.S. The U.S.-Japan security alliance has assured Japan of the security it needs, without Japan having to build up its own military forces and particularly a nuclear capability, which would destabilize the region.[4] With respect to the common security, Japan is invited to share burdens based on concepts devised in Washington and transmitted to Tokyo as received truth.[5] Since the end of the Cold War in 1991 the U.S. administration has supported Japanese rearmament, Japan's remilitarization has taken many forms, including expanded military budgets, legitimizing and legalizing the sending of military forces abroad, a commitment to join the American missile defense program and a growing acceptance of military solutions to international problems. This in turn promotes hostility between China and Japan and sabotages possible peaceful solutions in those two hotspots, the Taiwan Strait and North Korea, left over from the Chinese and Korean civil wars, and lays the foundation for a possible future of Sino-American conflict.

Since 1992, it has enacted twenty-one major pieces of security-related legislation, nine in 2004 alone. These began with the International Peace Cooperation Law of 1992, which for the first time authorized Japan to send troops to participate in United Nations (UN) peacekeeping operations.[6] The incursion by Chinese submarine into waters off Okinawa in November 2004,

China's search for natural gas in an area of the East China Sea which is viewed by Japan as lying within its exclusive economic zone[7] and a nuclear-armed North Korea have all led to Japan's feeling insecure and vulnerable. Japan thus signed on to develop a missile defense system with U.S. aid, and is easing constitutional limits on the development of its military forces.

Beijing has perceived the U.S. presence in Northeast Asia, calculating that U.S. maritime power will continue to play the role of a balancer, suppressing any third power, notably Japan, from emerging to dominate the region.[8] In this regard, the Chinese concern is the possibility of a joint U.S.-Japanese intervention in the Taiwan Strait, if there is an armed conflict. From China's view, the development of the theater missile defense (TMD) system serves the purpose of deterring its missile capabilities. Taiwan's effort to get a TMD umbrella is the most dangerous scenario in Chinese military planning. The strengthening of the U.S. military and political ties with China's neighboring countries is also perceived in the same vein.[9]

As a rapidly industrializing nation, China developed much more demand for petroleum and other raw materials, which brought it into direct competition with the world's largest importers, the U.S. and Japan. By the summer of 2004, the U.S. government became alarmed over China's growing power and its potential to challenge American hegemony in East Asia. In order for the U.S. to maintain its role as the leading *status quo* in East Asia, it urged Japan's rearmament and revision of article 9 of its constitution (renouncing the use of force except in the case of self-defense). As a bargain chip the U.S. also promised Taiwan that if China uses of force to prevent a Taiwanese declaration of independence, "America will help Taiwan defend itself." America's intention is also to use its alliance with Japan as a proxy in checkmating North Korea. Due to Japanese right-wing nationalism and fear that a burgeoning capitalist China threatens Japan's established position as the leading economic power in East Asia, Japanese officials also claim that the country feels threatened by North Korea's developing nuclear and missile programs.[10]

Japan's traditional problems with China, Korea and Russia may be exacerbated by Japan's concern for the security of sea lanes as a result of China's territorial claims in the South China Sea and East China Sea. China and other East Asian countries protested against a Japanese high-profile political elite's visit to the *Yasukuni* Shrine, and against Japan's revision of historical textbook about Japan's invasion in East Asia during World War II, and remain seriously skeptical of Japan's revision of its constitution, which allows Japanese government to send Self Defense Forces abroad for "peace-keeping." Japan's economy has long been in recession, and Japan's resurgent right-wing nationalism and its consistent refusal to open its agricultural markets to Asian countries makes Japan extremely wary of any trade deal with Republic of Korea (ROK), or opposed to implementing higher duties against exports from China. Japanese producers even plan to exploit a weaker *Yen* to regain some of the shares of world manufacturing that they have lost to ROK, Taiwan, and China.[11] All of these would seem that it is even more important for Japan to cling closely to the U.S.-Japan security alliance in spite of the opposition at home. With respect to China's military modernization, in 2005 U.S. administration authored an "out of area and out of business" military agreement with Japan. Consequently, Japan, with no official pacifism, joined the U.S. administration in identifying security in the Taiwan Strait as a "common strategic objective." Japanese Prime Minister Taro Aso even remarked in February 2009 that the five uninhabited islets *Diaoyu* Islands located between Taiwan and Okinawa were part of Japanese territory, and hence covered by the U.S.-Japan security treaty.[12]

In this regard, China passed the Anti-Secession Law, which indicates use of force as due resort for Taiwan's *de jure* secession from China, and accelerated its efforts to integrate Taiwan into Greater China as well. According to the discourse of realism, the national interest can be put into practice only by national power. China, as a regional and possible world power, depends on its combination of control of access to the largest untapped market in the world, possession of nuclear weapons, and a permanent seat on the UN Security Council. Chinese domestic economic growth, despite the current international economic downturn, is expected to continue for decades, reflecting the pent-up demand of its huge population, relatively low levels of personal debt, and a dynamic underground economy not recorded in official statistics. Besides, China external debt is relatively small and easily covered by its reserves, whereas that is not the case for both the U.S. and Japan. Well-established and persisting features of the U.S.-China bilateral economic relationship includes China's reliance on access to U.S. export markets, capital, and technology; U.S. dependence on inexpensive Chinese products; and the China's willingness to buy U.S. debt as well as hold U.S. dollar denominated assets. With the current financial crisis, China's importance as a purchaser and holder of U.S. debt will become more important for the U.S.[13]

With its renaissance China regards its relations with U.S. as partner, but the Taiwan issue still stands at the core of China-U.S. relations.[14] Beijing and Washington have significant compatible interests and agendas such as the Korean peninsula and the Taiwan Strait. The leadership in Beijing has made national economic development, which depends significantly on good relations with the Washington, a higher near-term priority than national reunification, which risks serious friction with Washington over Cross-Strait issues. Ma Ying-jeou's succession to the presidency in Taiwan in May 2008 brought significant reduction in the tension that characterized U.S.-Taiwan relations during the last decade. This in turn reduced the Taiwan issue as a point of friction in U.S.-China relations.[15]

The U.S. administration of President Barak Obama prefers a more multilateral approach to international issues. The U.S. and China have broadly compatible interests on major issues such as dealing with the current international economic crisis and the chronically crisis-prone Korean peninsula and Taiwan Strait. Washington and Beijing have strong common interests in avoiding a disruptive transition for a post-Kim Jong-Il North Korea.[16] For China, a more favorable security environment in the Korean peninsula would be more conducive to its efforts to concentrate on its own Four Modernizations; it does not want to get involved in a proxy war with the U.S. China remains interested in maintaining the balance of power in the Korean peninsula and in playing the role of a mediator in an area which is strategically important to China's security and where it is correspondingly keen to maintain peace and stability.[17]

North Korea's long-term objective has not been war, it is not able to sustain, but to demoralize ROK, that is, ROK, and undermine its relations with the U.S. by discussing the future of the Korea peninsula directly with Washington. The ROK sees in its alliance with the U.S. a way both to preserve its independence and to promote Korean reunification; in addition, ROK needs China to balance its relations with North Korea, Japan, and Russia.[18] ROK's President Lee Myung Bak has taken a hard-line approach, including reservations about the inter-Korean agreements to the North Korea *vis-à-vis* his two predecessors. Since Bak took office in February 2008, Pyongyang has cut off all direct contact between the two governments and banned ROK officials from the country.[19]

In the light of the North Korean nuclear and missile-launch crisis, the U.S. recognized the necessity for a multilateral approach, namely the Six Party Talks. [20] North Korea agreed to disable its main nuclear reactor in Yongbyon by the end of October 2008 in return for deliveries of fuel oil and other economic aid. Pyongyang has also been promised improved diplomatic ties with Washington and Tokyo. Former U.S. President George W. Bush had started a process to remove Pyongyang from the U.S. list of state sponsors of terrorism in return for the North Korea's denuclearization process.[21]

The U.S. move to take North Korea off the list of terrorism-supporting states, and North Korea's missile launch across over Japan's territory is a setback for Japanese government. Japanese concerns about its importance to the U.S., and Japan's role in the region more generally, reflect a potentially intractable weakness in Japan's position. With respect to power presentation in the region, China's relative rise *vis-à-vis* Japan is evident in economic power, in the hard power that China's newfound wealth can buy, and in China's position as a key player in regional and global processes and institutions, ranging from the Six-Party Talks on North Korea. [22] In this context, Japan's power presentation *vis-à-vis* China's in East Asia is almost *passé*.

In order to deter China and North Korea, Japan upgrades its *Boeicho* (Defense Agency) into a ministry and may possibly develop its own nuclear weapons capability; it could also free itself from its dependency on the American "nuclear umbrella."[23] As geopolitics goes regional, Washington's power presence in East Asia could be *passé* too, despite the U.S.'s strong bilateral security relationship, especially with Japan and ROK. There are already signs that the traditional U.S. leadership in dispute resolution is being superseded by China's cooperative approach. China has the most influences in negotiations over North Korea's nuclear Arsenal.[24]

With respect to the regional economic cooperation, there were two waves after World War II. The first wave of regional cooperation took place from the late 1950s through the 1970s. The most recent wave of regional cooperation has risen in the wake of the Cold War's conclusion. Some actors in the international system are actively promoting and participating in this process. The regional cooperation is consequently rather more multifaceted and multidimensional than in the past.[25] The countries in East Asia are diverse in historical background, political system, economic structure, and religious and socialcultural dimensions. In the first wave of regional cooperation in East Asia, Japan was the first economic miracle. It was followed by "The Four Little Dragons," namely Hong Kong, Taiwan, Singapore, and ROK, and in the 1980s by Malaysia and Thailand. China, Indonesia, and Vietnam appeared as poor East Asian economies. Market-driven regional cooperation has been occurring in East Asia since the mid-1980s through increased trade and investment linkages. This process has been driven by unilateral reforms in individual economies and by the logic of the "flying geese" pattern of relocating production processes to cheaper areas abroad as domestic costs rise.[26]

Before China and the ASEAN members established formal ties in 1991, their relations were marked by mutual suspicion, mistrust and, animosity largely because of China's support for the communist parties in ASEAN countries. Due to the reorientation of China's foreign policy and work for the establishment of a regional security dialogue and cooperation mechanism,[27] the normalization of relations with China in 1990 by Indonesia and then Singapore and Brunei Darussalam acted as a catalyst to set the path for China's admission into the ASEAN Regional Forum (ARF) in 1994 and a full dialogue partner of ASEAN in 1996.[28]

The end of Cold War provides a favorable external environment for Asia. Rich resources, abundant labor forces, and vast markets created unique advantages for Asia's sustained economic growth. The Asian way of regional cooperation keeps speeding up, which will raise the competitiveness of Asia comprehensively. Nowadays in Asia there are the territorial, ethnic and religious issues left over from history, the issue of imbalanced economic development, and such new problems as terrorism, and cross-border crime, as well as deterioration of ecological environment and spread of epidemic diseases.[29] In this context, China has put forth several proposals to develop new security arrangements based on principles of mutual cooperation and security, like bilateral security arrangements throughout the region.[30]

China's security policy for this area is "constructive engagement," but for all the East Asian states the major problem with China's security policy remains the lack of transparency. In 1995 China has announced that it will use international law and UN Convention on the law of the sea to examine the related claims. With respect to the South China Sea disputes, the Korean conflict and the Taiwan issue, the ASEAN has been taking a step-by step approach in engaging the Chinese. For small and medium-sized states, ASEAN has taken an active role in promoting multilateral dialogues on security with China, and it is also trying to engage and integrate China through multilateral channels like ARF. ASEAN hopes that its engagement with China in various dialogues will help the search for confidence-building measures, preventive diplomacy, and conflict resolution so as to preserve peace and security in South-East Asia and the larger Asia-Pacific region.[31]

The lesson of the Asian economic crisis of 1997 taught the Chinese leaders that the keen competition for markets and resources in the context of globalization and the enhancement of regional cooperation gave external factors more opportunities to influence the economic development of one country. Hence, the strengthening of coordination among governments concerned will become all the more essential. Therefore, the Chinese leadership prefers to create a multi-polar world, in which the major powers can develop friendly ties with each other and non-zero-sum games are the norm. China thus proposed the following patterns to establish the multi-polar order in Asia: (1) Economic cooperation as the key focus and development of comprehensive cooperation in a step-by-step approach, whereby trade and communications, agriculture, information and energy could be made priority sectors of cooperation, and then enlarged to other sectors; (2) Pan-Asia cooperation; (3) Step up bilateral cooperation to consolidate the basis of regional cooperation, which is an open one.[32]

In terms of regional cooperation in East Asia, the Japanese government is torn between its East Asian neighbors and the U.S., which is Japan's closest military ally, and has questioned whether regional cooperation could impede potential breakthroughs such as free trade area, but hesitated therefore about the regional cooperation,[33] till former Premier Minister Junichiro Koizumi stated that Japan is following a "two-track approach," namely building a framework in ASEAN as a whole and promoting bilateral efforts with ASEAN members that are ready to do so. "In the aftermath of the Asian financial crisis 1997, Tokyo wants more Official Development Assistance (ODA) going to Asia, which is more important for its security and prosperity," and firmly linked Japan's multilateralism to a regional multilateralism with its attendant identifications. In addition, Japan proposed the creation of an Asian Monetary Fund (AMF), which in turn could make the asianization of the *yen* possible. The expanding "asianisation of the *yen*" combines with Japan's growing institutional and political participation in the region to permit Tokyo to play a bolder hand in Southeast Asian affairs and work to maximize available resources. Japan has spread its interests towards Southeast Asia, "that single space which has been judged suitable for the attainment of a range of tasks," based upon variegated levels of interaction. Both the U.S. and China rejected Japan's idea for the AMF, for the very reason that they did not wish Japan to purchase greater regional leadership credentials by assuming this leading role.[34]

The financial crisis of 1997 reinforced the reality among Japan, China, ROK, and ASEAN that the region will have to work more closely to ensure its macroeconomic and financial stability to prevent a recurrence of the financial crisis.[35] From the ASEAN's view, it needs to strengthen cooperation among the other economies in East Asia, so that China does not become the only growth engine in East Asia. Cooperation amongst other Asian countries will produce a multi-focal, multi-connected pattern of growth, broader and more robust than a hub- and- spokes configuration where every link either starts from or ends in China. ASEAN offers a competitive production base, supplies Japan with many natural resources, especially energy, and contains some of the busiest and most efficient seaports and airports through which Japan can reach out to the world. ASEAN also occupies a strategic location midway between the growing markets of India and China. In developing a new framework for East Asian cooperation, ASEAN is taking an open, inclusive approach. ASEAN prefers a new regional grouping, namely the East Asia Summit, going beyond China, Japan and ROK, to include country that meets certain criteria. Beyond Asia, the key external linkage is with the U.S. In addition, ASEAN intends to establish an ASEAN Security Community to work on conflict resolution. The nuclear and missile-launch crisis sparked by North Korea has provided ASEAN with the opportunity, as chairman of the ARF, to play a role in defusing the tension in the region.[36]

GREATER CHINA: CHINA'S CORE FOR PROMTING EAST ASIAN REGIONAL COOPERATION IN THE ERA OF GLOBALIZATION

According to the worldview of China's decision maker, namely *heping fazhan hezuo hexie* (peace, developments, cooperation, and harmony), the development of multi-polarization and economic globalization bring new opportunities for world peace and development. The primary goal of China's development is to develop a moderately *xiaokang shehui* (well-off society) in a comprehensive way. The approach for Chinese development was and remains peaceful, open, cooperative, harmonious, and win-win. In this regard, China prefers to narrow the wealth gap and develop internally while pursuing peace and development externally. The enormous domestic demand and the broad internal market are the perpetual driving force behind China's economic development. In this context China must handle three key challenges: energy depletion, a deteriorating ecosystem, an imbalance between its economic growth and the wealth gap. The peaceful development approach is thus the *sine quo non* for China's modernization.[37]

Since 1979 China has pursued national reunification *via* modernization, which was based on the strategy initiated by Deng Xiaoping.[38] Therefore, China developed its opening-up policy toward foreign investment through the establishment of SEZs and the opening of coastal cities and delta areas.[39] In the meantime, Taiwan's economy was threatened, because other low-wage countries attracted capital and promised higher profits, which halted the successful continuation of export-led growth, and foreign capital was gradually transferred from Taiwan into mainland China's market. In order to maintain its economic growth after 1981, Taiwan's industry upgraded to high-technology, including information technology, biotechnology, electronics, and precision instruments.[40]

Taiwanese companies, from the perspective of comparative economic advantages, regard China's cheap and abundant labor, vast geographic land, huge domestic market, and strong engineering and technological capacity in selected industries as complementary to Taiwan's abundant capital, manufacturing experience, management skills, and some research and development capacity. These economic interactions, based materially on vertical division of labor, can encourage industries in China to concentrate on low value-added manufacturing while allowing Taiwan to accelerate industrial upgrade. China's traditional orientation toward heavy industries and large state-owned enterprises can therefore be balanced by Taiwan's small and medium-sized firms investing in China, whereby these firms can use their well-established production and marketing networks to help similar firms in China enter into the international market.[41]

At the end of Cold War Taiwan decided in November 1987 that Taiwanese citizens could be allowed to *tanqin* (visit relatives) in mainland China. This in turn sharply accelerated the growth in trade between Taiwan and China. In 1988 *guo wu yuan* (the Chinese State Council) promulgated a set of twenty-two measures to encourage investment from Taiwan, which guaranteed that Taiwan's and Hong Kong's establishments would not be nationalized, that their exported goods would be exempt from export tariffs, and that their management could have complete autonomy in running their firms in mainland China. The delta area (the Hong Kong–Shenzhen–Guangzhou triangle) has been planned by the Chinese government as *kaifang tequ* (an open district) to pioneer many innovations like out-processing and stock trading. After establishing sourcing networks, the Hong Kong and Taiwanese firms then engaged in cross-border production management.

The opening of China's market, the continued high valuation of the new Taiwan dollar, and the termination of Taiwan's Generalized System of Preference Status by the U.S. in January 1989, as well as China's definition in 1994 on the characteristic of Cross-Strait economic interactions as *zhongguo zhuti tong qi dandu guanshuiqu zhi jian de jingmao jiaoliu naru duiwai jingmao guanli tixi jinxing guanli* (the trade between China and its separate tariff zone is handled under the foreign trade management system) made the Chinese market increasingly attractive to Taiwanese businesses. The resulting trend was thus toward growing material interdependence among Hong Kong, Taiwan, and China. This interdependence was reflected in the crystallization of a subregional division of labor among Hong Kong, Taiwan and Guangdong as well as Fujian province in China.[42]

Hong Kong and Taiwan were therefore able to shift their labor-intensive industries to low-wage regions in southern China. This change has involved economic cooperation across the Taiwan Strait as well as in the Pearl River Delta. Without any official links between Taiwan and China, most of the flow of people and money targeted on Fujian province has passed through Hong Kong and Macao. The Cross-Taiwan-Strait area was subordinated to the developments in the Pearl River Delta within the Greater China bloc. The model of economic cooperation between Hong Kong and the Pearl River Delta has thus developed as *qiandian houchang* (front shops, back factories).[43]

With this new development, Taiwanese investment in mainland China has shifted from labor-intensive, low value-added, and short-term operations to more capital-and technology-intensive industries with longer investment horizons such as automobiles, computers, machinery, and petrochemicals. In this regard, Taiwan's government was afraid that the massive one-way outflow of capital and the relocation of high-tech industries to mainland China would accelerate unemployment and eventually lead to deindustrialization in Taiwan.

So, early in January 2001, Taiwan authorized *xiao san tong* (Mini-Three Links), namely direct trade, communications, and travel between the two small islands Kinmen/Matsu and the Chinese mainland.[44] Taiwan furthermore released in November 2001 the mainland policy *jiji kaifang youxiao guanli* (active opening, effective management). This policy was based on the upgrade of Taiwanese industries, but the upgrade of industries still has no breakthrough. In addition, Taiwan's then-ruling party *minjindang* (Democratic Progressive Party, DPP) was torn between economic interactions with China and political independence from China. These two major events gradually depressed Taiwan's economy, which again enhanced the investment of Taiwanese industries in mainland China (see Table 6.1).

After thirty years of reform and opening-up, China has radically liberalized its economy, and its ability to take foreign direct investment (FDI) is growing steadily. China's technology exports continue to grow rapidly, and one of the most important reasons is mainland China's production's getting a boost from Taiwanese companies that have moved their operations to China. Taiwanese firms are also important suppliers of components to leading computer companies in China, which they increasingly plan to use as a base for exporting goods to the rest of the world. Recognizing the engineering and technological capacity and skilled work force in some of China's large state-owned enterprises, Taiwanese companies have begun to ally with them to co-produce some relatively technology- and skill-intensive products such as major computer or vehicle components and parts. Taiwanese industries are fully aware that the only option whereby they can remain competitive in the global market is to relocate production plants to China, as it has been doing for some time. This trend accelerated after China's and Taiwan's World Trade Organization (WTO) accession.[45]

Under the *yiguo liangzhi zhengce* ("one country, two systems" policy), Hong Kong's role is planned as a free port and an international finance, trade, and shipping center.[46] Hong Kong's economic model was and remains based on being open to trade and investment flows from all over the world, and on providing a world-class business platform that those within the region and beyond may use and benefit from.[47] But after Hong Kong's handover to China, the direction of Hong Kong's development was once torn between internationalization and mainland orientation. The recovery of Hong Kong's economy, especially real estate, the stock market, and tourism industry which had been affected by the 1997 Asian financial crisis, the SARS epidemic, and bird flu, has much to be gained from economic integration with Pearl River Delta. Hong Kong's economic prospects will depend on successful interactions with China in such areas as finance, logistics, and tourism and on cooperation in developing new business opportunities. In order to give a hand to Hong Kong and Macao in their recovery from economic depression, and to set example of China's reunification for Taiwan, China released a series of measures, especially

Table 6.1 Taiwan Investment in Mainland China (Unit):(US $ million), %

Period	Official Data from Mainland China				
	Project	Contracted Amount	Average Amount	Realized Amount	Realization Ratio
1991-1992	9,807	8,253.53	0.84	1,894.10 (include date before 1991)	22.95
1993	10,948	9,964.87	0.91	3,138.59	31.50
1994	6,247	5,394.88	0.86	3,391.04	62.86
1995	4,847	5,849.07	1.21	3,161.55	54.05
1996	3,184	5,141.00	1.61	3,474.84	67.59
1997	3,014	2,814.49	0.93	3,289.39	116.87
1998	2,970	2,981.68	1.00	2,915.21	97.77
1999	2,499	3,374.44	1.35	2,598.70	77.01
2000	3,108	4,041.89	1.30	2,296.28	56.81
2001	4,214	6,914.19	1.64	2,979.94	43.10
2002	4,853	6,740.84	1.39	3,970.64	58.90
2003	4,495	8,557.87	1.90	3,377.24	39.46
2004	4,002	9,305.4	2.33	3,117.49	33.50
2005	3,907	10,358.25	2.65	2,151.71	20.77
2006	3,752	-	-	2,135.83	-
2007	3,299	-	-	1,774.37	-
Accumulated to 2007	75,146	-	-	45,666.92	-
Jan.-Nov. 2008	2,092	-	-	1,710.80	-
rate of change compared to same period of last year	-30.10	-	-	3.53	-
Accumulated to Nov.2008	77,238	-	-	47,377.72	-

Note: 1 Growth rate is the year-on-year growth rate. 2. The Figures do not equal the total due to rounding up.
Source: Ministry of Foreign Trade and Economic Cooperation, China, at http:// www.mac.gov.tw/big5/statistic/em/192/10.pdf (accessed on 18 March 2009)

the signing of CEPA with Hong Kong on 29 July 2003 and with Macao on 27 October 2003.[48]

The CEPA cooperation among China, Hong Kong and Macao let Hong Kong and Macao enjoy a head start to enter China's market and a wide range of market preferences, namely, measures to facilitate investment, a new zero tariff on many Hong Kong and Macao products, and the opening up of China's market to the Hong Kong and Macao services sector. These preferential arrangements are not committed to any other WTO members,[49] and they provide opportunities for Hong Kong to enhance its status as Asia's service hub. China has agreed to allow Hong Kong's banks to conduct personal *Renminbi* business. Since 4 August 2004 Macao's banks are also allowed to run *Renminbi* services (deposit, exchange, credit card, and remittance). It will enhance Hong Kong's and Macao's competitiveness and thus help further strengthen Hong Kong's position as an international financial center. The *gerenyou* (individual visit) scheme has also brought tremendous opportunities to Hong Kong's and Macao's tourism and other related sectors (see Table 6.2).[50]

Table 6.2 Summary of CEPA-induced employment/new jobs created in Hong Kong

As at year-end	Trade in Services		Individual Visit Scheme	
	Persons engaged (+)	New jobs created	Persons engaged (+)	New jobs created
2005	(no.)	(no.)	(no.)	(no.)
2006	4 295	2 880	17 815	-1 343
2007 and beyond	5 877	1 582	25 742	7 927
	7 957	2 080	-	-

Note: Persons engaged refers to the number of persons employed at the end of each period.
Source: Commerce, Industry and Technology Bureau of Hong Kong, *LC Paper No. CB (1) 1849/06-07(04) Legislative Council Panel on Commerce and Industry Mainland and Hong Kong Closer Economic Partnership arrangement (CEPA) Impact on the Hong Kong Economy Attached I*, June, 2007, at http:// www.legco. gov.hk/yr06-07/english/panels/ci/papers /ci0 6 12 cb1-18 4 9-4-e.pdf (accessed on 14 March 2009)

China also offered Taiwan on 17 May 2004 the possibility of joining the CEPA, in which greater market access to China for Taiwan's products, especially agricultural products, is guaranteed.[51] This offer drove Taiwan's DPP ruling government again into a dilemma. From the view of the Taiwanese government, this offer can further hollow out Taiwan's capital and industries, but if Taiwan doesn't join in this preferential arrangement, it may be marginalized not only by the market of Greater China, but altogether by the China -ASEAN Free Trade Area. The Taiwanese government hoped to negotiate officially with China for alternatives, but due to the different perceptions between China and Taiwan on *yige zhongguo yuanze* (the principle of one China), there was no response from China at that time, but the contact platform between the Chinese Communist party (CCP) and Taiwan then-opposition party Kuomintang (KMT) was established in 2005.

In regards to the framework of PPRD, China perceives the serious developmental gap among the eastern, middle and western parts of China, and the challenge of economic globalization, as well as the operation of China-ASEAN Free Trade Area in 2010. The PPRD was thus established on 1 June 2004 with full support from China. From China's view the PPRD group is comparable to the ten-nation ASEAN in terms of its population, scale of economy, total volume of external trade, and intake of foreign investment. Working as one it can produce powerful scale-economy effects for promoting this regional synergy, and it will raise the level of opening-up to allow regional enterprises to participate more fully in international competition and cooperation. China's accession to the WTO, the implementation of CEPA, and the anticipated establishment of the China-ASEAN Free Trade Area have created the *sine qua non* for the PPRD region to upgrade its industries and to tap international resources and markets.[52]

In addition, in the thirty years since China put the opening-up policy into practice, thousands of businessmen from Hong Kong and Macao came to invest in the PPRD region. The manufacturing industry in the PPRD provinces and regions needs to go to the world through the service industries in Hong Kong and Macao. In dealing with China's consistent economic growth, Hong Kong and Macao face changes in their economic mechanisms and a need to rely on the scientific and technological forces from China to support these transformations. China's building of the PPRD give Hong Kong a stage as the center of service industry and Macao as the region platform of business and trade service. Several major cross-boundary infrastructure projects, be they roads, railways, or bridges, will strengthen Hong Kong's and Macao's links with the PPRD.[53]

From Hong Kong's view, the major driving force behind closer cooperation between Hong Kong and PPRD provinces comes from the unique advantages each of them possesses, which enable Hong Kong to stagger its individual focuses and complement one another. The PPRD provinces are important manufacturing bases and consumer markets; in terms of resources and market access, they stand at the forefront of mainland China. Hong Kong, on the other hand, boasts advantages in the areas of capital finance, information, services, marketing, and so forth, and may serve as a high value-added services center to help upgrade the regional economy. With its highly open and cosmopolitan outlook, Hong Kong can also act as an intermediary for external economic co-operation, linking the PPRD region and the rest of the world.[54] From Macao's view, as a small export-oriented economy its dynamics greatly rely on its external cooperation. The CEPA provided institutional security to the closer cooperation between Macao and China. The PPRD would further provide Macao with new opportunities and richer resources.[55]

Since the implementation of the CEPA and PPRD, Hong Kong's and Macao's economies are better off, notably the service sector *via* an individual visits scheme, but the manufacturing industries did not benefit from CEPA and PPRD as expected. Unemployment, especially for low-level workers, is still unsolved. The wealth gap in Hong Kong and Macao is still wide, the provinces of PPRD are short of infrastructure, and the quality of human resources is relatively low, and these in turn are not good at the transfer of know-how. That is the reason why cooperation within the PPRD is not proceeding as easily as planned. In order to deal with this shortage, the CEPA II-IV was signed from 2004 to 2006, according to which Hong Kong's and Macao's investment in China and exchange of human resources among them are made easier, and almost all of Hong Kong's products can now be exported to mainland China with zero tariff.

The global economic recession since 2008 has forced over 10,000 Hong Kong factories to shut down in the Pearl River Delta region and more are expected to follow. Other sectors have also suffered. Entering the second half year of 2008, Macao's gaming and tourism sector started to slow down, and total investment in Macao continued to fall. In response, a supplement arrangement to the CEPA between the mainland China and Hong Kong will be signed during 2009, which will further increase the access to the Chinese mainland market for the services sector in Hong Kong. Besides, Hong Kong is allowed to use *Renminbi* for trade settlement, thus enhancing Hong Kong's role as the financial gateway to the mainland China. In addition, more mainland visitors' travel to Hong Kong and Macao are allowed under the individual visit scheme. The construction of the bridge connecting Hong Kong, Macao, and Zhuhai as well as the western part of the Pearl River Delta with an estimated investment of 72.6 billion *Renminbi* will also start before the end of 2009.[56]

With the steady progress of reform and opening-up, Beijing under State President Hu Jintao released a policy that stresses preventing Taiwan's opposition to achieving unification, and proposed a peace accord with Taiwan in November 2007. Taiwan also intended to draw a peace accord with mainland China including a mechanism of confidence building. The precondition for the negotiation is that mainland China removes military weapons targeting Taiwan, said be 1,000 short-range and intermediate-range missiles. Under the principle *jiuer gongshi* ("1992 consensus") the mainland China policy of the Ma Ying-jeou government is *butong budu buwu* ("no unification, no independence, and no use of force"). In addition, Taiwan and the mainland China could also find a *modus vivendi* based on non-zero-sum game and pragmatism. Ma's order for the priority of issues dealing with mainland China is, first, economic normalization between both sides such as the Economic Cooperation Framework Agreement (ECFA); second, Taiwan's diplomatic ties with foreign countries and membership in international organizations like Taiwan's participation in ASEAN+3 Free Trade Area; and then a peace accord with China. In this regard, President Ma Ying-jeou and his government back not only reactivation of the mechanism for institutionalized talks between Taiwan's Straits Exchange Foundation and mainland China's Association for Relations across the Taiwan Strait, but also to build comprehensive, normalized economic relations with mainland China.[57] On 15 December 2008, the mainland China and Taiwan started the first ever *da san tong* (Three Links), namely, direct flights, postal services, and shipping services since 1949. With the basic fulfillment of the Three Links between the mainland and Taiwan, free exchanges of people and goods have been realized except the flow of cash.

In furtherance of the policy of President Ma Ying-jeou of closer ties to China, Beijing proposed the CECA, Cross-Strait Economic Zone, and a *de facto waijiao xiubing* (diplomatic truce) under which Beijing has forgone opportunities to draw away some of the small number of governments that retain formal diplomatic ties with Taiwan. In addition, the Chinese mainland was "willing to have consultations" with Taiwan and made "fair and reasonable arrangement" for Taiwan's participation in international organizations for its good without the impression that there are *liangge zhongguo* (two Chinas) or *yizhong yitai* (one China and one Taiwan). As a result, former Vice President Lien Chan served in November of 2008 as Taiwan's representative to the Economic Leaders Meeting at the Asia-Pacific Economic Cooperation Forum (APEC). Taiwan was guaranteed direct access to World Health Organization (WHO) global health alerts in January 2009, and the International Health Regulations (IHR) applies to Taiwan.[58]

The global economic downturn depresses Taiwan's economy because of a drastic drop in external demand, especially in the European and the U.S. markets. In order to give a hand to Taiwan, PPRD-based Taiwan-funded companies are allowed to join in the 4 trillion *Renminbi* stimulus package of the Chinese government and its program *jiadian xiaxiang* (to subsidize electric appliances buyers in the rural areas); this in turn create more jobs in mainland China; in addition, China has developed a tourist scheme for Taiwan.[59] Hong Kong, Macao, and Taiwan depend so far materially on the *hongguan tiaokong* (macro economic control) of China; the functional interrelations within Greater China are transformed into the institutional way, which is headed by China. Cross-Strait rapprochement also has transformed the Taiwan Strait from a hotspot to a stabilizing force that is positive for the regional cooperation in East Asia.

MULTILATERAL INSTITUTION BUILDING: CHINA'S STRATEGY ON REGIONAL COOPERATION IN EAST ASIA

In the era of economic globalization the threats facing developing countries fall mainly into three categories: First, traditional security issues such as regional conflicts like territorial, religious, and ethnic disputes which remain a threat to the peace and stability of many developing countries. Second, nontraditional security issues are jeopardizing the livelihood of developing countries. The third is the existence of an unfair international economic order. There has been a growing call for multilateral cooperation.[60] The regional cooperation in East Asia, which is shaping the new arrangement of power, is motivated by the following factors. The first is the concern to reduce risks of financial contagion and unusual exchange rate instability, the damaging effects to which were made clear by the Asian financial crisis in 1997. A second key reason is the perceived need by other economies of the region for stronger cooperation with China, notably after its accession to the WTO. A third factor is the interest of business communities in getting preferential access to foreign markets.[61]

China perceives that Asia needs peace, stability, cooperation and development in order to avoid the competition for limited resources by abjuring overseas conquest and instead seeks greater economic cooperation in a win-win solution.[62] Chinese decision makers perceive China and the ASEAN states as developing countries in Asia, and have a considerable sense of common identity and hold similar views on values, human rights, democracy, and many issues in international affairs. After the economic crisis of 1997, ASEAN and China agreed to focus their cooperation on five priority areas, namely, agriculture, information and communications technology, human resource development, Mekong River Basin development, and two-way investment.[63] China, Japan, ROK and ASEAN also have built on the relationships developed at ASEAN+3 meetings by negotiating multi-lateral agreements on a range of subjects, such as regional security issues and humanitarian assistance in the event of natural disasters. From the Chinese view, East Asian Cooperation should focus on the economic area, especially on financial cooperation.[64]

In addition, China increases coordination with all Asian countries in trying to set up regional investment entities, a bonds market, and a financial cooperation system.[65] In this regard, the way to monitor and regulate short-term capital flow and reformation of the international financial system were discussed in the framework of ASEAN+3 Dialogue of Finance and Central Bank Deputies. This was proposed by the Chinese side in March 1998 and was launched under the auspices of ASEAN. Furthermore, ASEAN+3 states implemented in spring 2001 a series of arrangements to exchange currency among their central banks, a move designed to inoculate the region against future financial crises.

Financial cooperation of ASEAN+3 has deepened, resulting in agreements on bilateral swap arrangement (BSA) signed under the framework of the Chiang Mai Initiative. The parties concerned have agreed to establish and improve the collective decision-making mechanism and swap activation process on a bilateral basis and started a gradual process of multilateralism with the Chiang Mai Initiative.[66] The ASEAN+3 bilateral Swap Arrangement of Chiang Mai Initiative may be seen as a precursor to expand trade arrangements and greater financial and macroeconomic cooperation and coordination.

The energy sharing, except for financial cooperation, has been one of the most notable examples of regional cooperation. In January 2001 the leaders of Indonesia and Singapore opened a vital underwater gas pipeline between their nations. China's expanding economy will also require vast infusions of foreign energy, which prompted Beijing to tap into Southeast Asia's resources. Besides, China is already able to drive outward investment and the *zouchuqu* (go-abroad) policy, which is designed to expose Chinese firms to international business practices and for resource security, and encourages Chinese companies to invest in major engineering and construction projects, fuel, minerals, and other resources.[67]

There are natural affinities between PPRD and a portion of Southeast Asia, such as the headstream of Mekong River being in PPRD, and labor resource technologies are complementary. Therefore China is able to integrate the geo-economic and sociocultural advantages of CEPA and PPRD as a subregional economic zone to develop natural resources with ASEAN, and engages actively with its neighbor states in East Asian regional cooperation. In this regard, with the implementation of CEPA, the establishment of PPRD and eventually CECA, as well as the Cross-Strait Economic Zone, Greater China joins in the development with neighboring states in East Asia on natural resources and in the networking of transportation *via* track I (ASEAN+1, ASEAN+3) and track II (BFA). The Strategic and political goals are always part of China's economic "spill-over." China's rising exports and increasing demand for oil have also led its navy and its diplomats to pay more attention to the region's shipping lanes and the accessibility of the region's ports. Since 1998 China has stepped up its diplomacy toward Cambodia and Vietnam, both of whom possess key ports, and hopes to gain access to Vietnam's Cam Ranh Bay port as well as Cambodia's Sihanoukville port.[68]

As a big production base, the PPRD imports raw and processed materials from ASEAN. ASEAN becomes an important market for the PPRD in exportation. Besides, with CEPA's implementation, Hong Kong and Macao turned out to be active foreign trade bridges for the PPRD. In order to promote more two-way trade, China hosted the regular ASEAN-China exposition in Nanning (PPRD region) promoted fairs on investment policies in China and ASEAN member countries, and encouraged Chinese enterprises to make ASEAN a priority investment destination. In the economic crisis of 1997, Chinese leader promised not to devalue the *Renminbi* at her expense, which in turn avoided another round of competitive devaluations among Asian currencies, as an important contribution to stabilize the financial markets in Asia. This view was also shared within ASEAN.[69] It is positive for the following interactions.

China sees economic exchange and interaction as an important avenue to a lasting security in its surrounding area.[70] The Chinese pursue their military security strategies toward Southeast Asia in the two geographical arenas sharing with their Southeast Asian neighbors. The first area is the mainland of Southeast Asia itself, where China, particularly in the interior parts of the border regions, enjoys enormous advantages *vis-à-vis* its neighbors. The second strategic area is the maritime area. The South China Sea is the core of Southeast Asia. China with its harbor-rich southern coastline, its possession of *Hainan* Island and the *Xisha* (Paracel Island), and its claim to the *Nansha* (Spratly Group), is part of the Southeast Asian maritime scene. China and ASEAN, thus based on the principles of *qiutong cunyi* (agree to disagree) and win-win, signed four agreements in November 2002 on Declaration on the Conduct of Parties in the South China Sea, on Free Trade Area, and on Cooperation in areas such as drug trafficking, as well as on agricultural cooperation.[71]

Economic integration must be underpinned by a stable security environment. China and ASEAN signed further agreements in the Bali Summit 2003 the Joint Declaration on the Strategic Partnership for Peace and Prosperity and China's accession to the Treaty of Amity and Cooperation in Southeast Asia, which means nonaggression against each other. In addition, China has expressed its willingness to work with ASEAN for its early accession to the protocol to the Treaty on Southeast Asia Nuclear Weapon-Free Zone, which the U.S. consistently refuse to endorse, and is ready to set up a military security dialogue mechanism with other Asian countries as well as promote confidence-building measures in the military field. In this context, China supports ASEAN as the major driving force in ARF.[72]

As for the free trade area, the agreement of ASEAN-China Free Trade Area, will eliminate tariffs and nontariff barriers to goods and services, but give special and differential treatment and flexibility to the ASEAN member states Cambodia, Laos, Myanmar and Vietnam. China also decided to help Cambodia by writing off its debt, said be about $200 million.[73] In terms of the development of human resources, China shared US$5 billion with the ASEAN–China Cooperation Fund for development of human resources activities, increased its investment in the development of the Mekong River Basin by assisting in the implementation of the Quadripartite Agreement on the Commercial Navigation of the Lancang (in PPRD region)-Mekong River, participated *via* PPRD in networking of Kunming (in PPRD region)-Bangkok Highway and a Pan-Asia Railway, and also contributed a sum of US$ 5 million to help regulate some sections of the navigation channel within the territories of Laos and Myanmar.[74] In addition, China set up the Asian Regional Research center on Catastrophe and works with other East Asian countries to strengthen capacity building and improve efficiency and effectiveness in managing major natural disasters, such as the establishment an ASEAN plus Three Emergency Rice Reserve (APTERR) as a permanent mechanism in the region to ensure food security in time of crisis.[75]

In expanding its trade relations with Southeast Asia, China has been paralleled by a growth in its role as a source of regional investment. As for investment, the inflow of Chinese investments to ASEAN is promising due to the Chinese government's policy of encouraging its businessmen to go global with priority given to its neighbouring countries. In order to secure the resources necessary to fuel its growth, China is investing heavily in mining, natural gas, and logging opportunities throughout the region. China's WTO accession means more opportunity for the East Asian neighbors in China's markets. All countries in East Asia will benefit, and the scope is especially large for Japan and the newly industrializing economies (NIEs), yet still quite significant for the middle-income countries and the lowest-income countries.[76] Since China becomes a key player in promoting trade and investments within this region, regional trade agreements like the Agreement of ASEAN-China Free Trade by 2010 is signed, followed by ROK with ASEAN by 2011, and Japan with ASEAN by 2012.

Although a market-oriented and prosperous China clearly offers economic opportunities to the developing economies of Southeast Asia, particularly the nations of ASEAN, China also represents a source of economic competition for ASEAN. It becomes a direct rival in certain markets, such as Japan, and for certain products, especially raw materials and agriculture. Equally important for ASEAN is China's capacity to intake FDI, particularly from Japan, Hong Kong, and Taiwan, thereby reducing FDI in the ASEAN region. After China's accession in the WTO, the new pressure from competition in the third market will further sharpen China's competitiveness and its ability to win market shares. China's trade in East-Asia is growing both ways—imports as well as exports. Greater China is amongst the top five trading partners for almost every Asian country, including Japan, ROK and Singapore, and starting to generate outward investments itself; in addition, China is the fastest growing source of tourist for Asian country with growing purchasing power.[77]

Since the financial crisis 1997, Asian countries have now resumed the path of growth, which is coming from trade within Asia. Trade within Asia has increased about 50% out of the total trade in the region. Riding on this rapid development, Asia is now working toward greater regional economic cooperation in a multilateral institutional way. From the view of ASEAN, the result of China's engagement in East Asia enhanced mutual diplomatic, economic, and military exchanges; increased Chinese participation in regional and multilateral mechanisms and tactical flexibility on bilateral disputes, but ASEAN itself is faced with three coincidental challenges. The first challenge is that the enlargement of ASESN has increased the diversity of its members, with the result that some of them are unfamiliar with the ASEAN way. Another challenge to ASEAN was the economic crisis that hit most of the countries in the region, albeit to different degrees. This crisis caused members to look more inward, as they tried to deal with the tasks of reviving their economies and maintaining political stability.[78] "There is only one way out, not by looking west but by looking inward," Philippine President Maria Gloria Macapagal-Arroyo said in Laos. "A large East Asia bloc can secure ASEAN, China, Japan and Korea as economic leaders in the Asia-Pacific. We must ensure that China, Japan and Korea find it more convenient to be in our bloc than not."[79]

In order to enhance competitiveness, the ASEAN Free Trade Area (AFTA) became effective on 1 January 2002. The ASEAN Charter entered into force on 15 December 2008, which provides the legal and institutional framework for ASEAN's being the organization paving the way for realizing an ASEAN Community by 2015, which is comprised three pillars, namely, Political-Security Community, Economic Community, and Sociocultural Community. In addition, ASEAN engages actively with India, Russia, Japan, USA, Australia, New Zealand and EU to counterbalance China's power in the new power arrangement of East Asia. In spring 2003, Senior Party adviser Zheng Bijian in the BFA publicly articulated the China's foreign policy approach as *heping jueqi* (the peaceful rise of China), which implied that China must seek a peaceful global environment to develop its economy. In this regard, China's Asia Policy is *mulin fulin anlin* (good neighborhood, prosper the neighbor and safeguard the neighbor) on the basis of UN Charter and *heping gongcun wuyuanze* (the Five Principles of Peaceful Coexistence). From China's view Asian countries should maintain peace and stability; promote common development with win-win results; push forward comprehensive cooperation by starting with economic integration in institutionalized framework.[80]

Chinese State President Hu Jintao indicated furthermore at the conference of BFA on 24 April 2004, that China has been extensively involved in the various mechanisms of Asia-based regional cooperation *via* multilateral institutional building like free trade areas and security areas, and *via* bilateral preferential arrangement like free trade agreement, cultural interaction and personnel exchanges as well as military security dialogue mechanism. The Chinese enterprises are still encouraged to take Asia as their principal destination for the "going global" strategy. China continues to back ASEAN in playing the leading role of ASEAN+3 cooperation, and calls for better coordination among China, Japan, and ROK so as to bring into full play their respective strengths and roles. In addition, China has proposed conducting military spots exchange activities among the ASEAN +3 countries to enhance understanding and trust among the armed forces of these countries.[81]

Since China become ASEAN's strategic partner, and ASEAN gradually views China as more an opportunity than a competitor.[82] The cooperation between ASEAN and China furthermore extended to five priority areas, namely, politics, economy, social affairs and security, as well as regional and international issues. China supports the Initiative for ASEAN Integration (IAI), which drives ASEAN to deepen as ASEAN Economic Community,[83] and subregional cooperation in ASEAN such as Brunei Darussalam- Indonesia-Malaysia-Philippines East ASEAN Growth Area (BIMP-EAGA) to overcome the development gap within ASEAN, and construction of the Information Highway in the Greater Mekong Subregion (GMS) as well as exploration on the feasibility of conducting Pan Beibu Gulf cooperation. ASEAN thus hopes that China would sustain its constructive role in the search for a possible comprehensive political resolution of the crisis on the Korean Peninsula, and recognized China as a full market economy on 29 November 2004 at the 8th ASEAN+3 Summit in Vientiane, Laos.[84] ASEAN, in addition, backs the progress make in the implementation of the ASEAN-China trade agreements in goods, services and investment, which is targeted to be signed during the related summits with Dialogue Partners in April 2009.[85] In order to push forward the process of East Asia cooperation, the idea of establishing an East Asian Community (EAC), which is based on East Asian Economic Community (EAEC), is highly recommended.[86] In this regard, China proposed to push the establishment of the East Asia Free Trade Area (EAFTA) to deepen financial and investment cooperation, and to enhance further cooperation in the field of non-traditional security within the framework of ASEAN +3.[87]

The past thirty years of reform has brought China from the world's periphery to center stages. China is already the largest export market in East Asia, and accepts about US$500 billon of goods within the region every year. With respect to the global financial crisis since 2008, China prefers to coordinate macroeconomic policies and economic cooperation in East Asia, and is adopting various measures to expand domestic demand and maintain stable and rapid economic growth, which in turn maintains the economic and financial stability in the region. For example, China has been in cooperation with neighbor countries working on establishing bilateral currency exchange mechanisms and further expanding the swap scale. The ASEAN+3 Finance Ministers Meeting held in Phuket, Thailand, on 22 February 2009, agreed to increase the size of the Chiang Mai Initiative Multilateralisation (CMIM) from US$80 billion to US$120 billion and to develop a more effective surveillance mechanism to support the operation of the CMIM, and make the new Asian Bond Markets Initiative Roadmap as well as noted the on-going discussion to promote regional infrastructure financing. This again accelerates the construction of infrastructure strengthening cooperation in agriculture, and promotes bilateral and multilateral free trade agreements so as to increase the economic vigor and the driving force of growth in the region. Asian Development Bank President Haruhiko Kuroda believes that ensuring continued growth is the most important thing China can do to help Asia out of the global economic crisis.[88]

From China's view, parallel with aforementioned developments of regional cooperation, there are still some issues of joint development in the framework of track I; for example, ASEAN+1 and ASEAN+3 cannot yet be put into practice, since Greater China's development is closely related to Asia's prosperity. Thus, China engages actively in track II, namely the BFA, which was founded in 2001, and is the first large nongovernmental international organization headquartered in China. The forum provides a platform for high-level interactions between governments representatives, business leaders and academic scholars from Greater China and Asia to discuss not only joint strategies for Asian development, such as the possibility of monetary union and eventually the release of the Asia Dollar, and Asian competitiveness in the world, like the negotiation on the issues of WTO's Doha round, but also handling *quasi*-official contacts with Taiwan, for example, then-Vice President-Elect Vincent Siew attended the conference of BFA 2008 for the mainland China policy of then-President Elect Ma Ying-jeou.[89] In this regard, it could be a plus for shaping common interest of Greater China and Asian countries to be presented within and beyond Asia.

CONCLUSION

In the era of globalization the power constellation in East Asia is reconstructed *via* new multilateral institution building. In terms of regional cooperation, the end of the Cold War weakened the U.S. shaped power constellation in the region, which is based on a hob-and spokes system of bilateral alliance with the U.S. at the center. After thirty years of steady reformation and opening-up, China is capable to, despite the current international economic downturn, drive the cooperation with Greater China and ASEAN+3 under its macro economic control policy. The two hotspots, Taiwan Strait and Korea Peninsular, which made the U.S. as *status quo* power in East Asia, are manageable by China through a multilateral framework like Greater China and Six Party Talk. The participation of Greater China in multilateral institutional building such as

ASEAN+1, ASEAN+3 and BFA activate the economic and security cooperation in the region.

In order to enhance the scope and range of the cooperation in East Asia, China supports ASEAN as leader to promote the establishment of EAC and "ASEAN Security Community" with the function of conflict resolution. Could the membership of EAC for Taiwan and North Korea, and ARF as substitute of Six Party Talk are the result? It could be the interesting study for scholars in the near future.

By and large, China's policy on regional cooperation in East Asia, namely multilateral institutional building with ASEAN, ROK and Japan, and bilateral preferential arrangement for Hong Kong, Macao and Taiwan, maximize so far China's interest in national reunification *via* Modernizations and being as agenda setter of regional cooperation in East Asia.

NOTES

[1] The PPRD region, also known as "9+2," involves Fujian, Jiangxi, Hunan, Guangdong, Guangxi, Hainan, Sichuan, Guizhou, Yunnan as well as the Hong Kong and Macao special administrative regions. See at http://www. newsgd. com/specials/ panprd forum/ forumnews/200405280034.htm(accessed on May 30, 2004); China's Commerce Minister Chen Deming said at a press conference on the sidelines of the annual session of the National People's Congress "No preconditions for economic cooperation with Taiwan," March 10, 2009, at http:// www.china.org.cn/government/NPC_CPPCC_2009/ 2009-03/ 10/content_174149 (accessed on March 14, 2009).
[2] Christopher Hemmer and Peter J. Katzenstein, "Why is There No NATO in Asia? Collective Identity, Regionalism, and the Origins of Multilateralism," *International Organizaton*, Vol. 56, No.3, Summer 2002, pp.576-7.
[3] Henry Kissinger, *Does America need a Foreign Policy?*, New York (et.al.): Simon & Schuster, 2001, pp.117-9, 125, 160-1.
[4] Lee Hsien Loong, "The future of East Asian Cooperation," speech at the 11th International Conference on "The Future of Asia," Tokyo, May 25, 2005, at http://www. aseansec.org/17475.htm (accessed on June 1, 2005).
[5] Henry Kissinger, *Does America need a Foreign Policy?* p.119.
[6] Chalmers Johnson, *No Longer the "Lone" Superpower: Coming to Terms with China,* Working Paper of Japan Policy Research Institute, No. 105, March 2005, at http:// www. jpri. org/publications/workingpapers/wp105.html (accessed on May 26, 2005).
[7] "Koizumi warned over war shrine," *BBC*, November 2004, at http://newsvote.bbc. co. uk /mpa ppspagetools/ print/news.bbc.co.uk/2/hi/asia.../4031567.st (accessed on November 22, 2004).
[8] Tomohiko Taniguchi, "A Cold Peace: the Changing Security Equation in Northeast Asia," *Orbis*, Vol.49, Issue.3, Summer 2005, p.454.
[9] Phar Kim Beng, "China's strategic shift to common security," *Asia Times Online*, November 26, 2002, at http://www.atimes.com (accessed on June 24, 2005).
[10] Chalmers Johnson, *No Longer the "Lone" Superpower: Coming to Terms with China.*
[11] See James F. Hoge, Jr., "A Global Power Shift in the Making," *Foreign Affairs*, July/August 2004, at http://www.foreignaffairs.org/2004/...a-global-power-shift-in- the-

making.html? mode=print (accessed on October 28, 2004); Joshua Kurlantizik, "Is East Asia Integrating?" *The Washington Quarterly*, Vol.24, No.4, Autumn 2001, p. 27.

[12] "Aso trip delay not due to dispute," *China Daily*, March 18, 2009, at http://news. xinhuanet._com/english/ 2009-03/ 18/content_11029916.htm (accessed on March 18, 2009).

[13] Jacques deLisle, "The U.S. Elections and America's role in East Asia: views from the Region," *E-Notes-FPRI*, February 2009 at http://www.fpri.org/enotes/200901.delisle. use lectioneastasia.html (accessed on February 19, 2009).

[14] Wen Jiabao Attends Welcoming Luncheon of American Friendly Organizations and Delivers Speech on China-U.S.Relations, September 24, 2008, at http://www. fmprc. gov. cn/eng /wjdt /zyjh /t5 14790.htm (accessed on March 4, 2009).

[15] Jacques deLisle, "The U.S. Elections and America's role in East Asia: views from the Region."

[16] Jacques deLisle, "China Policy under Obama," *E-Note-FPRI*, February 2009, at http:/ /www.fpri.org/_enotes/ 2009 02. delisle.china po licyobama.html (accessed on February 16, 2009).

[17] Lee Lao To, "East Asian assessments of China's security policy," *International affairs,* Vol.73, No.2,1997, p.253.

[18] Henry Kissinger, *Does America need a Foreign Policy?*, pp. 116, 129.

[19] Choe Sang-Hun, "North Korea balks at South's call to resume talks," *International Herald Tribune*, July 13, 2008, at http://www.iht.com/bin/printfriendly.php?id =1445 05 9 0 (accessed on July 14, 2008).

[20] Kusuma Snitwongse, "A New World Order in East Asia?" *Asia-Pacific Review*, Vol.10, No.2, 2003, p.48.

[21] Song Jung-a, "North Korea to disable main reactor," *Financial Times*, July 13, 2008, at http://www.ft.com/coms/ s4fd334fc-50f9-11dd-b751-000077b07658,dwp_ =uuid =319b 98a6- 0c1a-1..., (accessed on July 14, 2008).

[22] Jacques deLisle, The U.S. Elections and America's role in East Asia: views from the Region.

[23] Chalmers Johnson, *No Longer the "Lone" Superpower: Coming to Terms with China.*

[24] Alan Boyd, "ASEAN, China all smiles for now," *Asia Times,* March 12, 2004, at http: //www.atimes.com/ atimes/printN.html (accessed on September 10, 2005).

[25] See Edward D. Mansfield and Helen V. Milner, "The New Wave of Regionalism," *International Organization* Vol.53, No.3, Summer 1999, pp.600-1; Schau Breslin and Richard Higgott, "New regionalism(s) in the global political economy. Conceptual understanding in historical perspective," *Asia Europe Journa,*Vol.1, 2003, pp.167, 172-3.

[26] Mari Pangestu and Sudarshan Gooptu, "New Regionalism: Options for China and East Asia," in Kathie Krumm and Homi Kharas, eds., *East Asia Integrates: A Trade Policy Agenda for Shared Growth*, Washington, D.C.: The World Bank, 2003, p.82.

[27] China's Position Paper on the New security Concept, July 31, 2002, at http://www. fmprc.gov.cn/ eng/ wjb/zzjg/gjs/gjzzyhy/2612/2614/t15319.htm (accessed on June 11, 2005).

[28] Ong Keng Yong, "Securing A Win-Win Partnership For ASEAN And China," keynote address at the ASEAN-China Forum 2004 "Developing ASEAN-China Relations: Realities and Prospects," Singapore, June 23, 2004, at http://www.aseansec. org/1625 6.htm (accessed on February 1, 2005).

[29] Wen Jiabao, "China Will Never Seek Hegemony," Asia Cooperation Dialogue Foreign Ministers Meeting, April 6, 2005, at http://www.fmprc.gov.cn/eng/wjd t/zyjh/t191 081. htm (accessed on June 20, 2005).

[30] Elizabeth Economy, "China's rise in Southeast Asia: Implications for Japan and the United States," October 6, 2005, at http://www.japanfocus.org/article.asp?id=414 (accessed on October 9, 2005).

[31] Lee Lao To, "East Asian assessments of China's security policy," *International Affairs*, Vol.73, No.2, 1997, pp.259-62.

[32] See Joseph Y. S. Cheng, "China's ASEAN policy in the 1990s: Pushing for regional multipolarity," *Contemporary Southeast Asia* Vol.21, No.2, 1999, pp.6-7, at http://proquest.umi.com/ pqdlikn?inde x=6& sid=21&srchmode=1&vinst= PROD & furt=4&s (accessed on May 15, 2004); Zu Rongji, "Work Hand in Hand to build a better Future for Asia in 21st Century," speech at first annual conference of BFA on April 12 ,2002, at http://english. People daily.com.cn/200204/12/ eng 200 20412_93946.shtml (accessed on May 15, 2004).

[33] Joshua Kurlantizik, "Is East Asia Integrating ?," pp.26-7.

[34] Julie Gilson, "Complex regional multilateralism: 'strategizing' Japan's responses to Southeast Asia," *The Pacific Review*, Vol.17, No.1, March 2004, pp.81-7.

[35] S. Pushpanathan, "ASEAN's strategy towards its dialogue partners and ASEAN plus Three progress," at http://www.aseansec.org/15398.htm (accessed on October 29, 2004).

[36] This security community is not related to traditional military cooperation. Indonesia's proposal was advanced in the context of the changing circumstances of ASEAN stability, chiefly in relation to international terrorism and also encompassing trans-national security issues, such as money-laundering and arms-trafficking. See Kusuma Snitwongse, "A New World Order in East Asia?," p.45; Lee Hsien Loong, "The future of East Asian Cooperation."

[37] See Li Zhaoxing "Peace, Development and Cooperation—Banner for China's Diplomacy in the New Ear," August 22, 2005 at http://www.fmprc.gov.cn/ en/zxxx/t208032.htm (accessed on August 23, 2005); State Council Information Office, White Paper "China's Peaceful Development Road," *Peoples Daily*, December 22, 2005, at http://english.peopledaily.com.cn/200512/22/print20051222_230059.html (accessed on December 23, 2005); Wen Jiabao, "China Will Never Seek Hegemony."

[38] Wu Bangguo, "On China's Economic Prospects in 21st century," at http://www.china. org. cn/English /News/Politics/0131/08.htm (accessed on February 1, 2000).

[39] Shi Guang Sheng, Speech delivered at the Press Conference of the First Session of the 9th National Peoples Congress, March 9,1998, at http://www.moftec. gov.cn/ mof tec/ official/html (accessed on May 10, 1998).

[40] This shift to a high-technology economy was fostered by tax incentives and venture capital at a time when other Asian countries were trying to undercut Taiwan, whose wages have risen. André Mommen, "The Asian Miracle: a critical reassessment," in Alex E. Fernández Jilberto and André Mommen,eds., *Liberalization in the Developing World Institutional and Economic Changes in Latin America, Africa and Asia*, London; New York: Routledge, 1996, pp.37-8.

[41] Xiangming Chen, "Taiwan Investments in China and Southeast Asia: Go West, but Also Go South," *Asian Survey* Vol.36, No.5, 1996, pp.457-8.

[42] The coastal development strategy had the following characteristics: First: The coasted-development strategy was targeted at the investors from Taiwan and Hong Kong. Second: Targeted at small investment projects from the small and medium-sized firms in Taiwan and Hong Kong. Third: Allowed investment in labor-intensive industries, which relied solely on raw material imports. Fourth: Instead of encouraging joint venture contracts, the present strategy preferred wholly owned foreign investment become of capital shortages. See On Kwok Lai and Alvin Yi So, "Hong Kong and Newly Industrializing Economies: From Americanization to Asianization," in Gerard A. Postiglione and James T.H.Tang, eds., *Hong Kong's Reunion with China*, New York: M.E. Sharpe, 1997, p.110; Ngai-Ling Sum, "The NIEs and competing strategies of East Asian Regionalism," in Andrew Gamble and Anthony Payne, eds., *Regionalism and world order*, New York: St. Martin's Press, 1996, p.232.

⁴³ "Tung to promote HK's Economic Integration with PRD," January 10, 2003, at http://www. china.org.cn/english/government/ 532 56.htm (accessed on May 6, 2004).
⁴⁴ Harvey Sicherman, "Taiwan's Chen Shui-Bian: a President's progress," *E-Notes-FPRI*, May 11, 2001, at http://www.fpri.org/enote/asia.20010511.sicherman.chenprogress.html (accessed on January 10, 2002).
⁴⁵ See Mari Pangestu and Sudarshan Gooptu, "New Regionalism: Options for China and East Asia," p. 93; Xiangming Chen, "Taiwan Investments in China and Southeast Asia: Go West, but Also Go South," pp.460-1.
⁴⁶ "Hu Says HK's Role Unchanged Under One Country, Two Systems," *Xinhua News Agency*, June 28, 2007, at http://www.china.org.cn/china/hk/2007-06 /28 /con tent_ 12 15294.htm, (accessed on March 28, 2009).
⁴⁷ Tung Chee Hwa addressed at the plenary session of the BFA annual conference 2003 "Asia Searching for Win-Win: Development through Cooperation" on November 2, 2003, at http://www.info.gov.hk/gia/general/ 200311/ 02/ 110219 2.htm (accessed on June10, 2004).
⁴⁸ Chen Zuoer, "Enhance coop. between mainland and HK, Macau, boost further reform, opening up," June 2, 2004, at http://www.newsgd.com/ specials/ panprdforum/ centralgov support/ 200406020065. htm (accessed on June 8, 2004).
⁴⁹ CEPA creates new opportunities for HK's many professionals, accounting, auditing, legal services, engineering, IT, and management consultancy, etc. See Tung Chee Hwa, "Building on CEPA to Enhance Our Service Hub Status," December 10, 2003, at http:// www.info.gov.hk/gia/general/200312/10/1210103.htm (accessed on December 20, 2003); Zhang Yuncheng, "Hong Kong tackles its Economic Woes," July 3, 2003, at http:// www.china.org.cn/ english/2003/Jul/68801.htm (accessed on July 13, 2003).
⁵⁰ See Tung Chee Hwa, "Building on CEPA to Enhance Our Service Hub Status"; "Agreements allow Banks in Macao to operate RMB Services," August 4, 2004, at http://www.macau.gov.mo/index _en.html (accessed on August 6, 2004).
⁵¹ Taiwan Affairs Office of CPC Central Committee and Taiwan Affairs Office of State Council, Statement on current cross-Straits relations, May 17, 2004, at http://www. gwytb.gov.cn:8088/ detail. asp?table=headlines&title=Headlines& off set =50&m_id= 154 (accessed on May 19, 2004).
⁵² Tung Chee Hwa, keynote speech at the PPRD held in Hong Kong, June 1, 2004, at http://www.info.gov.hk/gia /general/ 200406/01/0601252.htm (accessed on 7 June 2004).
⁵³ The blueprint of PPRD communications network construction includes 22 lines of highways. The network in the scheme, with Guangzhou and Hong Kong as its core, radiates to both inland and coastline areas. The Guangzhou as the center, the network will link Shenzhen, Hong Kong, Macao, Zhuhai, Zhongshan, Foshan, Dongguan together. The HK-Zhuhai-Macao Bridge under planning will better Hong Kong's economic radiation towards the west bank of Pearl River. This will bring PRD's economic radiating ability into full play, and confirm HK's role as the international air logistic hub. See Tung Chee Hwa, "Asia Searching for Win-Win: Development through Cooperation;" Zhang Chunxian, "Construct a perfect road and waterway network in Pan-Pearl River Delta region," April 1, 2004, at http://www.newsgd.com/specials/ panprdforum/ central govtsupport/ 200406020058.htm (accessed on June 8, 2004); "PPRD marks new breakthrough in China's regional cooperation," at http://www. newsgd.com/ specials/ pan prdforum/forumnews/200405280034.htm (accessed on May 30, 2004).
⁵⁴ The service industry is the mainstay of the Hong Kong economy, making up 87% of Hong Kong's total economic output. Tung Chee Hwa, keynote speech at the PPRD held in Hong Kong.

[55] Edmund Ho, "Pan-Pearl River Delta Cooperation in Line with Regional Economic Development," June 2, 2004, at http://www.macau.gov.mo/index_en.html (accessed on July 10, 2004).

[56] See Donald Tsang's speech at luncheon of Credit Suisse "Asian Investment Conference," March 24, 2009, at http://www.info.gov.hk/gia/ general/200903/24/ P200903240266_print.htm (accessed on March 28, 2009); Yuan Fang, "HK economy looks to mainland visitors for help," March 5, 2009, at http://www. china. org.cn/ govern ment/NPC_CPPCC_2009 /2009-03/05/content_173845 (accessed on March 28, 2009); "Bridge connecting HK, Macao and Zhuhai to be built," *Xinhua News Agency,* March 13, 2009, at http://www. china.org.cn/government/ NPC_CPPCC_ 2009/2009-03/ 13/content_ 174380...(accessed on March 14, 2009); "Gross Domestic Product (GDP) for 2008," Not.029/2009, March 27, 2009, at http://www.gcs.gov.mo/ files /news/ 2009 0327 (accessed on March 28, 2009); "HK's service sector to have more access to mainland market," *Xinhua News Agency,* March 13, 2009, at http:// www.china. org.cn/ government/NPC_ CPPCC_2009/2009-03/ 13/content_ 174381... (accessed on March 14, 2009).

[57] Ma Ying-jiou, Transcript of Interview with the New York Times and International Herald Tribune, June 18, 2008 at http://www.mac.gov.tw/english/ english/macpollicy/ ma 970618e.htm (accessed on March 4, 2009).

[58] See "Mainland willing to consult to Taiwan's participation in int'l organizations," *Xinhua News Agency,* March 13, 2009, at http://www.china.org.cn/government/NPC_ CPPCC_ 2009/ 2009/-03/ 13content_174380...) (accessed on March 20, 2009); "Emotional Wen bowled over by beautiful treasure island,"*China Daily,* March 14, 2009, at http:// www. china.org.cn/government/ NPC_CPPCC_2009/2009-03/14/ content_ 174 436... (accessed on March 14, 2009).

[59] "Cross-strait financial cooperation benefits mutually," *Xinhua News Agency,* March 9, 2009, at http://www.china.org.cn/government/NPC_CPPCC_2009/2009-03/09/content_ 174047... (accessed on March 14, 2009).

[60] Qian Qichen, "Multilateralism, the Way to Respond to Threats and Challenges," New Delhi Conference, July 2, 2004, at http://www.fmprc.gov.cn/eng/wjdt/zyjh/t142393.htm (accessed on June 4,2005).

[61] Mari Pangestu and Sudarshan Gooptu, "New Regionalism: Options for China and East Asia,"p.80.

[62] Lee Kuan Yew, "Win-Win Approach for China's Peaceful Rise," April 23, 2005, at http://www. Boao forum.org/ziliao/200505/13/t20050513_3826760.shtml (accessed on June 18, 2005).

[63] The five areas were agreed at the ASEAN-China Summit on 6 November 2001 in Brunei Darussalam. See at http://www.aseansec.org/5874.htm (accessed January 13, 2005); Joseph Cheng, "China's ASEAN policy in the 1990s: Pushing for regional multi-polarity."

[64] The Chinese side wishes to advance the following proposals:
1. To institutionalize the Meeting of Finance and Central Bank deputies, and convene meetings of finance ministers and central bank governors on basis of the deputy meeting,
2. To share information and experience of financial reforms readjustments in their respective countries within this mechanism and to set up an *ad hoc* committee for an in-depth study of supervision and regulation of international capital flow, the improvement of capabilities of guarding against and forecasting financial risks, the restructuring of international financial system and other question,
3. To coordinate positions and stances of East Asian countries on major international financial and economic issues through this mechanism so that East Asia does its part for the reform of the international financial system. At http://www.asean.or.id/ summit/ inf3rd/ prg_ch3 .htm (accessed on June 20, 2004).

[65] "When will 'Asian Dollar' come true?" *People's Daily*, April 26, 2004, at http://www. english.peopledaily.com.cn/200404/26/ eng20040426_141507.shtml (accessed on April 28, 2004).

[66] Wen Jiabao, "Work together For a Better Future through Stronger Cooperation,"speech at 9th ASEAN Plus three Summit, Kuala Lumpur, Malaysia, December 12, 2005, at http://www.fmprc.gov.cn/ eng/wjdt/ zyjh / t228272.htm, (accessed on December 30, 2005).

[67] Pangestu and Gooptu, "New Regionalism: Options for China and East Asia," p.94.

[68] Joshua Kurlantizik, "Is East Asia Integrating?," p.22.

[69] Details see Plan of Action to Implement the Joint Declaration on ASEAN-China Strategic Partnership for Peace and Prosperity.

[70] China's Position Paper on the new Security Concept.

[71] Harlan W. Jencks, "Counter-Encirclement or Hegemonism? PRC Security Strategy in Southeast Asia," in Joyce K. Kallgren, Noordin Sopiee and Soedjati Djiwandono, eds., *ASEAN and China An Evolving Relationship*, Berkely: University of California, 1988, p.64.

[72] See Isagani de Castro, "Big brother China woos ASEAN," *Asia Times*, November 6, 2002, at http://www. atimes.com/atimes/Southeast-Asia/DK06Ae02.html (accessed on November 8, 2002); ASEAN, "ASEAN-China Dialogue Relations," at http: // www. aseansec. org/ 5 874.htm (accessed January 13, 2005); Hu Jintao, "China's development is an opportunity for Asia," speech at BFA on April 24, 2004, at http://english.peopledaily. com.cn/ 2004 0424/ eng2004044_14 1419. shtml (accessed on May 2, 2004); "Plan of Action to Implement the Joint Declaration on ASEAN-China Strategic Partnership for Peace and Prosperity," November 30, 2004, at http://www. fmprc.gov.cn / eng /wjb / zzjg/ yzs/ dqzz y wt/t175815.htm (accessed January 9, 2005).

[73] Isagani de Castro, ibid.

[74] ASEAN, "ASEAN-China Dialog," at http://www.aseansec.org/ print.asp?file=/ dialog/ mchi. htm (accessed on March 10, 2004).

[75] Chairman's Statement of the 14th ASEAN Summit "ASEAN Charter for ASEAN People,"Cha-am, February 28- March 1, 2009, at http://www.aseansec.org/22329.htm (accessed on March 4, 2009).

[76] Kathie Krumm and Homi Khrars," Overview in East Asia Integrates," in *A Trade Policy Agenda for Shared Growth*, pp. 11-2.

[77] Robert A. Scalapino, "China's Role in Southeast Asia: Looking toward the twenty-first Century," in Richard L. Grant, ed., *China and Southeast Asia Into the Twenty-first Century*, Washington, D. C.: Center for Strategic and International Studies, 1993, p.58.

[78] See Tung Chee Hwa, "Building on CEPA to Enhance Our Service Hub Status"; Ong Keng Yong, "Securing A Win-Win Partnership For ASEAN And China"; Kusuma Snitwongse, "A New World Order in east Asia?" p.44.

[79] Alan Boyd, "ASEAN, China all smiles for now," *Asia Times*, December 3, 2004, at http://www.atimes.com/atimes/printN.html (accessed on October 9, 2005).

[80] Jia Qingling, "Building A Harmonious and Prosperous Asia for All Through Comprehensive Cooperation," speech at the BFA, April 23, 2005, at http://www/ boao forum.org/ziliao/200505/13/t20050513_3826679.shtml (accessed on June 18, 2005)

[81] See Hu Jintao, "China's development is an opportunity for Asia"; Wen Jiabao, "Work Together for a Better Future through Stronger Cooperation."

[82] S. Pushpanathan, "Building an ASEAN-China Strategic Partnership,"*The Jakarta Post*, July 1,2004, at http://www.aseansec.org/16253.htm (accessed on October 28, 2004).

[83] The initiative has four themes: 1.Collaboration with the Greater Mekong Sub-region program to accelerate ASEAN integration; 2. ASEAN as a single tourist destination; 3. ASEAN solidarity for peace and security, especially in the fight against terrorism; and 4. bold steps in sustainable natural resources management, including ratification of the

Kyoto Protocol by all ASEAN members. At http://www.aseansec.org/13198.htm
(accessed on October 30, 2004).
[84] See Press Statement of the Chairperson of the ASEAN+China Summit, the
ASEAN+Japan, the ASEAN+Republic of Korea, and the ASEAN+India Summit, Bali,
October 8, 2003, at http://www.aseansec.org/15287.htm (accessed on October 28, 2004);
"ASEAN recognizes China as a full market economy", November 30, 2004, at
http://new.xinhuanet.com /English/2004-11/30/content_2275961.htm (accessed on
January 9, 2005); Wen Jiabao, "Strengthening Cooperation for Mutual Benefit and a
Win-Win Result," speech at the 8th ASEAN+3 Summit in Vientiane, November 29, 2004,
at http://www. fmprc.gov.cn/eng/topics/ wenjiabaoaseanorg/t172730.htm (accessed on
February 1, 2005); Wen Jiabao speech at China-ASEAN Business and Investment
Summit, "Work together to Usher in a New Era of China-ASEAN Economic Cooperation
and Trade," October 31, 2006, at_http://www.china.org.cn/english /busi ness/187103.htm
(accessed on March 14, 2009).
[85] Chairman's Statement of the 14th ASEAN Summit "ASEAN Charter for ASEAN
Peoples."
[86] The idea of an EAEC was first mooted in the East Asian Vision Group (EAVG) Report
of January 2001 entitled "Towards an East Asian Community: Region of Peace,
Prosperity and Progress." In this report, the "integration of the East Asian economies,
ultimately leading to an East Asia Economic Community" was envisaged and trade,
investment and finance will be the catalysts in the community-building process.
Specifically, the EAVG called for the establishment of the East Asia Free Trade Area
(EAFTA) and the East Asia Investment Area (EAIA), among others. China was the first
country outside the ASEAN to declare support for the Concept EAEC. See Stephen
Leong , The East Asian Economic Caucus (EAEC): "'Formalized' Regionalism Being
Denied," in Björn Hettne, András Inotai and Osvaldo Sunkel, eds., *National Perspectives
on the New Regionalism in the South*, London (et.al.): Macmillan Press and St. Martins
Press, 2000, p.62; Pengiran Mashor Pengiran Ahmad, "East Asia Economic Community:
Prospects and Implications," keynote speech at "ASEAN Plus Three—Perspectives of
Regional Integration in East Asia and the Lessons from Europe," Seoul, November 30-
December 1, 2003, at http://www.aseansec.org/15656.htm (accessed on January 26,
2005).
[87] In the area of financial and investment cooperation, priority should be given in East
Asia to using the rich foreign exchange reserve and capital within the region, improving
investment and financing environment and building risk prevention and control capital
within the financial sector. To encourage investment cooperation of small and medium-
size enterprises will facilitate the participation of the private sector in East Asia
cooperation. Details see "Plan of Action to Implement the Joint Declaration on ASEAN-
China Strategic Partnership for Peace and Prosperity."
[88] See Wen Jiabao, "To Deepen Cooperation and Work Together to Overcome Current
Difficulties," December 15, 2008, at http://www.fmprc.gov.cn/ eng/wjdt/zyjh/
t526246.htm (accessed on March 4, 2009); Press Statement on the Global Economic and
Financial Crisis Cha-am, Thailand, March 1, 2009, at http://www.aseansec. org/_223
24.htm, (accessed on March 4, 2009); "China reaffirms opening up policy," *Xinhua News
Agency*, March 14, 2009, at http://www.china. org.cn/_government/NPC_CPPCC_2009/
2009 -03/ 14/content_174440..., (accessed on March 14, 2009).
[89] Long Yongtu, "BFA to Focus on Impact of Iraq War on Asian Economy," April 2,
2003, at http://www. bjreview.com.cn/Boao/0407-03.htm (accessed on August 10,
2004).

Chapter 7

How Economic Superpower China Could Transform Africa

Edward Friedman[*]

THE CONVENTIONAL WISDOM

Whereas all others have failed in uprooting the entrenched poverty of sub-Saharan Africa (hereafter Africa), if China could succeed there could be no doubt but that China had become an economic superpower. Actually, China's rapid rise to become a major power already is a world-transforming phenomenon. The consensus of Africanists, however, is that "China's presence signals more of the same for Africa." Contrary to the notion that a Chinese model is supplanting a Washington model, for Africanists, America's actual attempts to use "conditionality. . . to marketize Africa" is "not so different from the approaches of China," although the ideological camouflage varies. In fact, Chinese firms have purchased African firms that were privatized in line with the Washington Consensus. Neither China nor America can, in the dominant discourse, save Africa from the "resource curse" in which the profits from commodity exports serve only "the interests of . . . rentier elites."[1] That is, the suffering poor in Africa will not see their lives bettered by Chinese behavior in Africa since China's "interests in Africa is [sic] not much different from those of the neo-liberal Western powers."[2] This chapter challenges the conventional wisdom.

CHINA'S PROMISE

In fact, Chinese economic dynamism could catalyze new growth to fundamentally transform the African economy. What has already begun to occur is that a Chinese version of the East Asian development process is incorporating Africa into Asia, as, previously, Japan integrated Southeast Asian countries into Japan's "flying goose" pattern in which the leader pulls willing followers forward, creating economic tigers out of previously tortoise-like societies.

Of course, not all of Africa will equally benefit or grow at the same rate. Africa is large and complex, with some four dozen or so states with diverse demographic, economic and political problems. The general portrait to be sketched below does suggest which types of states are likely to be the ones that benefit most from China's deepening presence in Africa. In general, those governments will do best which have the capacity for effectiveness and which have commodities to export, as long as the society is not mobilizable by demagogues using xenophobic appeals to keep Chinese out and as long as the government largely ignores Chinese human rights abuses.

This projection is not a prediction. In general, political futures are unpredictable. In particular, in the post-Bretton Woods era of huge, unregulated, international financial liquidity, volatility is amplified and inequality is intensified. While the actual future is likely to make a mockery of all straight line projections, what follows is just such an extrapolation from trends in how China's political economy interacts with Africa's.

The rise of China opens new economic possibilities for Africa. Despots of poor African nations have championed China's rapid rise out of poverty. They have proclaimed that economic superpower China is a model for their nation in the post-Bretton Woods age of globalization. Lindsey Hilsum concludes an article on China and Africa, "China wants to buy; Africa has something to sell [energy and other resources]. If African governments could respond in a way which spread the new wealth—a large if, of course—then China might provide an opportunity for Africa which Europe and America have failed to deliver." "As a result of intensified trade links with China, Africa has enjoyed higher growth rates, better terms of trade, increased export volumes, higher public revenues."[3] A need for Europe or others to compete with "China is doing more to promote African development than any high flying [European] governance rhetoric."[4] That China's promise has already begun to be realized in Africa has not impressed the specialists. Yet a World Bank July 2008 report concluded that "China's investments ease Africa's poverty."[5]

Most important, China is in Africa for the long haul. The Government in Beijing finds it has a fundamental strategic interest in continuous access to African energy resources. Beijing does not want to be dependent on a politically fragile Middle East for the energy imports required to power China's economic and military rise. Because of Africa's huge proven reserves and minimal consumption, ruling groups in China see paying for secure access to African energy over the years ahead as a primary Chinese security interest.[6]

AUTHORITARIAN DEVELOPMENT?

Some might dismiss the embrace by African regimes of China's offers of infrastructural projects in return for Africa's oil and other resources as a cynical gesture to perpetuate African authoritarian power. However, almost anyone, not just African dictators, can be blown away by a visit to Shanghai, which has so many more skyscrapers than does New York City. Australian Prime Minister Kevin Rudd told the Brookings Institution on March 31, 2008 that "China's experience would be invaluable to other developing nations." It is natural for Africans to welcome Chinese overtures. The economic vigor carried into Africa by Chinese is mind-boggling. Millions of Chinese already reside in Africa, with more arriving every day. They "build dams, roads and railroads...or simply hope to get rich . . . " in businesses.[7]

Africans can imagine themselves as copying China's authoritarian development path. Zhang Weiwei explains "the Chinese model" as an alternative to "the American model" which promotes democracy in countries that lack democracy's supposed preconditions, thereby "fostering ethnic and sectarian conflict." Remembering that "three decades ago, China was as poor as Malawi," the question Chinese ask of Africans is how can Africa emulate China? The CCP regime claims to have used existing institutions (authoritarianism), maintained "macroeconomic stability" (the IMF model), and put "its emphasis on the role of the market, entrepreneurship, globalization and international trade." It is difficult for an outside observer to see anything here that the IMF would oppose. Where is a uniquely Chinese model? Is there more than a self-serving Chinese claim that authoritarianism can do better than democracy in the era of post-Bretton Woods globalization?

Zhang claims that the American model imposes "liberalization before safety nets were set up."[8] But China did worse; it liberalized while destroying safety nets. That's one reason why China is so unequal. China's extreme income polarization distinguishes it from all prior East Asian development states. Governments in Africa concerned with equitable development have to look elsewhere in Asia, not to China.

Given China's self-presentation, Africans could be excused for not understanding how China actually rose. Africans have long been told by others that they must take advantage of the opportunities of globalization. As the Chinese secretary general of an NGO, Network for International Exchange, speaking in just this way, put it in January 2007 at the Seventh World Social Forum meeting in Nairobi, Kenya, "we Chinese had to make the same hard decision on whether to accept foreign investment many, many years ago. You have to make the right decision or you will lose, lose, lose . . . [and] remain poor, poor, poor."[9] Integration with the world market, however helpful, is not a uniquely Chinese formula.

Inside China, there actually are numerous critics of the polarizing dynamics of China's development trajectory. These Chinese wonder where all the investment monies for Shanghai's large construction projects have come from. Part of the answer, to them, is that the wealth is taken from programs for China's needy. Between 2000 and 2005, illiteracy soared in China by a mind-boggling 30 million people. Huang Yasheng offers a sophisticated analysis of these dynamics. The yawning gap between rich and poor in China is felt by some CCP leaders to be endangering stability, as China surpasses Brazil as the world's most polarized major country.[10]

Consequently, many suspect that when authoritarian African leaders tout China as a model, their focus is not on raising their nation's poor out of poverty. Africa has not sent endless delegations of economists to explore the growth policies and institutions by which post-Mao leaders have ended poverty for hundreds of millions. China's growth is real. But Chinese explanations of that growth obscure how China has successfully adopted East Asian development state practices.

AN EAST ASIAN DEVELOPMENT MODEL?

Without denying that many groups in China are losers or sufferers of grievous harm during the reform era, China's rise is still real and globally transforming. When England rose in the age of the Industrial Revolution, the misery of English laborers led some well-known theorists to predict a proletarian revolution.   Rapid economic growth invariably has large costs, including expansionist chauvinisms. But this does not make the growth less real or negate the global transformative power of the rising nation. Those who today distinguish mere growth from real development or who expect societal conflicts to end China's rise are repeating the error of those who kept predicting the collapse of "capitalism" because it supposedly produced explosive immiserization and non-sustainable polarization. The transformative growth is real.

One way critics make it seem unreal is by discussing political democracy and obscuring economic transformation. To be sure, "authoritarian regimes in Africa will...utilize China's economic success to rationalize avoiding further political liberalization and genuine democratization."[11]   But it is difficult to believe that if authoritarian China were not a weighty factor in Africa that corrupt African tyrants would have meekly walked away from power because of sieve-like European Union good governance conditionality. Actually, there has been case after case where the IMF and other IFIs have found self-serving excuses for continuing to fund authoritarian regimes wearing merely the flimsiest of pseudo-democratic fig-leafs. This European conditionality did not break the cycle of poverty. Democracy-promoter Larry Diamond notes, "If international donors cannot get tough with a young punk autocrat in a tiny country [Gambia] of under 2 million people, can they do so anywhere?"[12] It is wrong to imply that Africa would be rich and democratic absent an allegedly negative Chinese political presence.

Whatever the narrowly self-interested motives of authoritarian rulers in Africa, China can, in fact, serve these poor nations both as a helpful model and, perhaps more importantly, as an economic motor of development, even though supreme leader Deng Xiaoping in 1985 told an African head of state that there was no Chinese model to emulate. Deng averred that all nations must adopt growth policies suitable to their own particular circumstances.[13]

True though that may be, it also is a good thing to learn from the best practices of the more advanced. Some Africans learn that the Chinese experience means concentrating on "huge infrastructural investments, production and trade"[14] and ignoring "social sectors," that is, slighting education and health for all.[15] In this perspective, polarization is the price of growth.

Others see the China model as defying "the conditionalities of the Bretton Woods institutions" and moving out of and against the dollar.[16] They want to zing it to the Americans, which is certainly not what China has done. Yet others dismiss the Chinese example as unsustainable "corporate globalization,"[17] no different than the Americans. These critics want to zing it to capitalism. Looking at China to settle scores with one's demons does not pinpoint the policy sources of China's phenomenal economic dynamism. Indeed, it obscures the Chinese path.

In fact, post-Mao China learned from East Asian neighbors: Japan, Taiwan, South Korea, Hong Kong and Singapore. The resulting synthesis was uniquely Chinese. This is taken by some Africans to mean just another instance of "export-oriented industrialization and inward foreign direct investment."[18] That formula does not convey the special scale and speed of China's success. Since economic reforms were initiated in China in 1979, more than two-thirds of all the poverty wiped-out on the planet earth has been in China. This monumental achievement suggests that there is much to learn from the Chinese experience. As a Congolese minister put it, "the Chinese are fantastic."[19]

Basically, what the Deng leadership did was to plug in to and learn from Japan-led East Asian development. Why then hadn't Africans earlier copied Japanese practices? That Japan was not taken as a model in the 1970s and 1980s could be because Japan is a democracy and therefore not attractive to authoritarian regimes. But democratic India also did not then see Japan as worth emulating. It is not only authoritarians that dismissed the Japanese experience. Besides, Japan's economic policies can be copied by any regime, democratic or authoritarian. Growth is not premised on a Good Housekeeping seal of approval on human rights practices. Growth stems from good economic practices. This is not a happy thought for well-meaning people who imagine democracy and human rights as the building blocks of growth.

The 1970s and 1980s rejection of the Japanese model was largely a reflection of broadly shared prejudices. Politically conscious post-colonial regimes were mesmerized by anti-imperialist theories such as "dependency." They concluded that development required delinking from the world market. That self-wounding prejudice against plugging into the dynamism of market-oriented winners such as Japan, which grew to have the world's second largest GNP, seemed, to both democratic and authoritarian post-colonial regimes, to be either an anomaly or a tool of imperialism, rather than the motor of economic growth that it in fact was.

When the New International Economic Order (NIEO) illusions of the 1970s were stripped away by the Third World debt crisis of the 1980s, Africans could begin to see the world differently. They could, by the 21st century, ask how a once-poor authoritarian China came to be such a big winner in the new moment of globalization, even though China's path merely reflects an adaptation of the East Asian development model pioneered by Japan. The era after the Third

World debt crisis and the implosion of autarkic Leninist regimes led most governments in poorer countries to see the wisdom of the Asian tiger development path which makes use of world market opportunities. The rise of China at that historic moment naturally caught their attention. Timing has a lot to do with China's appeal.

East Asians often describe their approach to growth as one of managing export-oriented industrialization (EOI). Cheap, unskilled labor is treated as an advantageous resource in producing and exporting the products of light industry. Yet top rank economists find that the success of China and India on this path blocks off that road for Africans. China and India dominate cheap labor, light industrial exports. China's monopoly of success in low wage manufacturing exports "may well have removed this strategy from serious consideration by any potential competitor in Africa."[20]

The painful proof supposedly is what happened when the Multi-Fiber Agreement (MFA) ended. The MFA gave to poor countries diverse quotas for exporting apparel to the OECD importing countries. When the MFA ended, instead of the poorest of the poor gaining market share, as dependency theory and NIEO advocates predicted, the exact opposite occurred. Manufacturers concentrated their factories in super-competitive China and India. All over Africa, apparel manufacturers lost orders, closed their factories, and laid off workers.[21] At that moment, Chinese practices hurt African growth. How then can Chinese behavior dynamize African growth? Is East Asia a model for growth or a competitor which defeats African growth?

NO CHINESE MODEL?

Maybe China's Supreme Leader Deng was correct: there is no Chinese model to emulate. The "wholesale replication of a Chinese 'model' is simply not possible."[22] The factors facilitating China's rapid rise do indeed include many idiosyncratic or conjunctural factors that are inimitable. Suffering during the late Mao era predisposed ruling groups in China to support the Deng policies of openness and reform, whereas the comfortable, corrupt, entrenched apparatus in Brezhnev's Soviet Russia, in contrast, blocked openness and reform.

One respected source for clues as to how China succeeded is the economist Joseph Stiglitz. He touts China as a model for how developing nations should rise and escape the prescriptions of Anglo-American neo-liberalism. The invocation of neo-liberalism as a bogey-man obscures the necessity of market-regarding policies and institutions to sustain economic growth.[23] As Zhang Weiwei mis-describes the China model in order to demonize democratization, so Stiglitz gets China's behavior wrong in order to demonize the Washington consensus.

While Stiglitz claims that the Clinton administration, in negotiating supposedly harsh terms for China's entry into the WTO, hurt China, in fact, China's entry into the WTO resulted in unprecedented FDI flowing into China and swallow capital returning to China such that Chinese exports exploded.[24]

China soon accumulated the world's largest foreign exchange reserves and, with it, enormous global clout, facilitating its rise to global superpower status. China also would swiftly move up the value-added chain in the direction of ever more advanced technology. These unprecedented achievements came after the publication of Stiglitz's volume with its warnings about the WTO. The amazing rise of China through WTO membership discredits his analysis.

Stiglitz's conventional misunderstanding has China a success and Russia an economic failure, not a view that can explain Russia's swift rise since 1999. Actually, in some ways, China has done worse than Russia. China's post-Mao gradual marketization, utilizing a two-tier price system, unleashed official corruption based on renting access to the cheap government price tier to get wealthy by selling on the market-oriented tier. This misguided policy, not part of East Asian development prescriptions, resulted in a plunder of property by officialdom which exceeded what the oligarchs in Russia did. China, consequently, is far more unequal than is Russia. In the eyes of Chinese ruling groups, this polarization threatens stability, a term which Stiglitz does not seem to understand means a CCP monopoly of power. Stiglitz does not comment on China's extreme polarization which is approaching or surpassing Brazilian levels, a danger Chinese call Latin Americanization.

Whereas Stiglitz concluded that China's two step marketization avoided inflation, by 2008 the consensus of analysts was that corruptly entrenched regional interests were an obstacle to grappling with rising inflation. Stiglitz praised the CCP for creating "an effective securities and exchange commission, bank regulations, and safety nets." Actually, these items are still an agenda for the future. Whereas the CCP laid off 60 million or so SOE workers, Stiglitz praised Beijing for "avoid[ing] massive unemployment." Whereas Stiglitz congratulated Beijing for not taking "fighting inflation to an extreme," in fact, China has, until recently, been an IMF poster child for balancing budgets and keeping inflation low. Stiglitz, in contrast, recommends "not follow[ing] IMF prescriptions."

Stiglitz, out to discredit the Washington Consensus, misses all the reasons why Africanists see key Chinese policies as in harmony with so-called neo-liberalism. "Chinese penetration...presents the ugly face of predatory capitalism." The Chinese "imperialist" "offensive" "is not an indicator of a new trajectory which would benefit the majority of the African people." [25] Africanists therefore discuss China's role in Africa as "post colonial exploitation." [26] Here the Chinese model might be embedded in its relations with near-by Cambodia. "In Phnom Penh, the capital of Cambodia, the economy is going strong, but the prime minister, Hun Sen, has organized the plunder of the nation's resources for the benefit of...China in exchange for Beijing's protection." [27]

Given its predatory practices, some analysts contend that what made China unique was that it cheated. Beijing did not allow workers to organize independent unions to bargain over conditions and pay. It subsidized exports. It ignored safety and environmental protections. It did not supply its people a social safety net. It stole intellectual property and ignored international rules, copyrights, and patents. It forced foreign businessmen to turn over technology to Chinese counterparts. If China is a model of anything, in this perspective, it is of a race to the bottom which will make the poor yet poorer.[28]

Actually, many governments cheat, lie and steal. Even the advanced do it. These numerous others not only do not rise, as China has done, but they often decline, stagnate or fall apart. Cheating does not explain China's rise. What does?

Stiglitz praises China for a shrewd gradualism and a wise sequencing of reforms. But the so-called gradualism was less a choice than a consequence of how far economic reformers could push given the resistance of left conservatives, hardliners who wanted to conserve as much as possible of what was created by the leftism of Mao.

China actually has been in a hurry. Its major economic reforms went quickly. Deng Xiaoping's wisdom was to not stop the Chinese people from racing beyond the politically-imposed cautionary experiments of anxious rulers. For example, after Deng was able to get CCP approval for a bit of experimentation with some decollectivization in a few places, villagers fled the collectives in mass. Deng deserves credit, as Kate Zhou has detailed, for not heeding the complaints of the left conservatives who wanted villagers stopped from exceeding the CCP's gradualism. In fact, compared to Russia, China's economic reforms were thorough and swift. When the CCP speaks of gradualism, it uses the term euphemistically. Gradualism does not mean slowing economic reforms, which went rapidly, but preventing political democratization.

Sequencing similarly is a story which does not support the Stiglitz depiction of a Chinese model. According to Huang Yasheng, the most important reform is democratization. This is because getting out of the trammels of a Leninist command economy cannot help but be painful. In a democracy, it is possible to have open conversations about this inevitable suffering, how to share the pain, and what to do about it. Without a legitimating consensus on sharing the pain, there is a continuing danger that the post-socialist regime will legitimate itself by deflecting the angers of the wounded into scapegoating foreigners, stirring up a victimization nationalism seeking vengeance that could produce dangerous foreign policies. Those tensions and risks rile China today. Some worry that left conservatives will one day mobilize the regime's scapegoating chauvinism in order to bring the openness project to a screeching halt.

For Huang Yasheng, in a proper sequencing, financial reform is second. In our globalized age of out-of-control international finance, it is crucial to get this sector right because so much else depends on finance. While Stiglitz has taught us all so much about the dangers of unregulated international finance (he was critical from the outset of the U.S. Treasury-backed IMF response to the 1997-98 Asian Financial Crisis), it is not obvious, given the central role of finance in post-Bretton Woods globalization, that Stiglitz's praise for Beijing's delaying financial reform is good advice. Many in Beijing worry that, with so many urbanites invested in the largely unregulated stock market which is manipulated politically, a crash could produce a destabilizing explosion of urban anger against the corrupt and selfish regime.

In addition, the chauvinistic scapegoating that pervades an undemocratic China focuses in part on international finance as a sector where the rulers have sold the nation out to America, with Chinese money keeping the dollar afloat and being ripped off in the process. In sum, Stiglitz's description of the Chinese reform process does not pinpoint lessons for others who wish to emulate China. It is not easy to describe a Chinese model when one ignores what China borrowed from others in East Asia.

China's location in East Asia cannot be copied. China's location made it attractive as a regional export platform to the new Asian middle class consumers who rose as Japan rose. Over 80 percent of China's investment came from a near-by Chinese diaspora that had been building wealth for over a century or was round-tripping Chinese capital. These crucial factors are peculiar to China. China's historically large population also made China attractive to investors as a market. Smaller nations cannot win the FDI that pours into China. The openness of America to China, granting its Mao/Deng partner, in opposition to Brezhnev's militarism, the world's largest MFA quota and MFN status, was also crucial for China's rapid rise.

Fortuitously, China opened to foreign investment in Special Economic Zones (SEZ) (that copied Taiwan's Kaohsiung export zone whose instantiation Chinese specialists inspected in Busan, Korea) just as the September 1985 Plaza Accord raised the value of previously artificially low-priced Asian currencies. Consequently, low-priced manufacturing exporters all over East Asia were suddenly priced out of American markets just as China opened up to investors on favorable terms. Other East Asians raced in to China to hold their market shares in America.

China benefited many times over from the good luck of fortunate timing. China's 1979 opening came after, and therefore avoided, the commodity price boom and bust of the 1970s, which left Warsaw Pact and Third World nations drowning in debt. That painful cycle initiated by 1970s OPEC price spikes subsequently produced the 1980s Third World debt crisis and the new belief that there was no alternative to competing in the world market in order to win foreign exchange. But China, having avoided the ups and downs of the 1970s, was better situated than other emerging market economies to take advantage of the global opportunity.

In politics, it is said, timing is everything. Wave after huge wave of good things have broken China's way. It has produced an extraordinary economic tsunami which has at lightning speed turned China into an economic super power, all facilitated by a government which built infrastructure, managed the currency brilliantly to avoid inflation (contra Stiglitz), and got out of the way of an explosion of entrepreneurial energies. Also China, uniquely among East Asian states, copied Singapore's openness to FDI by MNCs. Synthesizing diverse Asian experiences at a propitious moment, how can there be a China model?

Cultural predispositions in China lead many Chinese to presume that no others can replicate what a peculiarly wonderful China has achieved. Chinese describe themselves as pragmatically solving problems carefully and judiciously. But what makes success possible is China's inimitable quintessence, Chineseness. There therefore cannot be a Chinese model.

Confucian-embued ethical parents raise children who work hard, save, live frugally, value education, and share with their collectivity. China is establishing Confucian Institutes all around the world so that non-Confucians can appreciate the superiority of Confucian culture. Others are invited to gain from Chinese beneficence and then follow behind by accepting Chinese leadership. While all rising powers initially credit their culture and character for their sudden success, the persuasiveness of the Chinese depiction of Chinese uniqueness makes it difficult for Africans to imagine a Chinese model to emulate.

A CHINA MODEL?

Yet, there are overall lessons to be learned from China's success. Africans can see the importance of creating a larger common market and building the infrastructure to integrate economies across borders. Chinese construction firms can be of assistance in that African project.[29]

African leaders also can see the necessity of attracting foreign investment and stop demonizing the world market as neo-colonialism. Chinese investments can be embraced enthusiastically. Selling raw materials to China can be a first step up the economic ladder if the exporting nation builds human capital and wisely invests its hard currency earnings. South African President Thebo Mbeki, however, has warned against Africa "falling into a 'colonial relationship' with China."[30] Many see China as "The new colonialist."[31] Africans who still see China in the categories of the 1960s and 1970s may not understand how Chinese dynamism can help them.

Each African government should, as China did, seek to borrow from numerous instances of success those items which are suitable to its peculiarities. Each of the success stories, of course, actually contains both negative and positive facets. One must critically apprehend and indigenize international experiences. Each government, just as Deng suggested, should borrow and adapt what will work best for its own people. Each can go to the same large store with a shopping list and come out with the particular ingredients required for a recipe precisely suited to its own tastes. But whatever Africans borrow, they conclude, that "Chinese should be able to pull off the same magic" in Africa "where the rest of the world has failed."[32]

China can help Africans transform their economies for the better. A report to the U.S. Senate Committee on Foreign Relations concluded that "rapidly expanding Sino-African economic cooperation and the perceived relevance to Africa of China's rapid economic development process may cause Africans to increasingly view China as a more relevant political model for Africa than Western Democracies."[33] Chinese success in transforming African poverty will establish China as a global power.

Nonetheless, many in African NGOs, labor unions and civil society groups agree with nay-sayers in Europe and China and find no Chinese model to emulate. Instead, they conclude that China is largely a case of bad practices and not of best practices. The Government of China offers loans, aid, trade, investment, debt relief, scholarships and construction projects in such humongous amounts that corrupt, authoritarian African governments can gain the wherewithal to escape European good governance conditionality. Angola is a noted instance of such forum shopping.[34] Chinese policy helps the leaders whose policies have kept Africans poor to stay in power and continue wounding African peoples.

While African governments are delighted to see Chinese offers as an alternative to European restrictions, delays, failures, humiliations, and conditionalities, European critics find that the most corrupt elements in African regimes will use Chinese funds to hold on to power and avoid needed reform. Having just been bailed out of debt by OECD forgiveness, irresponsible African ruling groups can run-up new debt obligations to China. Will Chinese throw good money after bad, forgive the debts, or eventually be tough about re-payment? Corrupt African elites may benefit but, in this perspective, not the long-suffering citizens of African nations. Unaccountable and greedy ruling African groups will take Chinese monies for their personal aggrandizement, to pay and equip security forces to repress popular outrage, and to co-opt potential competitors, thereby further entrenching selfish authoritarian regimes. Africa will not be transformed by China's rise. That is the strong conclusion and conviction of most outspoken civil society groups in African democracies.

It is also the conclusion of Africanists and others of the anti-capitalist left. Although a 21st century China replaces a 19th century England in tapping African resources, "the fundamental dynamic remains the same." "[F]ew of those living in Africa's resource-producing countries will see any significant benefit from the depletion of their continent's natural bounty."[35] Such analysts still see the world market as the enemy of progress. They have hated OECD attempts to get Africa to abandon market-disregarding statism. They scapegoat neo-liberalism. They see Chinese firms bringing capitalism to Africa. They condemn Chinese greed, profiteering, and environmental destruction. They do not appreciate the expansion of wealth that accompanies market-oriented policies. In sum, the Africans and Africanists who do not see China transforming Africa for the better are legion.

In finding instead that China can dynamize an African rise, as this analysis does, one is not concluding that the political consequences will meet the ideals of democracy promotion or corruption eradication. But authoritarian China has risen rapidly while intensifying corruption. An analyst should not confuse his or her ideals with the actual sources and forces of rapid growth.

Certainly, democratic forces in Africa will be weakened by Chinese policies. When 2008 elections in Kenya were stolen and violence attended a post-election attempt to make the voters' will real, China declared that democracy was not suited to Africa. Equating democracy with chaos and ethnic strife, Chinese firms in Nigeria ordered their workers not to venture out for a month during Nigerian elections. It is a commonplace to the CCP, after it, on June 4, 1989 crushed a nation-wide democracy movement, that the post-Mao experience of a rising China is an "example" to the world of successful authoritarian development. People who value democracy fear that China's authoritarian development "will pose a potential global danger to democracy."[36]

But that obviously is not a negative to China's authoritarian ruling groups. The CCP regime propagandizes against democracy. At the November 2006 China-Africa summit in Beijing, the PRC distributed literature arguing against democracy, portrayed as a political system that exacerbates societal tensions and brings instability, suggesting that democratization was not the wave of the future.[37] The Chinese firms in Africa have not enjoyed dealing with local democratic institutions, with labor unions, independent media, or oppositional political parties, all of which oppose local Chinese abuses. For the CCP, authoritarianism is the better road ahead.

Because of China's policy of so-called non-interference, anxious and corrupt African authoritarians use Chinese assistance to avoid changes in the direction of law, accountability and human rights. The Chinese model that is being borrowed therefore is said by critics to be one not of authoritarian growth but of authoritarian stagnation. The CCP intends to defeat the global forces of human rights so as to promote a world in which China's authoritarian system and its leaders can be more comfortable. Chinese policy in Africa is said to reflect this most basic interest of the CCP. Be that as it may, promoters of good governance, democracy and human rights err by not seeing that authoritarian development is possible. Following China, however, does have political consequences.

Despite Beijing insisting that no strings are attached to Chinese money, actually, those funds do come with political strings. As do all governments, the CCP regime has interests. The recipient is expected to break relations with democratic Taiwan. It is expected to vote on United Nations bodies to protect China from embarrassment on human rights issues. One certainly does not speak out on behalf of a Tibetan people begging for minimal rights from a repressive and discriminatory armed Chinese occupation. The CCP finds major political gains in courting African governments.

China clearly does interfere. It threatened Zambia with retaliation if its citizens voted for a candidate seen in Beijing as unfriendly to China. It leaned on the Government in Sudan to change policy on Darfur a bit to help deflect the complaints of rights activists portraying the 2008 Beijing games as the genocide Olympics. It sent weapons to the Mugabe regime to crush the popular will of the people of Zimbabwe in 2008. Consequently, many analysts see Beijing as acting on a Chinese set of interests. It does not prioritize ending poverty in Africa. This complaint about Beijing's political interests, however accurate, conflates politics and economics.

CHINA AS A MOTOR OF DEVELOPMENT

The issues of economic growth and political freedom are separate items. China can be a spark to greatly reducing poverty in Africa whatever its political system preferences. Japan, after all, did not make democratization a precondition for Japanese FDI in Southeast Asia. Tokyo's policies served Japanese interests. Likewise, China is willing to pay to have Africa treat China "as leader of the developing world."[38] It will fund friends which support China "in the struggle against America 'hegemony'"[39] Beijing has put billions into a "fund to encourage Chinese companies to invest in Africa."[40] It has offered debt relief. It is opening its burgeoning markets to African goods and offering friendly nations interest free loans. It is training medical personnel. It is teaching the Chinese language to African students. It is providing Chinese businesses with information and technical support to lower their cost of doing business in Africa. China is building a basis for deep business cooperation with Africa that can be of huge benefit to Africans precisely because it serves major Chinese interests. But just as the CCP claims, Africa can benefit economically, too.

Whereas satisfied European and American investors saw few profit making opportunities in Africa, entrepreneurial Chinese have found lots of such possibilities. Chinese firms need to be taken more seriously. Even Chinese cars are beginning to compete with European manufacturers in Africa.[41] Since its entry into the WTO and an amassing of unprecedently huge amounts of foreign exchange, Beijing has promoted a "going out" policy of helping Chinese firms to become globally competitive. Africa is a testing ground of this policy.[42] Africa matters to China.

That China acts in a self-interested way does not mean that poor Africans cannot be lifted out of poverty by Chinese economic policies. That other nations, including Mao era China, have in the past provided similar help to African nations without Africa being transformed misses the two unique features of the post-Mao Chinese impact, the post-socialist timing which makes Africans receptive now as never before, and the unique force of the sudden, continuing, and enormously weighty rise of 1.4 billion entrepreneurial Chinese acting on the basis of a proven Asian development model.

Africans can march ahead by joining in. If China promotes infrastructure development so that Africa is no longer a place where "the power supply is poor, telephone service is erratic, and internet access is limited"[43] and if Africans become socialized to Chinese best practices, then Africa will greatly benefit from ties to Asia.

It was the Japanese who first applied "the lessons of export-led development."[44] They promoted a "flying goose" pattern.[45] In this perspective, the lead nation in a sector, whether it is today's Japan, China or India, whether the sector is electronic goods, apparel or software, is rapidly moving up in technology and value-added production. It therefore is regularly superannuating a prior generation of goods. It is continuously producing industrial sectors and market shares which it can subsequently move to lower-priced labor countries. Other geese will then fly behind the lead goose and will be pulled ahead, increment by increment, by the lead goose. African governments have to treat the 100,000 plus African (a rapidly growing number) "traders in south-east China and Hong Kong" and African students from China as a resource to plug into the Chinese engine.[46] China shows how a region's diaspora can catalyze development at home.[47]

From this African point of view, "This 21st century is the century for China to lead the world. And when you are leading the world, we want to be close behind you. When you are going to the moon, we don't want to be left behind."[48] Many African geese are willing to benefit from the lead goose today as they never were in the era of Japan's rise.

Economists who, in contrast, see China hurting Africans because China is supposedly a unique juggernaut that is monopolizing low wage light industry will be proven wrong. Economic laws are not negated by China's rise. Higher wages and costs and a higher valued currency in China will force much lower end production out of China. Indeed, this already is beginning to happen. The trend is inexorable. The flying geese of Japan's Asia can become the flying geese of China's Africa, part of a continent taking China as a powerful economic pole and economic motor, the extension of Asian dynamism to Africa. China can transform Africa.

The analysts who see Chinese governmental aid and state enterprise investment lost down a rat hole of African regime corruption do not see that growth can accompany corruption. They miss the powerful dynamism of Chinese society. Tens of thousands of young, poor Chinese have flocked to Africa to use ties to Chinese businesses back home in order to get a business started from scratch in Africa. Millions more will be coming, as hundreds of millions in China continue to flee the stagnant farming sector to join a frenzy of entrepreneurialism. Chinese growth is revved forward by millions of Chinese out to make a buck in business, people who engage in cut-throat competition which creates a virtually unbeatable China price. Young Chinese looking for adventure and opportunity are racing to Africa. They will give their energies and talents working for a pittance to turn a profit. They will make use of their connections to Chinese networks of entrepreneurs who are losing out at home because of higher Chinese prices and are therefore open to moving enterprises to lower wage Africa.

This flying goose networking reaching out to Africa under China's aegis, made possible by recent revolutions in communication and transportation, which made the world smaller and decreased transaction costs, has the potential to ignite rapid growth in Africa tomorrow as it did under Japan's aegis in Southeast Asia yesterday. The Chinese strategic need for African energy guarantees that the Chinese commitment to Africa will persist. The focus of most analysts on the Chinese state ignores how post-Mao China is a very different world than that of the statist Mao era command economy. In the reform era, the work of non-governmental private sector actors all over the society creates wealth, jobs, brands and enterprises. One should pay more attention to the rise of the firms in China and the frenzied energies of would-be Chinese entrepreneurs.

Europeans and Americans cannot do what Chinese are doing. Coming from richer countries, they insist on better living conditions and thicker profit margins. While Chinese may cluster in Chinatowns and spark a racist backlash, they work harder in harsher circumstances. They accept thinner margins. Their numbers, coming from the 300 million or so still locked into the rural stagnation that Mao era policies caused, are also infinitely greater than the handful of Euro-Americans moving to Africa. Backed by a government with a seemingly bottomless pool of foreign exchange and a serious commitment to succeeding in Africa, China's energies can transform the continent. The subsidies, cheap money and assistance to business in Africa from the Chinese government will have a huge impact because of the efforts of hard-working, globally-mobile, entrepreneurial Chinese.

In the Chinese version of the Japanese flying goose project, African nations can benefit from playing a role in a world economy largely structured by an Asian motor. India, Malaysia, Taiwan and Japan are all also increasingly active in Africa in order to try to compete with China.[49] The post-Mao regime has unleashed a new globalizing dynamism. "The rise of Asian-African business networks...mimicking the 'flying geese' paradigm . . . is a potential harbinger" of cooperation and rapid growth for Africa.[50] A transformed Africa could be the consequence of integrating into the East Asian development process. But not all in Africa will benefit equally.

After all, Marcos in the Philippines frittered away the Japanese opportunity. Burma, Cambodia, Vietnam and Laos long kept East Asian market dynamism out of their countries. The key to success is openness to grasping the opportunity. A key is what each African country does. The goal should be to plug into Chinese dynamism, make money, and then re-invest that EOI wealth in human capital so that the nation can continually move up a value added ladder. The onus is on the host government to get its house in order. That is, the big question is which African governments will initially take advantage of the opportunities inherent in China's rise? Which will be willing to join the flock of flying geese and benefit from intra-Asian rivalries which are also creating new opportunities for Africa in very large ways? Only a few may grab the opportunity and benefit at first. But successes will attract emulators.

China then is less a model and more a "catalyst for development."[51] It revives hope that poor authoritarian regimes can "scale the development heights."[52] It is "an inspiration."[53] Without the political will to enter into the Chinese endeavor, however, African governments cannot succeed.

Some analysts argue that few African governments are set-up so as to be able to take advantage of the China-structured opportunity. No matter how many tens of billions of Chinese investment pour into Africa, whether the money is from the Chinese state or from Chinese society, these observers find, the wealth will be frittered away and flee out of Africa. There already are instances of billions disappearing. The outcome then could be that China will get the energy it needs for continuing its rapid rise but, at the end of the process, in Nigeria, the Congo, Angola and numerous similar countries, nations will stagnate, population will grow, and the people will no longer have precious and scarce resources to use to rise out of poverty.

In this view, China's defeat of European good governance conditionality in the name of non-interference, a slogan attractive to African nationalists, will unintentionally, yet inevitably, defeat development in Africa. Critics worry that

Chinese policies are strengthening corrupt national leaders who will enrich themselves but not invest in the education, health and infrastructure that would allow the general citizenry to keep rising. China's rise, in the view of many well-informed analysts, cannot transform Africa. I respect the knowledge and skepticism on which such negative projections are based. It creates a virtually hegemonic discourse.

But surely it can no longer be seriously argued that the rise of commodity prices brought on by Chinese spending is bad for African nations with commodities to export, except, of course, from an environmental perspective. The many, many tens of billions in investment that China and Chinese are pouring into Africa are prodding Russia,[54] India, Japan and even Europe to try to match the Chinese tenders to African governments. This is very good for Africa. However much the weight of corrupt dictators is strengthened by a Gresham's Law effect in which India, Japan, *et al* copy China in putting aside good governance criteria in courting bad African governments so that law, accountability, rights and democracy are put to the side, it is still inconceivable that African growth will not speed up. Indeed, it in fact already has. With so many huge wealth opportunities suddenly available, and so much more in the offing, however much is wasted or is serving only elites, the extraordinary wealth and dynamism of the Chinese-initiated entrepreneurial frenzy should most likely transform large sectors of Africa. Corrupt ruling groups, as in China, will seek to get rich from growth.

SPECIAL ZONES TO START THE CHINESE MOTOR

Beijing's policies offer a clue as to how the Chinese economic motor would energize African development. Mauritius established an Export-Processing Zone in 1970 which attracted a wave of FDI that sustained export-led growth until the end of the MFA in 2005 devastated its apparel manufactures and benefited China. Therefore, in October 2007, Mauritius contracted with China's Tian Li Group to set up an economic cooperation zone with Tian Li investing $500 million in the project. Meanwhile, some local factories moved from Mauritius to Madagascar where wages were much lower. Flying geese are already at work inside of Africa.

In addition, Mauritius is trying to attract Chinese tourists to its beautiful beaches and to move into banking, biotechnology and services. To win with China in a globalized age of rapid change requires a resilient state capable of facilitating continuous upgrading.[55] In general, the huge amount of capital that flees Africa could be attracted back by new wealth opportunities facilitated by China if African governments can do more to nurture their human capital.[56]

As in China, where most regions did not at first grasp the reform opportunity, the success of a few SEZ will, over time, attract, out of greed and jealousy, emulators. The Chinese government has facilitated the construction in Africa of five large Taiwan style SEZs in diverse parts of the continent to channel Chinese business spending. Business in these zones would soar as

Chinese trade and investment flew in. Africans would then flock to the successful SEZs and learn marketable skills. Some zones might be disappointments, but not all. Afterwards, the winners in prospering zones would disperse across the continent and do business throughout Africa. Other Africans would want to emulate them. Their leaders and people would want to get rich. Governments then would build infrastructure connecting the SEZs to areas with resources or markets. Initial spots of hot-housed wealth would then spread their economic reach ever wider. More and more Africans would be attracted to dynamic locales. Blots of wealth would appear and widen and link up and cover ever more territory. This is precisely what happened in China.

In sum, China has begun to transform Africa by adapting Japan's flying goose pattern of wealth expansion from Southeast Asian realities to the particularities of African development using SEZs pioneered in Taiwan but funded in Africa by Chinese corporate groups. In 2008, Nepal's incoming prime minister declared, "We build special economic zones like China." "The SEZ stimulated Chinese economic development and we want to learn from China."[57] Others note, "This is China's development model being transplanted to Africa, drawing on the success of the economic zones in China...which resulted in sweeping liberalization of the Chinese economy."[58] Just because experts on China incorrectly argued that such extraordinary success was impossible for China in the late 20th century is no reason to repeat the error in the 21st century and not see that similar possibilities actually also exist for Africans.

I may be naïve in under-estimating the limitless power of corrupt African regimes which lack effective state capacity to fritter away opportunities. I respect the knowledge of Africanists who conclude that "It would be overly optimistic to believe that China's long-term resource agenda dovetails with Africa's requirement to alleviate the extreme poverty that blights the continent."[59] I think these critics underestimate the proven success of Asian development policies. Is it not the case that analysts since 1978 have continually underestimated China's capacity for economic success? Isn't the same error being repeated in the conventional wisdom about China and Africa? China's outward move into Africa already dwarfs that of the World Bank, IMF, EU and others. Most analysts do not appreciate the enormous scale and momentum of China's extraordinary rise.

But that amazing explosion of Chinese wealth and its international impact is only beginning. The result for Africa will soon be much, much larger. As the China of today was inconceivable in 1976 or 1989, so is the transformed Africa of tomorrow almost inconceivable today. China's huge impact on Africa may not win the undying love of African peoples. It may not bring democracy or equity or end corruption. But China's transformative energies should begin to raise Africa out of poverty.

Of course, as mentioned above, not all observers see the Chinese model in terms of entrepreneurial energies, flying geese and export zones. There are ways of seeing other aspects of the Chinese rise which obscure the features which are focused on in this chapter. According to then Russian president-to-be, Dmitry Medvedev, Russia should follow the Chinese "model." That is, Moscow should nurture Russian companies "seeking to expand into global markets" so that Russia could upgrade technology and know-how and diversify and win foreign markets. "National champions" in steel, nickel and aluminum, among others, that is, in economic sectors considered to be strategic, should be helped "to compete on a global scale." Medvedev understood the China model to have a realpolitik core of enhancing military strength, a strategy which required learning how newly risen Chinese firms had benefited from globalization in terms of the state's strategic interests.[60] Medvedev may be right and yet ignore other aspects of China's developmental dynamism.

Medvedev is correct that CCP leaders are dedicated to enhancing China's hard power. But there are many facets to China's rise. Africans should choose to see in China what is useful for Africans. No matter where one comes down on the issue of whether the Chinese motor in Africa has the horse power to greatly diminish entrenched poverty, some African governments already dismiss nay-sayers about China, condemning them for trying to deny Africans of an opportunity for success made possible by China's fabulous economic rise. These governments vie to house China's SEZs. China is both a powerful inspiration and a real motor of development into which some African nations can plug, thereby re-charging their economies. Africans would not be acting in their own self interest if they denied themselves of the higher octane that Chinese energies can provide to Africa. This is where some of Africa is going. We should wish these Africans well.

DEMOCRATIC BLINDERS TO SEEING THE FUTURE

Non-Chinese long blinded themselves to China's economic power. The industrialized democracies hid from themselves the importance of authoritarian China's post-Mao rise. That authoritarian success story conflicted with the hegemonic European discourse of the end of the Cold War in which West Europe and the European Union, the camp of freedom, peace and prosperity, defeated Brezhnev's stagnant, militaristic tyranny leading to the implosion of both the Soviet Empire and the Soviet Union. Market democracies, not authoritarian regimes with state nurtured development policies, seemed the wave of the future. China's rise was invisible. Consequently, Japan in 1995 was shocked by superpower China's large, new influence in Asia. Europe, around 2006, was likewise shocked by superpower China's large new influence in Africa.

As China came to challenge Japan in Asia, so it is now beginning to challenge Europe in Africa. However, as Japan's transformation of Southeast Asia did not end kleptocratic government in Indonesia or brutal military dictatorship in Burma, likewise, China can not transform all of Africa. In addition, the influx of Chinese construction workers and entrepreneurs into Africa could spark a backlash as locals complain about jobs lost to foreigners who are, to put it gently, culturally insensitive.[61] The projection of this chapter depends on millions more Chinese going to Africa. The number is rapidly rising. Chinese already out-number Portuguese in Angola.[62] Obviously, backlash countries will not enjoy the full benefit of Chinese dynamism.

But for those who join China's flying geese flock and lock into China's SEZ networks and who welcome entrepreneurial Chinese, a huge transformation should be in the offing. In fact, given that China's population is more than ten times that of Japan's, and given that China's rise should continue and strengthen and broaden in the foreseeable and ever more globalized future, the transformative impact of China in Africa could yet turn out to be far larger than that of Japan in Asia.

Fixated on how China, "a second superpower," "will pose a potential global danger to democracy," many observers blind themselves to the beneficial economic impact of superpower China. "Given its huge population, if it grows at anything like its present pace, China will before long become an economic and military power of the first rank." "China is exerting growing influence around the world...." "One also hears a great deal about the Chinese model these days in Africa."[63]

This chapter tries to explain why. It is an attempt to open eyes to how China could transform Africa. We should see that an opponent of democracy can still bring material benefit to hundreds of millions. But it does not do it all by itself. China has not risen alone or in a vacuum. The Chinese rise has benefited from changeable and powerful background factors and contextual forces which are too often invisible to observers. China's model for success is dependent upon external international matters. China has soared in a post-Bretton Woods era of unimaginable volatility when uncontrolled and unregulated international finance was available in hitherto unimagined volume and when the American market appeared to be insatiable and the American dollar seemed as good as gold.

There has been developing, however, a contradiction between unregulated finance, on the one hand, and the openness of the American market and the strength of the U.S. dollar, on the other. These forces are under great tension. What this contradiction portends for the future is unknowable. The volatility of this age is beyond imagining. It can rapidly give the lie to any optimistic projection. The straight-line extrapolation of this chapter is not a prediction about an inevitable future. So many other factors are in operation besides the Chinese contribution of entrepreneurial frenzy, flying geese, and export zones.

But let's bracket these speculations on the possible end of an era whose negation could diminish or deny the positive impact of China's rise on Africa. Let us instead focus on the early 21st century era in which Africa can benefit, and has already benefited, from China's extraordinary growth, an economic rise dynamized by an adventurous, risk-taking, entrepreneurial, money-making society which is pulling much the rest of Asia further into Africa. Let's treat China, for Africa, as both a model (of East Asian style flying goose and export zone success) and a motor of development for whoever allows its nation to be pulled into the economic dynamism of a lead goose, or lead geese. African governments have barely begun to join the East Asian flock. But that is where many are going. It is most likely how ever more African governments will act, treating China as a model and motor for Africa's 21st century success. As inconceivable as it may seem to Africanists, African democrats, and outside analysts incapable of imagining a transformed Africa, my educated bet, based on observing a long record of successful, persistent and transferable globalized Asian dynamism, is that China's rise, despite the conventional wisdom to the contrary, is a motor of development which will help transform much of Africa for the better.

NOTES

[*] The author thanks the following journal for permission to reprint previously published article: "How Economic Superpower China Could Transform Africa," *Journal of Chinese Political Science*, vol. 14, no. 1, 2009, pp. 1-20. I am grateful to Howard French, Michael Schatzberg and Crawford Young for sharing their critical views on African development.

[1] Giles Mohan, "China in Africa," *Review of African Political Economy*, 115, 2008, p. 164.

[2] Giles Mohan, and Marcus Powers, *New African Choices?*, 115, 2008, p.31.

[3] Lindsey Hilsum, "We Love China," *Granta* 92, 2007.

[4] Helmut Reisen, "Is China Actually Helping Improve Debt Sustainability in Africa?" OECD Development Centre, July 2, 2007.

[5] T. Miller, "China's investments ease Africa's poverty," *South China Morning Post*, July 12, 2008.

[6] Lei Wu, and Lu, G. S. "Some Reflections on the Problem of the Development of Sino African Energy Relations" (in Chinese), *Shijie jingji yu zhengzhi*, September, 2008.

[7] Serge Michel, "When China Met Africa," *Foreign Policy*, May/June 2008, pp. 39-46.

[8] Wei-Wei Zhang, "The allure of the Chinese model," *International Herald Tribune*, November 2, 2006.

[9] Walden Bello, "China Provokes Debate in Africa," *Foreign Policy in Focus*, March 9, 2007, pp. 1-6.

[10] Yasheng Huang, *Capitalism with Chinese Characteristics*, (New York: Cambridge University Press, 2008)

[11] Firoze Manji, and Stephen Marks, eds. *African Perspectives on China in Africa*, (Fahamu: Oxford, 2007), p. 44.

[12] Larry Diamond, *The Spirit of Democracy*, (New York: Holt Paperbacks, 2008), p. 262.

[13] Chris Alden, *China in Africa*, (New York: ZedBooks, 2007), p. 131.

[14] Leni Wild, and David Mepham, *The New Sinosphere*, (U.K.: Institute for Public Policy Research, 2006), p. 58.

[15] Firoze Manji, and Stephen Marks, eds. *African Perspectives on China in Africa*, (Fahamu: Oxford, 2007), p. 112.

[16] Manji and Marks, eds. *African Perspectives on China in Africa*, p. 136.

[17] Manji and Marks, eds. *African Perspectives on China in Africa*, pp. 149, 166.

[18] Manji and Marks, eds. *African Perspectives on China in Africa*, p. 139.

[19] Daniel Nyeribe Michael, "Issues in Nigeria-China Relations," *Daily Champion* (Lagos), April 30, 2006.

[20] Marcel Kitissou, ed., *Africa in China's Global Strategy*, (London: Adonis and Abbey Publishers, 2007), p. 185.

[21] Chris Alden, *China in Africa*, (New York: ZedBooks, 2007), p. 125.

[22] Marcel Kitissou, ed., *Africa in China's Global Strategy*, p. 36.
[23] Joseph Stiglitz, Globalization and Its Discontents, (New York: Norton, 2002), Chapter 4, pp. 89-132.
[24] Stiglitz does not note that the EU, Mexico and India insisted on more concessions from China than did the USA.
[25] Henning Melber, "China in Africa," *Current African Issues* No. 33, 2007, Uppsola, Nordiska Afrikainstitut, pp. 6-8.
[26] D. Herman, "China focused on oil, not Sudanese needs," *Christian Science Monitor*, July 27, 2007.
[27] François Hauter. "Chinese Shadows," *The New York Review*, 54.15, October 11, 2007.
[28] For an introduction to cheating and Chinese economic growth, see Misha Glenny, *McMafia*, (New York: KnopfBooks, 2006), chapter 4.
[29] T. Miller, "China's investments ease Africa's poverty," *South China Morning Post*, July 12, 2008.
[30] Dino Mahtani, "Demand for new reserves is stronger," *Financial Times*, November 9, 2007.
[31] Alec Russell, "The new colonialists," *Financial Times*, November 17, 2007. While most analysts define neo-colonialism as post-independence exploitation using economic means in a formally independent country, Africans imagine neo-colonialism as having a militarily interventionist dimension. The French, Belgians and British have frequently intervened militarily in Africa in the post-independence era. So is China. It builds weapons factories in the Sudan and delivers weapons to friendly regimes. Africans are anxious about Chinese "boots on the ground," and not just in Peace Keeping Operations, as stories abound about Chinese security forces at Chinese extraction projects.
[32] Serge Michel, "When China Met Africa," *Foreign Policy*, May/June 2008, p. 41.
[33] Congressional Research Service, *China's Foreign Policy and 'Soft Power' in South America, Asia, and Africa*, Committee on Foreign Relations, United States Senate, April, 2008, p. 130.
[34] Or, perhaps more accurately, China's investments facilitated a surge in Angola's export earnings which then sky-rocketed as oil prices soared after 2002, giving Angola the wealth to ignore IMF lenders, see Erica Downs, "The Fact and Fiction of Sino-African Energy Relations," *China Security*, 3.3 Summer 2007, pp. 42-68.
[35] Michael Klare, *Rising Powers, Shrinking Planet*, (New York: Metropolitan Books, 2008), pp. 149, 150.
[36] Marc Plattner, *Democracy Without Borders*, (Lanham, Maryland: Rowman and Littlefield Publishers, Inc., 2008), pp. 141, 142.
[37] Serge Michel, "When China Met Africa," *Foreign Policy*, May/June 2008, p. 45.
[38] Joshua Eisenman, "China's Post-Cold War Strategy in Africa," in Joshua Eisenman *et al.*, eds., *China and the Developing World*, (Armonk, New York: M. E. Sharpe), p. 29.
[39] Joshua Eisenman, "China's Post-Cold War Strategy in Africa," p. 33.
[40] Joshua Eisenman, "China's Post-Cold War Strategy in Africa," p. 35.
[41] John Miller, "Africa's New Car Dealer: China," *Wall Street Journal*, August 28, 2007. For a report which focuses on "a fundamental underlying problem" in China's engagement with Africa and minimizes "the prospects of China's corporate engagement in Africa," see Bates Gill and James Reilly, "The Tenuous Hold of China Inc. in Africa," *The Washington Quarterly*, summer 2007, pp. 37-52.
[42] Marcel Kitissou, ed., *Africa in China's Global Strategy*, pp. 87-100 and 108-131.
[43] Harry G. Broadman, "China and India Go To Africa," *Foreign Affairs*, March/April, 2008, p. 104.
[44] Alden, *China in Africa*, p. 97.
[45] Alden, *China in Africa*, p. 48.

[46] Alden, *China in Africa*, p. 86. For a description of African business in China, see Brigitte Bertoncello and Sylvie Bredeloup, "The emergence of new African 'trading posts' in Hong Kong and Guangzhou," *China Perspectives*, January, 2007, pp. 94-104.
[47] Kitissou, ed., *Africa in China's Global Strategy*, pp. 190-2.
[48] Alden, *China in Africa*, p. 68-69.
[49] David Pilling, "Tokyo shows mettle in the race for Africa's ore," *Financial Times*, May 22, 2008.
[50] Alden, *China in Africa*, p. 126.
[51] Alden, *China in Africa*, p. 4.
[52] Alden, *China in Africa*, p. 35.
[53] Alden, *China in Africa*, p. 59.
[54] Kester Kenn Klomegah, "Russia: Chasing China in Africa," IPS, June 18, 2008.
[55] Vinaye Dey Ancharaz, "David v. Goliath: Mauritius facing up to China," *African Economic Research Consortium*, January, 2008.
[56] Greg Mills, and Chris Thompson, "Partners or Predators? China in Africa," *China Brief*, 8.2, January 17, 2007, pp. 7-10.
[57] Russel Hsiao, "Nepal Following China's Economic Path," *China Brief*, 8, July 3, 2008, p. 1.
[58] Alec Russell, "Island wants to be east Asia's gateway into Africa," *Financial Times*, March 7, 2008.
[59] J-P Thompson, "China's Crucial Role in Africa," *Africa Files* 6, August-November, 2007, pp. 1-11.
[60] Catherine Benton, "Copy China, Says Medveder," *Financial Times*, February 1, 2008.
[61] Rory Carroll, "China's Goldmine," *The Guardian*, March 28, 2006.
[62] Indira Campos, and Alex Vines, "Angola and China," Chatham House, London, Center for Strategic and International Studies), March 2008.
[63] Marc Plattner, *Democracy Without Borders*, (Lanham, Maryland: Rowman and Littlefield Publishers, Inc., 2008), pp. 140-142.

Chapter 8

The Role of Greater China in Latin America

Thomas Cieslik

INTRODUCTION

Within the global integration of national economies, Greater China is gaining gradually more influence in all regions of the world. This chapter focuses on the People's Republic of China (PRC) geopolitical and economic influence in Latin America and discusses the struggle for diplomatic recognition in Central America and the Caribbean. It is the last region in the world in which the majority of nation states recognize the Republic of China (ROC), commonly known as Taiwan, as the sole legitimate government of the whole of China and not only the actual jurisdiction of the island groups of Taiwan, Penghu, Kinmen and Matsu. However, since June 2007, Costa Rica broke off diplomatic relations. Taipei now fears, that other nations could follow to establish relations with Beijing. Consequently, the claim of international legitimacy will become obsolete.

THE NEW FOREIGN POLICY OF CHINA

Chinese foreign policy is still following the legacy of the three principles of Sun Yat-sen to overcome the devotion of the Unequal Treaties after the Opium-Wars. Sovereignty, emancipation and anti-hegemony have been postulated as principal goals of Chinese foreign policy after the foundation of the PRC to overcome humiliation, the loss of its cultural and moral authority and victimhood in the period of the centurial colonialism until the end of the Second World War. Both imperialism and the Second World War with the Japanese occupation have been a long with the Cold War the three historical experiences that shaped the formulation of contemporary Chinese foreign policy.[1] Therefore, maintaining independence and safeguarding national sovereignty is one of Chinese highest priorities in foreign policy activities. According to the official statement of the Chinese government, the PRC also opposes hegemonism and safeguards world peace, which includes the support of the Treaty on Non-

Proliferation of Nuclear Weapons, which the PRC signed in 1992. In the context of a multi-polar world system the PRC upholds five principles of peaceful coexistence: respect to sovereignty, mutual non-aggression, non-interference in each other's international affairs which means also to prevent any other country to interfere in these affairs. Moreover, equality and mutual benefit as a result from political, economic cooperation and finally peaceful coexistence, which guarantees the living in harmony regardless the difference in social, political or ideological systems.[2] On the basis of the five principles, China looks forward to contributing to the construction of a new international order after the end of the Cold War that is founded on the principles of the UN Charter. Nevertheless, China focuses a special role on developing countries in Africa, Asia and Latin America to support these nations on their road to independence and development. The official statement of the government clearly stresses: "Whenever the developing countries suffer external aggression and interference, China is ready to give its support."[3] China has several times proven that it is willing to back countries and their governments in the United Nations Security Council. Within Chinese understanding of sovereignty, Beijing rejects any international attempt to recognize the government of the ROC. Taiwan is considered as an inalienable part of Chinese territory. The ROC is called as a renegade republic; the declaration of independence would be seen as an act of hostility against Beijing. In spite of recent rapprochements (direct charter flights, economic cooperation, e.g.) between Taipei and Beijing, the PRC White Paper on Taiwan from the year 2000 is still valid and aims the reunification and the use of force in the case of any Taiwanese unilateral declaration of independence.[4]

In short, its main goal is the creation of its sovereignty, independence and international recognition as an equal member of other great powers in the world. It is principally based on diplomacy and the rejection of warlike actions. China has participated in the non-aligned movement during the East-West-Conflict, it defended its independence as a communist developing state during the 1960s in the border conflict with the Soviet Union and has rebuild confidence after the massacre on Tiananmen by economic integration and political participation in regional forum and cooperation with ASEAN and other Asian nations. After the substitution of Taiwan in the United Nations and its full membership in the Security Council, many countries have switched diplomatic relations from the ROC to the PRC. Meanwhile, the PRC has begun to be an influential player in world politics that represents consequently the interests of non-intervention, multipolar balance, and state's sovereignty. Moreover, in the last years, with growing economic wealth and more participation in global issues, Chinese foreign policy has changed from a traditional representative of the non-aligned movement toward a pragmatically operating global power that seeks mutual security and balance of power in the international system according to neo-realistic theory. The principle of non-intervention enjoys high priority to the Chinese government and the leading Communist Party. The protection of its own claim to power includes the acceptance to deal with any government in the world, no matter if dictatorship or democracy.

A turning point in Chinese politics has been the XVth Chinese Communist Party Congress in 1997. It gave a clear signal to continue the modernization process of the country that started with the leadership of Deng Xiaoping. But it also defined its new role, giving up the traditional role as a developing country toward a regional power that accepts and takes responsibility for regional and global affairs. The economic and social reform agenda remarked ambitious goals in the transition process by supporting with precaution the liberalization process during the Asian Financial Crisis. In this context, China has started to demonstrate its responsibility for global issues. China's role as mediator in the North Korean Nuclear Energy Crisis or in the transition of Cambodia has underlined the assertive foreign policy that focuses on co-existence and dialogue. Since the takeover in Hong Kong in 1997 Chinese foreign policy has ushered to take influence in world affairs in order to represent national interests. After the change from President Jiang Zemin to President Hu Jintao the new government under Prime Minister Wen Jiabao has defined Chinese foreign policy as a "peaceful rising,"[5] but includes the continuation of the "go-out strategy" to develop new sources of raw materials and the take over of foreign companies to ensure the sustainability of Chinese rising. The National Development and Reform Commission drafted this concept, and the Chinese Development Bank financed state's companies like the China National Petroleum Corporation, the China Minmetals Corporation, the China Construction Corporation or the China Metallurgical Group Corporations as players in the global trade, but actually tools of the Chinese government to fulfill its principal objectives.

International relations are stamped by Western and euro-centric tradition. With the ascent of China as a global player and its emphasis on a multipolar world, Chinese intellectuals have founded theses that go beyond traditional concepts of international security. Recently the new Chinese world order vision of the *"Tianxia* All-under-Heaven"-concept is discussed. *Tianxia* has been the key to governance and self-understanding of over two millennia of Chinese empire and experiences its renaissance in the twenty-first century of new universally valid approach.[6] The prominent philosopher at the Chinese Academy of Social Sciences, Zhao Tingyang, published in April 2005 the memorandum "The Tianxia System: A Philosophy for the World Institution" that describes a Chinese-inspired world utopia as an exemplary case of normative policy making toward current global problems. It examines a new Chinese hegemony (including its diaspora) and hierarchical empire that overcomes "a failed and disordered world of chaos."[7] Though Callahan identified serious theoretical problems, he identified Chinese potency to play with its soft power as a source of a global model of world politics. "Beijing says that China will peacefully rise as a responsible power within the present international system, and not challenge the structures and norms of world order. But the success of *The Tianxia System* shows that there is a thirst in China for "Chinese solutions" to world problems, and a hunger for nationalist solutions to global issues, especially when they promote a patriotic form of cosmopolitanism."[8] Zhao's main argument points out that each of the imperial system like the Roman, British and American inspired with its utopian ideal its governance regime like the Pax Romana, the civilizing mission, the white man's burden, the free world, and so on. The western universalization and manifestation of these models to be the best for the world may be likewise, but it's an alternative for Chinese politics. Like the American model, the Chinese understanding may not be attractive at all but thus it has impacts on governmental decision in the future because it is re-founding legitimacy for the Communist Party. Zhao's social theory model, however, rejects classical democracy, but included people in a hierarchical way by the Confucian-Leninist elite and would not exclude them like the West has done from the historical perspective during colonialism and after. Therefore, this theoretical background is basically likeable toward the left-populist leaders in Latin America, because it allows emancipation from western American style and its hegemony.

In the context of a return toward Confucianism as a guide in the implementation of politics, the Chinese Communist Party adopted the idea of the harmonic world order in its party platform at the XVIIth party's assembly on October 2007. This reflects not only the will to guarantee social peace but also to discipline inner party's criticism. This logical thought has become also part of foreign policy: Peace making is predominantly the creation of harmony in order to overcome political international tension. Therefore, respect and rationality would help to reduce contradictions and conflicts. Many authors consider that part of China's post-Cold War grand strategy is the avoidance of conflicts, primarily with the United States. Its pursuit of natural resources affects this strategy in various ways of course,[9] but its "impact on world order, in both system-shaping and norm-construction, is dynamically changing with the development of China's engagement in and benefit from world order."[10]

In general, Chinese foreign policy is nowadays realistic and pragmatic. It wants to play a new international role as a nation of responsibility that fosters construction of harmonic world order. From the perspective of the neo-realistic school, however, international relations are orientated to the question, which is winning, who is losing? International relations are the environment in which China needs to look for its own advantages. And so, it does not intend to implement ideologies like the Soviet Union and the United States did during the past. It does not intend to promote human rights, democracy and global capitalism like the United States or countries of the European Union do. It is not devoted to moral values, but advocates pragmatic friendship among the governments and looks for international cooperation and mutual respect. Therefore, Chinese government reaffirms constantly the sovereignty of its country and its decision on internal issues. The unity and self-determination of the Chinese nation includes the completeness of its sovereignty, rejecting consequently international approaches to recognize independence of Chinese provinces like Taiwan, Tibet or East Turkistan (Xinjiang). Chinese Nationalism is the thriving engine to practice its foreign policy, to its mission as the leading culture in the region and to enhance political and economic development.[11] The clear position on non-intervention in international politics and an active diplomacy around the world that demonstrates the new image of a successful, economically expanding nation is the way how China expresses its new rapidly growing self-consciousness. In short, the Foreign Ministry spokesman Qin Gang states the current Chinese foreign policy in eight points:[12]

1. China will not seek hegemony. China is still a developing country and has no resources to seek hegemony. Even if China becomes a developed country, it will not seek hegemony.
2. China will not play power politics and will not interfere with other countries' internal affairs. China will not impose its own ideology on other countries.
3. China maintains all countries, big or small, should be treated equally and respect each other. All affairs should be consulted and resolved by all countries on the basis of equal participation. No country should bully others on the basis of strength.
4. China will make judgment on each case in international affairs, each matter on the merit of the matter itself and it will not have double standards. China will not have two policies: one for itself and one for others. China believes that it cannot do unto others what they do not wish others do unto them.
5. China advocates that all countries handle their relations on the basis of the United Nations Charter and norms governing international relations. China advocates stepping up international cooperation and do not play politics unilaterally. China should not undermine the dignity and the authority of the U.N. China should not impose and set its own wishes above the U.N. Charter, international law and norms.
6. China advocates peaceful negotiation and consultation so as to resolve its international disputes. China does not resort to force, or threat of force, in resolving international disputes. China maintains a reasonable national military buildup to defend its own sovereignty and territorial integrity. It is not made to expand, nor does it seek invasion or aggression.
7. China is firmly opposed to terrorism and the proliferation of weapons of mass destruction. China is a responsible member of the international community, and as for international treaties, China abides by all them in a faithful way. China never plays by a double standard, selecting and discarding treaties it does not need.
8. China respects the diversity of civilization and the whole world. China advocates different cultures make exchanges, learn from each other, and compliment one another with their own strengths. China is opposed to clashes and confrontations between civilizations, and China does not link any particular ethnic group or religion with terrorism.

The first statement that China would not seek hegemony is controversial due to the fact that in its own sphere of interest in East Asia, China is necessarily interested in reducing the influence of foreign powers like the United States or its ally Japan. Moreover, its political and economic initiatives in both Africa[13] and Latin America, which are of course not traditional zones of interests, China represents clearly its business and political interests that may reduce the influence of other nations and could be part of building up a new form of (soft) hegemony that is not based on hard resources like military. China's foreign policy strategy focuses on a "win-win-partnership" that is officially not a renaissance of colonialism or imperialism based on exploitation and humiliation. China's strategy includes the support of African nations through financing and constructing necessary infrastructure. But as a permanent member and veto power in the United Nations Security Council, however, China could bind these nations in the future to behave toward Beijing's interests.

THE ROLE OF LATIN AMERICA IN CHINA'S FOREIGN POLICY STRATEGY

Historically, China has defined itself as the Celestial Empire. It neglected in general its periphery and focused only on Southeast Asia for its tribute missions due to the fact that China was the only superpower in its view of the world. The relations between China and Latin America are quite new. The diplomatic relations have been built up since the recognition of the PRC in the United Nations through the Resolution 2758 passed by the General Assembly, withdrawing the Republic of China the legitimate government on October 25, 1971.

Table 8.1 Diplomatic Relations of American Nations with the People's Republic of China

Year	Country
1960	Cuba
1970	Chile, Canada
1971	Peru
1972	Mexico, Argentina, Guyana, Jamaica
1974	Trinidad and Tobago, Venezuela, Brazil
1976	Suriname
1977	Barbados
1979	United States
1980	Ecuador, Colombia
1983	Antigua and Barbuda
1985	Bolivia, Grenada (until 1989), Nicaragua (until 1990)
1987	Belize (until 1989)
1988	Uruguay
1997	Bahamas, St. Lucia (until 2007)
2004	Dominica
2005	Grenada (restored)
2007	Costa Rica

The economic integration of the Asian Pacific Economic Cooperation (APEC) with the three Latin American countries Mexico, Peru, and Chile have supported this approaching process in the last years. Beijing tracks three main strategies in its Latin America policy. First, the diversification of its economy and markets, then the encouragement of its export industry, and finally the participation in the exploitation of raw materials in order to reduce the vulnerability of Chinese dependence on resources helping China's rising. In 2001, the Chinese President Jiang Zemin visited Brazil, Cuba, Venezuela, Chile, Argentina, and Uruguay, and in 2004 President Hu Jintao traveled to Chile (the host of the APEC summit) and Argentina. Hu Jintao offered USD 20 billion in investments in construction projects, railways, oil and gas. Additionally, China has become one of the most important importers of Argentinean soybeans. These Chinese commerce activities contributed to the economic recovery of the Argentinean industry in 2003 and 2004. Hu Jinato also visited Brazil, Venezuela, and Cuba. China invested USD 500 million in the nickel industry of Cuba. Since 2000 around 50 percent of Chinese nickel comes from Cuba, which is an important material to produce stainless steel. During his stay President Hu Jintao was also in Lourdes, which was the largest oversea espionage base of the Soviet Union. This journey opened new dimensions in the trans-pacific relations. China promised to invest around USD 100 billion in Latin America in the next ten years and reduced trade restrictions for products from South America, but it has aimed yet in 2007. Chinese investment in Latin America remains relatively small at some USD 6.5 billion through 2004, but that amount represents half of China's foreign investment overseas. China's *Xinhua News Agency* reported that Chinese trade with the Caribbean exceeded USD 2 billion in 2004, a 40 percent increase from the previous year. Behind the United States (USD 560 billion) and the European Union (USD 250 billion) China has become in 2007 the third main trade partner in the region. Today, China may become the most important trade partner for Peru, for Mexico it is already the second largest and for Brazil the fourth largest.

With Chile the Chinese government signed in 2006 the first Free Trade Agreement. Chile is the largest producer of copper as while China the world's biggest consumer. The treaty frees 92 percent of Chile's export to China from customs tariffs, and removes Chilean tariffs on 50 percent of Chinese export. For example, in 2004 Chile provided 49.1 percent of all Chinese copper imports. During the state visit of Hu Jintao the Chinese national metal commerce company *Minmetals* agreed with the Chilean *Corporación Nacional del Cobre (CODELCO)* in investment cooperation of USD 2 billion. Furthermore, CODLECO promised to develop the copper deposit *Gaby* in the North of the country. It might be a model for China and Latin America to evaluate the functionality of this treaty in order to enlarge and deepen economic relations. In November 2008, China signed with Peru also a Free Trade Agreement in the frame of the APEC Summit in Lima. China imports especially iron core, copper and lead from Peru. In this occasion of the Summit, China releases for the first time a document on its Latin American strategy on November 5, 2008 (see annex) that depicts the meaning of the composition of a strategic partnership.[14]

A delegation of 12 ministers and some 600 business leaders accompanied the Chinese President Hu Jintao. The large number of ministers indicated the political importance of this journey. In a speech at the Peruvian Congress, the Chinese President stated that China and Latin America should maintain high-level contacts. Moreover, for the first time the Chinese government has emphasized its willingness to include into the cooperation military training, peacekeeping and assistance for the development of armies. Today, China spends military assistance to Barbados, Bolivia, Brazil, Costa Rica, Ecuador, Mexico, Paraguay (sic!), Peru, St. Vincent and Grenada, Trinidad and Tobago, Uruguay, and Venezuela.

Before the APEC Summit, President Hu Jintao traveled with his delegation to Cuba and Costa Rica.[15] Especially Costa Rica plays an important role for the PRC strategy to earn diplomatic recognition in Central America. Costa Rica broke off diplomatic relations with Taiwan in 2007 as the first country in this region. Moreover, negotiations between the PRC and Costa Rica for a Free Trade Agreement are underway.

Not only the Venezuelan President Hugo Chávez but also other Latin American leaders consider for ideological reasons China as an alternative partner in order to establish a multi-polar world that may reduce U.S. hegemony. The current left governments in Argentina (Mrs Christina Fernandez de Kirchner), Brazil (Lula), Bolivia (Evo Morales), Paraguay (Fernando Lugo), Ecuador (Rafael Correa), Nicaragua (Daniel Ortega) and of course Cuba (Raúl Castro), tend to establish a strategic alliance with Beijing that helps to promote both national and Latin American interests in the United Nations.

Latin America has become an important role in the strategy of the PRC energy diplomacy. According to data from the International Energy Agency (IEA), China has become the world's largest oil consumer.[16] With four times as many as people as the United States, the PRC will overtake the USA to become the world's largest energy consumer after 2010. In spite of a high demand of coal, which makes still a two-third share of total primary energy consumption, the import of oil has especially become for transport necessities and to continue with its economical growth essential. The IEA calculates that the net oil import could quadruples from 3.5 mb/d in 2006 to 13.1 mb/d in 2030. Furthermore, it estimates that China is expected to import as much oil as the United States does today. Currently, around 60 percent of Chinese oil import supply comes from the Middle East, mainly from Saudi Arabia, Iran, and Oman,[17] a region that is politically and economically instable, and like Saudi Arabia, Iraq and the Arabian Emirates partners of the United States. Therefore, Beijing considers Africa and Latin America as market alternatives. Latin America has traditionally be a continent under the U.S. sphere of influence since the Monroe-doctrine, established in 1823. After the terror attacks of September 11, 2001, U.S. foreign policy has being concentrated in the Middle East and Central Asia, neglecting Central and South America. Rhetorically, but also politically and economically, (left) populist leaders in Latin America have developed an emancipation policy against U.S. hegemony in the region. The Free Trade Area of the Americas, promoted by the Bush administration, has been rejected at the OAS

(Organization of the American States) summit in Mar del Plata in 2005. Due to rising energy prices, Latin America has become an important spot on the international energy market. It is estimated to hold around 13.5 percent of the world's proven oil reserves, which opens new opportunities for China in order to reduce its dependence on the Middle East. "China's limited progress in accessing local energy resources due to poor relations with neighboring states [like the disputes with Japan and Vietnam over the East China Sea, T.C.] have forced China to search for energy further afield. [...] The competition for energy resources in Latin America is unlikely to be confined to the economic sphere as seen by developments in other regions where China is attempting to access energy resources. For example, China's military cooperation with Myanmar, Sudan and the Central Asian republics cannot be separated from its attempts to access energy resources in these states. While not a zero-sum game, growing interlinkages and interdependence between China and Latin America is likely to come at the cost of the U.S. relations with its neighbors, which will only undermine U.S. ability to access the region's energy resources."[18] Within Latin America, Venezuela is the fifth world's largest crude export nation. It sells around 50 percent to the United States and the Venezuelan President Hugo Chávez looks to reduce the dependence from the U.S. market due to political reasons. He considers the United States as a political enemy in his plan to develop the socialism of the 21st century in Latin America. During a state visit in December 2004 he said: "We have been producing and exporting oil for more then 100 years but they have been years of dependence from the United States. Now we are free and we make our resources available to the great country of China."[19] However, China has to conquer geographical barriers in its way to tap energy resources from Venezuela, Brazil or Argentina. Both the construction of pipelines to the Pacific coast and the enlargement of the Panama Canal could be real options.

First, in spite of the political and ideological conflicts between Colombia and Venezuela, both countries have already finished the construction of one undersea gas pipeline in October 2007. Moreover, Chávez' is planning to unify the continent like the European Union. Its integration process started with the European Coal and Steel Community through energy cooperation. The president shares the vision of Simon Bolivar and his fight for the independence of South America in the 19th century and the creation of a unified power bloc that is not following the leadership of the United States. In several statements he has repeated the idea to consider oil and gas pipelines as part of the energy integration of South and Central America. And this would open Venezuela the door to economic cooperation with East Asia, especially to China, which Chávez considers as an attractive market. In January 2005, Vice President Zeng Qinghong visited Venezuela and signed an investment project in oil and gas fields. China committed to invest in Venezuela's energy infrastructure by investing USD 350 million in 15 oil fields, USD 60 million in gas fields and in railway and refinery infrastructure. In exchange, China will get daily 100,000 barrels of oil and annually 3 million tones of fuel oil. Furthermore, the China National Petroleum Corporation got also development and investment opportunities for exploration and exploitation at the fields of Zumano in Eastern Venezuela. This region contains approximately 400 million barrels of oil.

Before his visit to Beijing in September 2008, Chávez announced that he wants his country to ship one million barrels per day by around 2011, about 13 percent of its current demand. Venezuela supplied China with 5.17 million tones of crude—just 177,000 barrels per day—from January to July 2008, though it was an increase of 94 percent on the same period last year.[20] In 2004, for example, China received only 70,000 barrels of oil per day. The joint venture projects between the Venezuelan state oil company PDVSA (Petróleos de Venezuela, S.A.) and the largest Chinese oil and gas company PetroChina that is the listed arm of state-owned *China National Petroleum Corporation* (CNPC) have become closer in the last years. CNPC has started its activities in South America in 2004; it bought for USD 200 million a sub-company of the Peruvian PlusPetrol. The CNPC also direct the consortium *Andes Petroleum*. In September 2005 it purchased for USD 1.4 billion oil- and gas installations of the Canadian enterprise EnCana in Ecuador. Furthermore, *Andes Petroleum* bought the shares of EnCana at an Ecuadorian pipeline.[21] In May 2008, PDVSA and PetroChina agreed in a significant deal to build a refinery in the Guangdong province. And the PRC lent USD 4 billion to Caracas to create an investment fund for development projects, which it will repay in fuel. In spite of the Chávez offensive energy diplomacy, the PRC looks officially for aloofness. Chinese Foreign Ministry spokeswomen Jiang Yu explained that the PRC did not want to be drawn into the diplomatic rivalry between Caracas and Washington and the energy ties between Beijing and Caracas would not affect the oil supply to other countries.[22]

Second, since Hutchison Whampoa Limited, one of the largest companies listed on the Hong Kong Stock Exchange, operates and controls the port in Panama, the geo-strategic Panama Canal could be come a key of Chinese global operations. Li Ka Shing runs the company. The tycoon has strong ties to the rulers of the Communist Party in Beijing. History has frequently proven that the control of important waterways is an advantageous political tool in international politics.

Apart from energy, Latin America and China have also established deeper political, military and trade relations. "Latin America is a clear trade winner from Chinese global integration."[23] China has been replacing quickly the United States in the market of raw materials and manufactured products. Latin America is a commodity oriented export continent. The PRC published in 2003 a white paper named *China's Policy on Mineral Resources*: "There is a fairly large gap between the supply and demand in oil, high-grade iron, high-grade copper, fine-quality bauxite, chromite and sylvite. The degree of difficulty in looking for mineral resources by geological means in the eastern regions has increased, and the increase range of proved reserves there has slowed down. The production in some mines has entered the middle or late phase, and their reserves and output are decreasing year by year. [...] The scope of international exchange and cooperation in the field of mineral resources should be further broadened. [...] The Chinese government shall [...] encourage the signing of long-term supply contracts with foreign companies, and import minerals from diversified sources. [...] The Chinese government encourages domestic enterprises to take part in international cooperation in the sphere of mineral resources, and in exploration, exploitation and utilization of foreign mineral resources."[24] The vulnerability on key-minerals for Chinese economy is obvious. Therefore, the Chinese government is willing to promote and protect investment in mineral resources outside China, which also includes the development of cooperation in prospecting and exploitation according to the white paper. Jörg Husar developed in his book "China's engagement in Latin America"[25] that Chinese cooperation with Latin America is characterized through asymmetric interdependence and, therefore, Chinese actions are focused on the mitigation of this vulnerability. China has mainly transactions with countries whose relations are characterized by an asymmetric interdependence like Brazil, Argentina, Chile and Cuba. And president Hu Jintao has visited these countries. Only these four countries unify 23.2 percent of Chinese worldwide imports.[26] An important tool of economic cooperation is foreign direct investment. China concentrated it in Brazil, Mexico, Chile, Argentina, Peru, and Venezuela. Furthermore, it invested USD 350 million in the Inter-American Development Bank. Chinese investment is based on three directions. First, infrastructure projects that avoid supply shortages; second, investment projects that help to control the resource exploitation; and third, financial investments that encourage Chinese export.[27]

Table 8.2 Chinese Foreign Direct Investment (FDI)

	Arg.	Bra.	Chile	Ecua.	Guy.	Col.	Mex.	Peru	Ven.
Iron and iron ore		▓						▓	
Oil and energy								▓	▓
Fishing and fish meal production	▓	▓	▓	▓					
Silviculture and wood processing	▓	▓	▓						
Industrial manufacture	▓					▓			
Agriculture							▓		
Textile industry							▓		
Science and technology	▓								▓

Source: Lehmann, Vera; Husar, Jörg: Ziele, Strategien und Instrumente der chinesischen Lateinamerikapolitik, in: Albiez, Sarah; Kauppert, Philipp; Müller, Sophie (eds.) (2007): *China und Lateinamerika. Ein transpazifischer* Brückenschlag, Berlin: wvb, 243-280, 266, p. 267. In Argentina, China did FDI in the production of motorbikes and TV, in Colombia motorbikes. In Mexico, China constructs so called textile cities like maquiladoras.

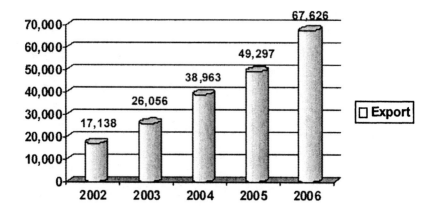

Figure 8.1 Chinese Foreign Trade with Latin America (in million USD)

Source: UN Comtrade [United Nations Statistic Division] (2007): Comodity Trade
Statistics Database, http://www.comtrade.un.org, in: Sangmeister, Hartmut; Zhang,
Yingyi (2008): Die China-Connection: Chinesische Wirtschaftsinteressen in
Lateinamerika, Ibero-Analysen, 22 (September), p. 14.

**Table 8.3 China's Top 10 ex- and import countries in Latin America 2002-
2006**

China's import from Latin America	In million USD	China's export to Latin America	In million USD
Brazil	40.420,18	Mexico	25.464,66
Chile	18.209,36	Brazil	19.491,03
Argentina	14.722,78	Panama	11.957,88
Mexico	9.763,92	Chile	9.228,63
Peru	8.200,33	Argentina	4.813,17
Venezuela	5.297,12	Colombia	3.741,15
Costa Rica	4.056,02	Venezuela	3.733,29
Jamaica	1.003,85	Peru	2.636,19
Colombia	734,04	Guatemala	2.104,12
Uruguay	544,59	Ecuador	1.959,05

Source: UN Comtrade UN Comtrade [United Nations Statistic Division] (2007):
Comodity Trade Statistics Database, http://www.comtrade.un.org, in:
Sangmeister, Hartmut; Zhang, Yingyi (2008): *Die China-Connection:
Chinesische Wirtschaftsinteressen in Lateinamerika, Ibero-Analysen*, 22
(September), p. 15.

Table 8.4 The Meaning of Chinese Demand for Primary Products in Latin America

Country	Aluminum, iron, zinc, uranium, manganese	Copper	Gold, platinum	Nickel	Oil, gas	Coffee, cacao	Soy beans	Meat	Fish, shrimp, fish meal
ARG					10-25%				
BOL	5-10%		5-10%				>25%		
BRA							10-25%		
CHILE		>25%							
COS. R.									
DOM. R.				>25%					
ECU					>25%				5-10%
HON						10-25%			
JAM	>25%								
COL					>25%	10-25%			
CUBA				>25%					
MEX					10-25%				
NIC						>25%			
PAN									5-10%
PAR						>25%	5-10%		
PERU		10-25%	10-25%						5-10%
TT					>25%				
URU								10-25%	
VEN					>25%				

Source: Trinh, Tamara (2006): *Chinas Rohstoffhunger. Auswirkungen auf Afrika und Lateinamerika, Deutsche Bank Research, Aktuelle Themen*, 359, Frankfurt/Main, in: Sangmeister, Hartmut; Zhang, Yingyi (2008): *Die China-Connection: Chinesische Wirtschaftsinteressen in Lateinamerika, Ibero-Analysen*, 22 (September), p. 24. The share of selected primary products on the total export of one country to China divided into three groups (very important (>25%), important (10-25%), less important (5-10%)).

Especially China and Brazil are deepening their trade relations. Brazil is the key player in Latin America. China is Brazil's third largest trade partner, and for China Brazil is the top trade partner in Latin America. Since the presidency of Lula da Silva, Brazil has made enormous steps toward global participation and leadership as an emerging power. Its economic success is based on its agriculture industry. Within the G 33 bloc of developing countries at the World Trade Organization and its bid to become a permanent member in the United Nations Security Council, Brazil favors strategic alliances with China, South Africa, and India in order to enhance the South-South Cooperation. During the state's visit in 2004, President Hu Jinato signed an agreement on cooperation in satellite development programs. Additionally, the Brazilian oil company Petrobras and the Chinese Sinopec agreed to construct a 2000 kilometer long oil pipeline that should help to double Brazilian oil export to China. Furthermore, China announced a USD 10 billion energy deal and cooperative studies to joint operations in exploring, exploiting and refining oil around the world.

China focuses also its interests on the Caribbean states. With Cuba, Jamaica, and Trinidad and Tobago, China looks for trade and investments into their natural resources. Where raw materials do not exist, China trades with diplomatic recognition. It has started successfully with the two micro states Dominica and Grenada in 2004 respectively in 2005. In exchange for establishing diplomatic relations, both states received significant amounts of aid and investment from Beijing. Now, Beijing intensifies its relations to Haiti, though officially it recognizes the ROC as the sole representative of China. The PRC is engaged in the United Nations Stabilization Mission in Haiti (MINUSTAH) since October 2004. Up to 100 riot police officers have been sent by Beijing in order to support the peacekeeping mission. With this measure China tries to convince the government to break relations with Taiwan. Moreover, China is also interested in a deeper economic engagement. Agents of state-owned companies are investing in land for planting jatropha, which is a drought-resistant plant that produces feedstock oil for bio-fuel processing. One hectare contains around 1900 litre of fuel. This could help reducing greenhouse gas emissions and could boost the Haitian economy.[28]

But Chinese influence in Latin America has also negative consequences. Lax visa regulations in some Latin American countries like Ecuador spark human trafficking. The International Relations and Security Network of the *Eidgenössische Technische Hochschule Zürich* (Swiss Federal Institute of Technology) reported that Chinese organized crime would be the first to take advantage of new visa regulation policy of the Ecuadorian government that drooped strict restrictions.[29] According to statistics from Ecuadorian police, some 2,875 Chinese entered the country from January to June 2008. After the removal of the restrictions on June 20, some 7,837 Chinese arrived by the end of 2008. The report states that Chinese consider the entry for travelling easily to the United States. The newspaper *El Universo* estimates that these human trafficking mafias would have earned USD 750 million in 2008. The left-populist Ecuadorian government, however, seeks the benefits from this new visa policy with the Chinese government for a Chinese logistic company will support trade, tourism and the development and construction of a deep-water port in Manta.

CHINA IN THE "BACKYARD" OF THE UNITED STATES: IMPLICATIONS FOR NEW CONFLICTS?

Do Chinese activities in Latin America challenge the United States hegemony? Is Latin America looking in China as an alternate ally against United States hegemony? What are the reasons for Chinese expansion and what might be the answer of the United States? Does the U.S. give up its inattention toward Latin America? Under the George W. Bush Administration Latin America was quite neglected. U.S. foreign policy tended toward Central Asia and the Middle East, culminated in the war on terrorism against Al-Qaeda, the Taliban regime in Afghanistan and Saddam Hussein in Iraq. The neo-conservative U.S. policy looked for nation-building and demonstration of U.S. hegemony. The over-stretching of the empire[30] a long with economic depression, a huge deficit in public spending and stagnation in the peacemaking process in the Middle East have catapulted the U.S. in a serious crisis. The victory of the Democratic Senator Barrack Obama as the 44th President of the U.S. at the presidential Election Day on November 4, 2008, was a symbol for the Americans to a new start in (international) politics with multi-lateral approaches to cope with the current challenges. Obama has never been in Latin America, but he stated that he is willing to deal with the contemporary problems like migration, war on drug trafficking and security. Though he is favor of protectionism of U.S. economy and has a positive attitude toward the re-opening of some chapters of the North American Free Trade Agreement (NAFTA) with Canada and Mexico, he knows that an intensification of the economic crises in Latin America and the dependence on the U.S. economy, especially of Mexico (some 85 percent of its total exports goes to the U.S.) and Central America, would increase migration and security problems. Meanwhile President George W. Bush treated Latin America as a low priority region for U.S. global and security interests, the new President Obama may focus on better communication and integration of Latin American governments in the U.S. concept for maintaining global hegemony.

Gonzalo Paz analyses that China is testing the water how the United States would react in his geo-space of interests. It is a response to U.S. activities in East Asia like in Central Asia, South Korea, Japan, and still Taiwan. The fear of encirclement has been transformed into a response strategy of offensive economic alliance building in order to establish the balance between the main powers in a multi-polar world. Indeed, China is following only the historical principles of Sun Yat-sen like nationalism, freedom from the imperial domination, democracy as a constitutional system and government for the people as well as social welfare. These values should help to create sovereignty for Beijing and keep world security. "The first Chinese venture is not ending U.S. hegemony, but it might be starting a new trend, to some extent allowing many Latin American and Caribbean countries to diversify their external trade and international relations, if they decide to use this new alternative. [...] Politically, moreover, the offensive is promoting multipolarity, multilateralism, and transregionalism, ideas that may be simply a cheap and useful sideshow, but which have a certain political payoff. However, for the foreseeable future, the dragon wants to keep the backyard's dog sleeping."[31]

In 2004, China stepped remarkably into Latin America and has been a turning point in the relationship between Latin America and China that have been shaped through organizations like the APEC, the Pacific Economic Corporation Council and then as dialogue partners (with Japan and South Korea) to Mercosur, the Rio Group or the Forum of the East Asia-Latin America

Cooperation. This international regime was founded after the Asian Financial Crisis in 1998, similar to the annual Asian European Meeting. It is an intergovernmental transregional agreement and shares the idea of promoting cooperation and on the long run institutionalization.[32] The 12th Asia-Pacific Economic Cooperation (APEC) summit was held for the first time in South America in Santiago de Chile. The first in Latin America was held 2002 in Los Cabos (Baja California, Mexico). In addition, in 2004 China officially achieved the observer status at the Organization of American States (OAS). The continent has been always considered as the backyard of the United States. Since the establishment of the Monroe Doctrine in 1823 the United States considers Central and South America its sphere of political and economic influence. The jump into this new geopolitical and geoeconomic space has opened a new chapter in international politics. China's President Hu Jintao spent more time in Latin America than U.S.-President George W. Bush. And even the Latin American presidents like Lula da Silva (Brazil), Nestor Kirchner (Argentina), Evo Morales (Bolivia) and Hugo Chávez (Venezuela) have been traveling through China than the U.S. administration. Historically, the economic relations between these two regions have been insignificant. Now, investment and trade have been constantly increased. In 2004, some 50 percent of Chinese companies' investment in foreign markets were directed to Central and South America.[33]

For the first time China and the United States discussed their relations on Latin America in a meeting in April 2006, before of the state visit of President Hu to the United States some days later. One official American source was quoted that both sides do not want to get their wires crossed.[34] China and United States are depending on the agenda setting. Latin America has never played an important role to U.S. activities during the Cold War so long the countries were not opposing U.S. interests in general. At the moment there is no direct U.S. response to Chinese activities. Both East Asia and Latin America may continue to dense its network and full the vacuum, however it might be likely that the new U.S. President Obama will try to recover the traditional sphere of interest in order to establish new routes of U.S. world geopolitics. Especially when China would repeat the mistakes of other colonial powers to see Latin America as a continent that can be exploited like Spain or the United States did it in the past, Latin America could defend its new emancipation from the U.S. against hegemonic activities of Beijing. But this is at the moment only one prospective option.

Emancipation, national reconstruction and being competitive against other rising powers and securing global consumer market shares are the modern challenges in world politics for nation states. China is quite sensitive against hegemonic structures in the international system. The U.S. *Pax Americana* is considered as a threat to traditional interests of China. The deployment of U.S. troops in Central Asia in the context of war on terror underlines Chinese fear to become encircled. The continuation of mistrust against Japan as a still potential threat, especially in its competition for markets in East Asia is an obstacle in a collective security system. Within this perception strategic alliances—no military alliances—have been options to maintain a balance of power. The Shanghai Organization for Cooperation (together with Russia) for example is still a tool to counter U.S. hegemonic behaviour. Chinese activities in Latin America are a logical consequence of this strategy. Despite this strategy, the Chinese government should not underestimate that on the long run U.S. influence is still predominant. "The future growth potential of Chinese investment and trade will always be constrained by the economic advantages conferred by U.S. geographic proximity to Latin America. Furthermore, they [observers, T.C.] indicate that migration patterns to the United States from Central and South American countries have given the United States greater cultural ties and longer-term economic importance to the region than China could ever have. Adherents of the view maintain that the United States should avoid overreacting to China's economic initiatives in Latin America. They assert that China's emerging presence in the region is not a threat to the United States, but is consistent with the long-standing U.S. policy of integrating China into the world system."[35] Moreover, the political assessment is quite vague, "because once the "China hype" has died down, the Latin American side will have to achieve a substantial diversification of export products for the Chinese market if it is to enjoy a secure future."[36] And if Latin America would succeed in diversifying its economy, the U.S. would likely be again the first contact due to its geographic proximity.

The U.S. itself should find fitting answers to the Chinese challenge in its traditional sphere of influence like the acceleration of free trade agreements, the adoption of more comprehensive relationships like the Plan Colombia that combats narco-terrorism, strengthens institutions, reactivates economy and provides peace, and more pressure on liberal reforms and the usage of sustainable public diplomacy: "Regrettably, Chinese aid and commodity imports may buy time for state industries, powerful presidents, and influential oligarchs. Most of all, such commerce could delay needed reforms and industrialization that might lift Latin America's near majority underclass out of poverty."[37]

CHINA VS. TAIWAN: THE STRUGGLE FOR DIPLOMATIC RECOGNITION IN LATIN AMERICA

Chinese integration in the global markets has challenged both Taiwanese and Central American politics. Taiwan had to expand its position as investor, in order to support Central America's economic development to compete with Chinese textile and other manufactory industry.[38] But the PRC strengthens its financial efforts to win political recognition. "The PRC has pursued its objective with sturdy patience. By the 1990's, a public declaration of accord with Beijing's "One China Policy" had become almost a pre-condition for economic agreements."[39] The following twelve countries from Latin America and the Caribbean are still maintaining diplomatic relations with Taiwan (in parentheses the year of recognition) and recognizing it as the sole legitimate government of the whole of China and not only the actual jurisdiction of the island groups of

Taiwan, Penghu, Kinmen and Matsu: Belize (1989), Dominican Republic (1957), El Salvador (1961), Guatemala (1960), Haiti (1956), Honduras (1965), Nicaragua (1990), Panama (1954), Paraguay (1957), Saint Kitts and Nevis (1983), Saint Lucia (1984-1997 and again since 2007), Saint Vincent and the Grenadines (1981). Relations were broken off with the Bahamas in 1997, Dominica 2004, Grenada 2005, and recently with Costa Rica in 2007. Worldwide, eleven states more have diplomatic relations with the Republic of China, four in Africa (Burkina Faso, Gambia, São Tomé and Príncipe, Swaziland), six in Oceania (Kiribati, Marshall Islands, Nauru, Palau, Solomon Islands, Tuvalu) and finally one in Europe (Vatican City).

Very interesting is the case of Costa Rica.[40] Only this country has a significant share of Central American export business to the PRC because of its chip- and computer industry. Costa Rica could raise its export volume from U.S.D 14 million in 2001 to USD 1.1 billion in 2006.[41] China has become Costa Rica's second biggest trade partner. Only in 2007 the bilateral commerce registered an increase of 33 percent over the previous year with a volume of USD 2.8 billion.[42] Moreover, the PRC bought from Costa Rica state bonds in an amount of USD 300 million. That Costa Rica switched allegiance from the ROC to the PRC could have a domino-effect. Costa Rica's President Oscar Arias emphasized the motive that China is a global player and that the PRC is representing the geopolitical reality.[43] Taiwan's foreign minister, James Huang, offered his resign after the loss of another ally in an interview. He said: "We tried our very best to try and maintain ties with Costa Rica, but eventually we failed. This is not something that a country which stands for peace and democracy should do, cut ties with its partner of 60 years."[44] The new bilateral relations have experienced yet good prospects with the consequence that in September 2008 the first China-Central America Trade Cooperation Forum in San José was inaugurated.

Deeper economic relations between China and Latin America could reduce the Central American dependence on the U.S. economy. In fact, Beijing could open new possibilities for Central America. The new Chinese middle class consumes qualitative and luxury goods like exotic fruits, coffee and chocolate. Also tourism could be a booming market. The direct flight connection with Mexico and the Approved Destination Status for Chinese group tourism could be enlarged with the Maya-route in Central America. Moreover, export-joint-ventures in the electronic and textile industry might be attractive for Chinese Foreign Direct Investment.[45] But despite these arguments pro China, Central American politicians and public do not see all trends positively. These nations do compete with China for market shares in the textile industry for example; and not all are really capable of competing due to low wages and the under-evaluation of the Chinese currency. Therefore, the Free Trade Agreement with the United States was considered as a possible solution to face this problem. Besides, many Central American countries complain the flood of Chinese cheap manufactured products that had reduced the trade surplus significantly. And besides, cultural misunderstanding and different views on legal systems are also obstacles for a conflict-free economic cooperation.

Traditionally, the Central American nations have been influencing one another's policies, especially on international affairs, for example in the creation of the CAFTA, the Central America Free Trade Agreement with the United States, signed in 2004, or in its relations to Europe. The in 1984 launched San José Dialogue has been the cornerstone of these relations, culminated into the EU-Central America Political Dialogue and Co-operation Agreement, which were signed in 2003. The Central American governments, especially those that are rule by left politicians, like in Nicaragua, Honduras (President Zelaya) and now El Salvador (the neo-marxist party and former guerilla FMLN (Farabundo Martí para la Liberación Nacional and runs with Mauricio Funes as presidential candidate in 2009) see in relations with Beijing better economic options and political support. These political move has also foiled Taiwan's intention to become a member as a sovereign country under the name "Taiwan" of the World Health Organization (WHO). In a WHO session in May 2007 Nicaragua and Panama were absent, Haiti was abstained and Costa Rica voted against.

The next candidate that could break relations with Taiwan is Nicaragua. The Central American country has already had diplomatic ties with Beijing in the 1980s when it was under the rule of the Sandinista National Liberation Front. After the victory of November 2006, Daniel Ortega has become again president of Nicaragua. Therefore, Taiwanese authorities are making huge efforts to prevent a second switch. For example: They offered generators to ease the chronic power shortages. But also Chávez has been generous with his political comrade Ortega by shipping cheap oil to Nicaragua. Taiwan has been alarmed and intensified diplomatic activities. Taiwanese President Chen attended Ortega's inauguration in January 2007 and is ready to make major concessions to maintain its increasingly tenuous links to Managua.

Panama is another candidate. In June 2007, the Panama Canal International Advisory Board visited Shanghai in order to study the deep-water port of Yangshan. Panama's President Torrijos invited Beijing to support the expansion of the Canal. Due to the influence of Hutchison Whompoa and the establishment of cultural ties through several sister-city relationships, a switch is likely, too. In Nicaragua, Panama and other Caribbean states, Venezuela has the capacity to pressure these states to recognize China officially due to its economic potency in the region.

A further candidate for switching allegiance is also Paraguay. Its new left-populist President Fernando Lugo will probably reverse diplomatic relations with Taiwan. Since 1957 Paraguay has diplomatic relations with the ROC. Paraguay has voted every year in support of resolutions to admit Taiwan to the General Assembly of the United Nations. In the past, Taiwan has sent millions of dollars to the impoverished country for low-income housing, agricultural development and scholarships, and even USD 20 million for a new Congress building. Taiwan has become the biggest bilateral creditor after two Taiwanese banks offered Paraguay USD 400 million loan. Even now, Paraguay's Senate considers accepting new donation from Taiwan, but it is a relict from the dictatorship of General Stroessner. President Lugo emphasized in interviews that his government wants to maintain diplomatic relations with all countries of similar interests and will not accept conditions, but it will no longer vote at the UN for Taiwan.

The only counter strategy of Taiwan to halt the PRC triumphal procession in Latin America is raising aid and financial support a long with frequent and highly publicized exchanges of official visits that President Chen Shui-bian did in his administration. Moreover, Taiwan continues also aggressively pursuing bilateral free trade agreements with its allies in Central America. Successful negotiations were finalized with Panama in 2003 and with Guatemala in 2005, trade negotiations with El Salvador and Honduras were completed in May 2007, while preliminary talks with the Dominican Republic began in October 2007. For example: Since the free-trade agreement with Panama went into effect in January 2004, trade between the two countries has grown from around $130 million to $250 million annually, but mainly it favors Taiwan. Taiwanese strategy, especially with CAFTA (Central American Free Trade Agreement) in place, helps Taiwanese manufactures to reduce dependence on Chinese market and is a gateway to the United States.

Before Taiwanese President Chen Shui-bian left his office, the Barbados Prime Minister Owen Arthur blamed him that the Taiwanese government had fund the election campaign of the Democratic Labour Party in order to support a change in the government that would switch diplomatic allegiance toward Taiwan. Though the Democratic Labour Party won the elections, the new government under Prime Minister David Thompson still keeps relations with the PRC. Whether the new Taiwanese President Ma Ying-jeou (since May, 20, 2008) from the Kuomintang would continue the traditional diplomacy toward Latin America is not quite clear. Because of first successes in approaching to Mainland China, the new government is unlike Chen not really interested in provoking frequently the Communist government in Beijing.

Diplomatic relations with the PRC or the ROC does not really preclude sustained economic trade with the other. And it is a fact that many nations that recognize China still do business with Taiwan and vice versa. But global reality undermines the claim of the ROC to be the sole legitimate government of China.

CONCLUSION

In the context of the Olympic Games 2008 in Beijing, China has worked on the improvement of its image. The catastrophic view on the torch relay with the Tibet protests has threatened the show to demonstrate Chinese pride and success. Chinese foreign policy is pragmatic. Unlike European countries, China does not link moral values and human rights with political and economic actions. The majority of journalists from the Western world have written China as an aggressive country that destroy Tibetan culture, exploited not only its own population, but also natural resources in Africa and Latin America, cooperates with other dictatorships and supports the politics of rouge states like Iran and North Korea by using its veto power against sanctions of the United Nations Security Council. The economic policy that China is implementing especially in

Africa is described as a sort of "Mother Courage Economy," [46] respecting traditional values without motivation of missions. China uses globalization for its purposes and through this mechanism it is able to implement new ways of culture and political operations. Since the Cuban Revolution 1959/60 the PRC has approached ideologically to Latin America. After its integration into the United Nations the political and economic most important countries have established with the PRC diplomatic relations. Only Central America and some Caribbean islands have still maintained diplomatic recognition of the ROC, mainly due to its economic development aid and financial assistance.

Economically, the PRC considers Latin America as an important market in order to satisfy its demand for commodities and raw materials in order to overcome its vulnerability of dependence on global markets. This strategy of diversification is a logical consequence of its principles on foreign policy based on independence, sovereignty and equality. Whether Latin America is able to adjust these asymmetric alliance must be seen critically due to the lack of political willingness to set necessary market reforms that may support economic freedom, promote social cohesion and overcome the unequal distribution of wealth and poverty. Latin America needs itself to reduce its dependence on raw material exporter toward an economic region that is investing in manufacturers and high technology.

Depicting the future of Chinese foreign policy in the future is speculative. Too many indifferent factors would not allow meaningful conclusions. However, academics from the University of Trier and Society and Technology Research Group of the Daimler Research in Berlin have developed three main scenarios for preparing and constructing future policy recommendations and strategies. [47] The thriving factors that shape scenarios are global regulatory politics, the global and national economic development, the national political system and dealing with resource scarcity. The first scenario describes the end of the "China threat syndrome." China would be in a difficult transformation process toward democracy, and is cooperative in the international system to manage multilaterally global economy in an integrative way. The second scenario emphasizes China as a "snarling dragon" in a world that is characterized by anarchy and powerless international organizations. The struggle for raw materials would force military interventions of the Chinese technocratic elite in fragile and failing states. And the countervailing power U.S. would try to contain Chinese influence globally. The third scenario details an "awaken dragon" that is a multilateral ruler toward deepen global institutionalisation ruled by technocratic experts. The highlight would have been the foundation of the new supranational organisation "wèi rénlèi fúwù" (the servant of humankind) that would make other international institutions gradually obsolete due to their inefficiency. The last scenario indeed recollects ideas of the *Tianxia* model. "China is not a standard *status quo* state now, and will not be so in a foreseeable future either. But China has transformed from the world order's antagonist and revolutionary defier to a critic and advantage-taker, and further to today's supporter and proactive shaper." [48]

Latin America is a stroke of luck for Chinese problems like scarcity of raw materials and food production due to the exhaustion of arable land. The new economic cooperation allows market access due to the economic integration of Latin American countries into the North American Free Trade Agreement (NAFTA), Mercosur and the established Free Trade Agreements between Europe and Chile, respectively Mexico. "In the political realm, China has tried to promote itself as champion of a multipolar world, portraying the United States as hegemonic and the America vision as unilateralist. This vision, coming after the disappointing effect of the years of the "Washington Consensus" and the war on Iraq (mostly perceived in Latin America as bypassing international law embodied in the UN), has been warmly welcome in Latin America. China is moving easily from "Third World-ism" to champion of multilateralism."[49]

Summarizing the current situation of Chinese foreign policy toward Latin America the author comes to the conclusion that the initiatives of Beijing to establish trade agreements for energy security and to seek diplomatic recognition in Latin America is part of the global game to construct a multipolar world where China defends national interests abroad by reducing U.S. influence and creating a balance of power system. Furthermore, the Taiwan question could be solved in Latin America, assumed that Beijing continues to invest strongly in the region and pressures diplomatically Central American states to give up the diplomatic recognition of Taiwan for economic and political reasons.

NOTES

[1] Möller, Kay (2005): Die Außenpolitik der Volksrepublik China 1949-2004, Wiesbaden.
[2] China's Foreign Policy, http://english.people.com.cn/china/19990914A128.html.
[3] Ibid.
[4] Medeiros, Evan S.; Taylor Fravel, M. (2003): China's New Diplomacy, Foreign Affairs (November/December).
[5] Liu, Guoli (2004): Chinese Foreign Policy in Transition (New York: Aldine de Gruyter), p. 1 and Costa Tanan, Claudiney (2007): Die Außenpolitik Chinas unter Hu Jintao und das neue Konzept des "Friedlichen Aufstiegs": Chancen und Gefahren für Lateinamerika, in: Albiez, Sarah; Kauppert, Philipp; Müller, Sophie (eds.) (2007): China und Lateinamerika. Ein transpazifischer Brückenschlag, Berlin: wvb, 185-216.
[6] Callahan, William A. (2008): Chinese Vision of World Order: Post-hegemonic or a New Hegemony?, International Studies Review, Vol. 10: 4 (December), 749-761, 751pp.
[7] Zhao, Tingyang (2005): Tianxia Tixi: Shijie Zhidu Zhexue Daolun [The Tianxia System: A Philosophy for the World Institution], Nanjing: Jiangsu Jiaoyu Chubanshe, 1.
[8] Callahan, 759 (see endnote 6).
[9] Friedberg, Aaron L. (2006): "Going Out": China's Pursuit of Natural Resources and Implications for the PRC's Grand Strategy, NBR Analysis, Vol. 17:3 (September).
[10] Pan, Zhongqi (2008): China's Changing Image of and Engagement in World Order, in: Sujian Guo, Jean-Marc F. Blanchard (eds.): "Harmonious World" and China's New Foreign Policy, Lanham, MD: Lexington Books, 39-63, 56.
[11] Fehlbier, Tobias (2006): Konstanten chinesischer Außenpolitik, Beiträge zur Internationalen Politik und Sicherheit, Nr. 2, 17-26.

[12] Beijing likens Cheney criticism to nosy neighbor, March 1, 2007, http://www.washingtontimes.com/news/2007/mar/01/20070301-104826-2978r/
[13] Sieren, Frank (2008): Der China Schock. Wie Peking sich die Welt gefügig macht, Berlin: Econ.
[14] http://www.chinaconsulatesf.org/eng/xw/t521025.htm
[15] Hongbo, Sun (2008): Hu's visit to deepen Latin America ties, China Daily, November 18, http://www.china.org.cn/international/opinion/2008-11/18/content_16782272.htm.
[16] World Energy Outlook 2007, http://www.iea.org.
[17] China Oil Web, http://www.chinaoilweb.com.
[18] Bajpaee, Chietigj (2005): Chinese Energy Strategy in Latin America, China Brief, Vol. 5, Issue 14 (June), www.weltpolitik.net/print/3340.html.
[19] Quoted at Institute for the Analysis of Global Security, In Search of Crude China goes to the Americas, January 18, 2005, http://www.iags.org/n0118041.htm, in: Hänni, Tobias (2007): Wirtschaftliche Beziehungen zwischen Lateinamerika und China, June 21, http://www.weltpolitik.net/print/3319.html.
[20] Buckley, Chris (2008): Venezuela's Chávez to visit oil-hungry China, September 16, www.reuters.com.
[21] Lafargue, Francois (2006): China's Strategies in Latin America, Military Review, May-June, 80-84, 81, http://findarticles.com/p/articles/mi_m0PBZ/is_3_86/ai_n 166897 56/print.
[22] Buckley (see endnote 20).
[23] Santiso, Javier (2006): China: A Helping Hand for Latin America?, Policy Insights, No. 23 (June), OECD Development Centre, www.oecd.org/dev/insights.
[24] Information Office of the State Council of the PRC (2003): China's Policy on Mineral Resources, I, IV, http://www.china.org.cn/e-white/20031223.
[25] Husar, Jörg (2007): Chinas Engagement in Lateinamerika, Saarbrücken: Verlag für Entwicklungspolitik.
[26] CEPAL (2005): Panorama de la inserción internacional de América Latina y el Caribe, 2004. Tendencias 2005, Santiago de Chile, 162.
[27] Lehmann, Vera; Husar, Jörg: Ziele, Stragien und Instrumente der chinesischen Lateinamerikapolitik, in: Albiez, Sarah; Kauppert, Philipp; Müller, Sophie (eds.) (2007): China und Lateinamerika. Ein transpazifischer Brückenschlag, Berlin: wvb, 243-280, 266.
[28] Erikson, Daniel P.; Chen, Janice (2007): China, Taiwan, and the Battle for Latin America, in: The Fletcher Forum of World Affairs, Vol. 31:2 (Summer), 69-89, 81-82, http://www.iadialog.org/PublicationFiles/Erikson-Chen-1%20(2).pdf.
[29] Logan, Samuel (2009): Ecuador: Back door to America, ISN Security Watch, January 29, www.isn.ethz.ch.
[30] Burbach, Roger; Tarbell, Jim (2004). George W. Bush and the Hubris of Empire, Zed Books Ltd.
[31] Paz, Gonzalo (2006): Rising China's "Offensive" in Latin America and the U.S. Reaction, Asian Perspective, Vol. 30:4, 95-112, 109pp.
[32] http://www.focalae.org/user/index.asp.
[33] EFE, published by El Pais (Uruguay), February 7, 2005.
[34] Paz, 107 (see endnote 31).
[35] Dumbaugh, Kerry; Sullivan, Mark P. (2005): China's Growing Interest in Latin America, CRS Report for Congress, RS22119, April 20, 6, www.usis.it/pdf/other/RS22119.pdf.
[36] Maihold, Günther (2006): China and Latin America, in: Stiftung Wissenschaft und Politik (ed.): China's Rise: The Return of Geopolitics? Berlin: Stiftung Wissenschaft und Politik, 37-45, 45.

[37] Johnson, Stephen (2005): Balancing China's Growing Influence in Latin America, Backgrounder, The Heritage Foundation, No. 1888 (October 24), 6.

[38] Cieslik, Thomas (2004): China sucht nach mehr Einfluß in Lateinamerika—Taiwan kämpft um die Aufrechterhaltung seiner diplomatischen Anerkennung, China aktuell, Vol. 10: 10 (October), 1115-1120.

[39] Buck, Karl (2007): China's engagement in Latin America and the Caribbean: Expectations and bad dreams, in: Albiez, Sarah; Kauppert, Philipp; Müller, Sophie (eds.) (2007): China und Lateinamerika. Ein transpazifischer Brückenschlag, Berlin: wvb, 51-86, 54.

[40] Watts, Jonathan (2007): Victory for China as Costa Rica cuts Taiwan ties, The Guardian, June 8, http://www.guardian.co.uk/world/2007/jun/08/china.jonathanwatts.

[41] Minkner-Bünjer, Mechthild (2005): Zentralamerikas, China(alb)träume: Herausforderungen und Zukunftsaussichten, Brennpunkt Lateinamerika, No. 17 (September 15), 197-208, 199.

[42] Xinhua News Agency, November 17, 2008.

[43] China's first ambassador to Costa Rica, http://www.chinadaily.com.cn/china/2007-08/17/content_6031613.htm.

[44] Blanchard, Ben; Jennings, Ralph (2007): Costa Rica switches allegiance to China from Taiwan, Reuters, June 7, http://www.reuters.com/article/worldNews/idUSPEK 14344320 070607.

[45] Minkner-Bünjer, 206 (see endnote 41).

[46] Sieren (see endnote 13).

[47] Szenarioprojekt China 2020 (2008): Szenarien für die chinesische Außenpolitik im Jahr 2020+, Friedrich Ebert Stiftung: Internationale Politik und Gesellschaft, 90-106.

[48] Pan, 57 (see endnote 10).

[49] Paz, 102 (see endnote 31).

Chapter 9

Greater China and Its Neighbors in Comparative Perspective: Lessons from Europe?

Katja Weber*

INTRODUCTION

Recent reconciliation efforts across the Taiwan Strait under Taiwan's new president Ma Ying-jeou, and Chinese President Hu Jintao's warm spring visit to Japan in May 2008, give reason for cautious optimism that Greater China and its neighbors are seeking improved relations and are interested in promoting regional security, peace and prosperity. Up to this point, the main mechanisms for stabilizing the region have been a "hub and spokes network" consisting of five bilateral alliances (between the US and Australia, Japan, South Korea, the Philippines and Thailand), along with the Association of Southeast Asian Nations (ASEAN) and, more recently, the ASEAN Regional Forum (ARF).

Anyone familiar with the region, however, readily concludes that existing security provisions are not enough and that plenty of obstacles remain. Aside from the problems on the Korean peninsula (the North Korean nuclear crisis, and now the uncertainty surrounding Kim Jong Il's succession), the Taiwan Strait issue remains volatile, not to speak of terrorism or the proliferation of weapons of mass destruction (WMD). Moreover, different threat perceptions complicate cooperative efforts where China is concerned about Japan's greater assertiveness in the military realm—Japan's dispatch of Self Defense Forces (SDF) to provide logistical support to coalition operations against international terrorism in Afghanistan; SDF in Iraq; the deployment of a Theater Missile Defense (TMD) system to intercept ballistic missiles in outer space; the building of multi-functional flexible forces to deal with new threats like the proliferation of WMDs, terrorism; and greater defense cooperation with the U.S.)—and Japan, similarly, worries about China's increased military power, its steadily rising defense expenditures, and the relative lack of transparency regarding China's defense budget. Add to this outstanding territorial disputes between Japan and China over the East China Sea, Japan and Russia over the Northern territories, China, Taiwan and Vietnam over the Paracel Islands, to mention but a few of a long list of contested areas in the region, and the fact that, in spite of the encouraging events mentioned at the outset, reconciliation steps taken by China, Japan and its neighbors in the eyes of many citizens of these countries have been insufficient, causing the history problem to resurface. Finally, there is the great heterogeneity regarding culture, language, religion, and political systems.

This suggests that non-like-minded neighbors need to be further reassured and that the countries in the region need to find additional ways to engage each other to promote greater coordination and cooperation. As this chapter will show, the problem of creating regional security is not new, but has been confronted by other countries before. In the aftermath of World War II, and once again at the end of the Cold War, Europeans created order and thereby enhanced their stability. They did so by (1) transcending historical legacies, (2) including former enemies into security structures, and (3) tying the U.S. to the European continent. Or, put differently, Europeans promoted peace and stability by giving rise to multi-faceted, multi-tiered security structures and, over time, creating a complex web of governance.[1] Recognizing that there are significant differences between Asia and Europe, the chapter argues that the process of European security provisions, nevertheless, provides useful lessons for Greater China and its neighbors, particularly when it comes to the institutionalization of trust in the form of multi-level governance structures—a development that appears inevitable in the long run.

WEST EUROPEAN SECURITY PROVISIONS IN THE AFTERMATH OF WORLD WAR II

In the aftermath of World War II, Europeans sought to transcend the many years of bloodshed, reestablish trust, and build institutions that would facilitate cooperation. As is readily apparent in the German case, to deal successfully with historical legacies is a complex process. It, in fact, took Germany decades to overcome its violent past, asking for forgiveness, reeducating its people, offering financial compensation, building memorials, etc.

More specifically, there appear to be three essential elements to reconciliation: remembrance/truth seeking, restitution/justice, apology/settling the past.[2] Historical legacies, therefore, not only need to be addressed but dealt with in a particular manner to remove the big stumbling block these issues still represent for regions like Asia-Pacific. Since confidence building takes time, Europeans—and foremost among them the Federal Republic of Germany and France—sought to remove outstanding obstacles to cooperation and create institutional structures that would promote mutual respect, trust and tolerance.

Following the end of the Second World War, the United Kingdom, France, and the United States tried to determine how the USSR would react to the defeat of Germany and Japan.[3] Would the Soviet Union cooperate with the United States and allow for free elections in Poland and the rest of Eastern Europe as indicated at Yalta, or would it pursue an expansionist policy and thereby pose a threat to the security of independent countries?

History books readily reveal that, as a result of the installation of Soviet puppet governments in some of the East European countries, as well as the serious military imbalance between the Soviet Union and the west, the West Europeans, by 1946, already felt threatened by the Soviet Union. To make matters worse, some countries—foremost among them France—additionally feared a resurgent Germany. To enhance their security these countries promoted greater cooperation among themselves, very importantly, sought to integrate Germany in international institutions to contain its power once and for all, and asked for U.S. support. Thus, over the course of more than fifty years, the West Europeans brought about a variety of cooperative structures with varying memberships and varying degrees of institutional commitment which, following the end of the Cold War, many East European countries were allowed to joined. Or, put differently, the Europeans, over the course of several decades, gave rise to multi-level governance structures to promote peace, stability and prosperity.

Convinced that there was a dual threat, the West Europeans had different security needs in the early post-1945 period than the U.S., which largely viewed the Soviet Union as posing a political threat to international peace. This explains why the West Europeans acted first to improve their security. In early 1947 British foreign minister Ernest Bevin took a decisive step to coordinate a West European defense system by offering a treaty to France. In his mind such a treaty should not only win French support by promising British assistance in the event of renewed German aggression, but also decrease the uncertainty regarding French behavior by pulling France away from the USSR. After drawn-out deliberations, on March 4, 1947, a Treaty of Alliance and Mutual Assistance was finally signed at Dunkirk, in the form of an old-fashioned military alliance.

Only days after Dunkirk, the American position began to change. U.S. decision-makers started to attribute recent unrest in Greece and Turkey to Soviet infiltration attempts and therefore persuaded President Truman to take action to stop Soviet influence from spreading. On March 12, 1947, the American president (in what became known as the Truman Doctrine) asked Congress for financial assistance to aid free peoples who are susceptible to pressure from the USSR or pressure from domestic Communist movements. And, as an additional measure to stem Soviet infiltration, U.S. Secretary of State George Marshall, on June 5, 1947, introduced a plan (Marshall Plan) to stimulate European economic recovery via massive U.S. financial assistance.

Still viewing the Soviet threat as political in nature, however, the U.S. was determined to avoid "entangling alliances" and made clear to the West Europeans that they would have to demonstrate their willingness to engage in self-help before any further U.S. commitment would be discussed. Again, Bevin took the lead and, on January 22, 1948, called for the creation of a Western union. Several troubling events in early 1948 (the Communist takeover of the government in Prague; a telegram by General Clay from Berlin warning that war "could come with dramatic suddenness"; rumors about a Soviet-

Norwegian nonaggression pact; talk that Denmark feared an armed invasion by the USSR) underlined the need for greater security cooperation and, on March 17, 1948, led to the signing of the Brussels Treaty in which the United Kingdom, France, and the Benelux countries vowed to build a common defense system and to strengthen economic and cultural ties.

Since the Europeans now had fulfilled their end of the bargain, Truman gave permission to start secret North Atlantic Treaty (NAT) talks with the UK and Canada. While the negotiating parties were discussing several versions of a pledge, the Soviets, feeling provoked by western occupation policies in Berlin, responded with a partial, and soon thereafter full, blockade of the city. The United Kingdom initiated an airlift (which the U.S. later joined) and, on September 27, the defense ministers of the Brussels Treaty powers decided to create a Western Union Defense Organization as a first step to a larger association that the United States should join. At the same time, NAT talks were progressing and, on April 4, 1949, Belgium, Canada, Denmark, France, Iceland, Italy, Luxembourg, the Netherlands, Norway, Portugal, the United Kingdom, and the U.S. signed the North Atlantic Treaty. Within a year of its creation, NATO became much superior to traditional military coalitions and, through a high level of integration, a unified command, joint planning, and combined military training, set itself apart from most previous military arrangements.

Although, on May 9, 1949, the USSR lifted its blockade on Berlin, improved East-West relations did not follow. On the contrary, on September 23, President Truman announced the detection of an atomic explosion in the Soviet Union and responded by signing a Mutual Defense Assistance Act to facilitate cooperation among the Western allies. Then, on June 25, 1950, North Korea attacked South Korea. Convinced that the Korean War was initiated by the USSR, and that it might even be a "dress-rehearsal" for Europe, the Western powers grew anxious about their serious military inferiority vis-à-vis the Soviet Union and began to discuss German rearmament.

Terrified by the increase in Soviet belligerence and deeply troubled by the prospect of a remilitarized Germany, in the fall of 1950 France called for the founding of a European army in which the contingents of the members (including Germany) "would be incorporated...on the level of the smallest possible unit."[4] That is, fearing that Germany could become militant again and act opportunistically, France sought to contain Germany through integration and control. Initially opposed by other countries (the U.S., the UK, and the Benelux countries preferred to integrate Germany in NATO), the proposal for a European Army—also known as the European Defense Community (EDC)—was eventually accepted by them only to be rejected finally by the French themselves. Following Stalin's death on March 5, 1953, and the signing of the Korean armistice on July 23, 1953, many French perceived a reduction in Soviet threat and thus, on August 29, 1954, the French National Assembly voted against the ratification of the EDC and made its demise official. The result of four years of security debates was a strengthened NATO, i.e., agreement was reached that the Western European Union (WEU) would be restored within

NATO, that Germany would join the WEU and hence, become a member of NATO.

At about the same time an EDC was being discussed, two Frenchmen, Jean Monnet (a businessman) and Robert Schuman (foreign minister), in consultation with West German Chancellor Konrad Adenauer, proposed to bring the coal and steel industries of France and Germany under one interstate organization with significant supranational characteristics. Other countries were invited to join and on April 18, 1951, France, West-Germany, the Benelux countries, and Italy signed the Treaty of Paris, creating the European Coal and Steel Community (ECSC). Although bringing about a Free Trade Area for basic materials such as coal, coke, iron, ore and steel would yield economic benefits, the main purpose of the ECSC was to tackle the French-German problem and make war between France and Germany impossible.

Each member state, by ratifying the ECSC Treaty in August 1952, declared its willingness voluntarily to curtail its freedom of action by delegating some aspects of its sovereignty to a "High Authority" and, thus, started a long process of institution-building that led to the creation of a sophisticated structural arrangement which, with the signing of the Maastricht Treaty in 1992, became known as the European Union (EU). In a little more than five decades, the Europeans have moved from a free trade area to a customs union to a common market with a common currency, and have discussed the further curtailment of their autonomy in the context of a Common Foreign and Security Policy, a European Security and Defense Policy, Europol, etc. It furthermore needs to be stressed that integration took place at varying speeds where those EU member states that were ready to move forward did so, while allowing others to exempt themselves from policies that they were not yet ready to adopt.[5]

One needs to keep in mind, however, that the EU does not operate in a vacuum. In the security realm, ever since its founding in 1949, NATO has protected Europe and continues to do so. Like the EU, the North Atlantic Treaty Organization has come a long ways in institutionalizing both cooperation among its members and, as will be discussed below, with its post-Cold War partners. Other international actor that help promote peace in Europe are 1) the Organization for Security and Cooperation in Europe (OSCE—formerly known as the CSCE) which, since the signing of the Helsinki Accord in 1973, has taken a particular interest in human rights issues; 2) the Council of Europe (where Heads of State exchange ideas); and 3) the United Nations (UN).[6]

EUROPEAN SECURITY PROVISIONS FOLLOWING THE END OF THE COLD WAR

The end of the Cold War brought a need to reassess threat and to adapt security provisions to deal with new challenges such as ethnic unrest in the former Yugoslavia, terrorism, and the proliferation of weapons of mass destruction, to name but a few. Similar to what happened after World War II, where France, but also the U.S. and the United Kingdom, reached out to Germany and brought it into western security structures, in the aftermath of the Cold War both the European Union and NATO extended a hand of friendship to many of their former enemies and allowed them to become members of these two "prestigious clubs." Moreover, NATO established "a set of interrelated formal bilateral and multilateral committees and meetings designed to manage security issues with non-member states."[7] For instance, in the Euro-Atlantic Partnership Council (EAPC) NATO members meet regularly with partner countries to discuss political and security-related issues. The Partnership for Peace (PfP) seeks to promote security cooperation with each partner country via joint defense planning, military exercises, etc. Regular bilateral meetings are held in the context of the NATO-Russia Council, the NATO-Ukraine Commission and the Mediterranean Dialogue.

Since national solutions and existing security arrangements are increasingly inadequate for dealing with the multi-faceted security challenges of the post-Cold War environment, a more complex European security architecture is taking shape in which NATO, the European Union and the Organization for Security and Cooperation in Europe work along side each other. "In the Balkans [the situation is even more complicated in that] NATO works not only with the EU, OSCE, and the UN in post-conflict reconstruction efforts, but also with a range of public and private non-governmental actors ranging from the International Committee of the Red Cross to private contractors."[8]

The numerous actors involved in promoting security, however, do not always see eye-to-eye on what policies to pursue to enhance the stability of the region. Although it is obvious to the Europeans that they need to do more to assure their security, there is no agreement what the right formula might be.[9] Does the answer lie within a Common Foreign and Security Policy (CFSP) which—as was readily apparent during the Gulf War (1991), the problems in the Balkans, Bosnia, Kosovo and, most recently, the Iraq War—presently does not exist? A European Security and Defense Identity (ESDI) within NATO? A European Security and Defense Policy (ESDP) which, combined with a European Rapid Reaction Force (ERRF), would allow Europeans to act militarily without the U.S.? Matters are further complicated by a serious capability gap between the U.S. and Europe, particularly with respect to high tech equipment, investment and procurement.

To sum up, given that with the disintegration of the Soviet Union the West's arch enemy disappeared, NATO and the EU invited several Central and East European countries to join them and, by "dangling" the membership carrot, sought to assure that these countries would create democratic structures, protect human rights and uphold the rule of law. With Russia, which could not simply be absorbed into the Western security umbrella, both NATO and the EU created bilateral arrangements to facilitate disarmament, non-proliferation, border security, etc. Thus, over the course of about fifteen years, the western allies gave rise to an increasingly complex security system in which they incorporated potential rivals. Of course,

[a]t one level, this was a method employed among Euro-Atlantic states during the Cold War itself. Vanquished centres of power (Germany), those in the

ascendant (the US) and those on the wane (the UK and France) jointly managed their common security and in the process jettisoned historical animosities as well as maintaining the institutional edifices of west European stability, the EU and NATO.[10]

This system of governance assumes the existence of multiple actors (both public and private) with varying degrees of power and formality who operate on multiple levels and fulfill a multiplicity of tasks to deal with an increasingly complex international environment. [11] Or, put differently, "Europe is characterized by...multiple centres of power, a multiplication of actors involved in the provision of security, and highly developed forms of institutionalization and community building, with these forms being extended across the continent, functionally within the sphere of security and geographically through enlargement and partnership."[12]

Aside from actors' interests, norms, rules and ideas are crucial in shaping security policies. "International organizations such as NATO, the EU and the Council of Europe...are [increasingly becoming] receptacles of congruent ideas [that] interpret and project them as appropriate norms of international behaviour."[13] At the same time it needs to be understood that, given the varied nature of security threats in the post-Cold War environment, the provision of security increasingly requires a broad spectrum of tools including financial and technical assistance, economic cooperation, nation-building, etc., in addition to more traditional military measures.

SECURITY PROVISIONS OF GREATER CHINA AND ITS NEIGHBORS IN THE AFTERMATH OF WORLD WAR II

When the U.S. defeated Japan in 1945, China and Korea were liberated from Japanese rule. Yet, whereas the Europeans relied on multiple institutional arrangements with varying degrees of commitment to assure their security, in Asia-Pacific bilateralism trumped all other security provisions. [14] Australia, Japan, South Korea, the Philippines, and Thailand all relied predominately on the American "hub and spokes network" to deal with external threats.

To avoid putting all their eggs in one basket, in 1954, the U.S., France, Great Britain, New Zealand, Australia, the Philippines, Thailand and Pakistan founded the Southeast Asia Treaty Organization (SEATO). Its main purpose was to prevent communism from gaining ground in the region. However since, "[u]nlike NATO, SEATO had no independent mechanism for obtaining intelligence or deploying military forces, [its] . . . potential for collective action was necessarily limited."[15] SEATO held annual joint military exercises and engaged in consultation, but suffered from a lack of "credibility" and therefore was disbanded in 1977.

Since many Asian countries, particularly in the Southeast, perceived internal challenges as the main threat to their security, and not the USSR, they saw no need for a military pact. When the "communist victories in Indochina and the subsequent Vietnamese invasion of Cambodia" increased the risk of domestic upheaval in the region, Indonesia, Malaysia, Singapore, Thailand and the Philippines, in 1967, decided they would be much better served by an arrangement equipped to deal with sub-regional disputes peacefully, and thus, gave rise to the Association of Southeast Asian Nations (ASEAN).[16] From the outset, in its 1967 Bangkok Declaration, ASEAN spelled out norms for its members that guide their behavior to this day. Of particular importance in this regard are: mutual respect for independence, sovereignty, and territorial integrity; non-interference in the domestic affairs of one another; the settlement of differences by peaceful means; and the renunciation of the use of force.[17] To reinforce the norms of mutual non-interference, in 1971, ASEAN called for a "Zone of Peace, Freedom and Neutrality (ZOPFAN)" in Southeast Asia. For outside threats, much like Australia, Japan and South Korea, to this day, ASEAN continues to rely on security guarantees from the U.S.

ASEAN has come a long way since its founding days and, with respect to security matters, bilateral military ties among member states have evolved significantly. Aside from intelligence sharing and joint-counterinsurgency operations, ASEAN now also holds joint naval and air exercises and regular defense ministers meetings. [18] Over the years, ASEAN, furthermore, has expanded its membership (Brunei, Vietnam, Laos, Myanmar, and Cambodia were added over time) and, as will be seen below, now also engages in security talks with key non-members in the region.

In the early post-World War II era China sided with the Soviet Union. In 1950 the two countries signed a Treaty of Friendship and Alliance, but when Mao began to advocate a Chinese model of revolution instead of a Soviet one, the relationship between the two countries became strained. The situation deteriorated further when Mao criticized Khrushchev for backing down in the Cuban missile crisis and in 1969 there were even armed clashes along the border between the two countries. Having come to think of the Soviet Union as a foe instead of a friend, and given its close geographic proximity, in 1972 China sought closer relations with the U.S. At the same time, China was a member of the Non-Aligned movement where it still holds observer status today.

SECURITY PROVISIONS OF GREATER CHINA AND ITS NEIGHB ORS FOLLOWING THE END OF THE COLD WAR

In the post-Cold War era, the countries in Asia Pacific confront new transnational challenges (terrorism, the proliferation of weapons of mass destruction, etc.), greater uncertainty regarding the behavior of the Great Powers in the region, and the fear of U.S. isolationism. Much like in Europe, these changed circumstances necessitate a reassessment of existing security structures in the region.

If the U.S., pre-occupied with its missions in Iraq and Afghanistan, pays less attention to Asia, how will China, Japan (and possibly India and/or Russia) react? Will they compete for power and in the process start a new arms race? Will China's growing power upset the balance of power in the region and, down the road, lead to renewed military aggression? Will we see a return of Japanese militarism, should the U.S. no longer play the role of regional balancer?

Given the serious reliance of the countries in the region on the U.S.' security guarantee, in the short-term, they need to do everything in their power to keep the U.S. involved and thereby prevent a power vacuum. As stated above, however, this sole reliance on bilateral relationships with the U.S. is insufficient and could prove very dangerous. "[Having] outlived any usefulness in its original form the 'San Francisco System'...is being transformed to a more complex structure of security relationships involving the U.S., its Asian friends and allies and other key Asian security actors outside the U.S. strategic orbit."[19] Or, in other words, to reduce their dependence on the U.S. in the years to come the countries in the Asia-Pacific region also need to complement their hub-and-spokes networks more effectively with trilateral and multilateral arrangements. First of all, the importance of the U.S.-Japan-China triangle should be elevated by encouraging Chinese stake-holding in the region, while reemphasizing Japanese global relevance.[20] At the same time, existing multilateral arrangements like ASEAN and the ASEAN Regional Forum (ARF)—which will be discussed in more detail below—need to be adapted. In this post-Cold War environment in which shifts in the regional balance of power are externally driven, ASEAN can no longer insulate the region from outside influence and thus, needs to find new ways to constrain others through dialogue and consultation.[21] ASEAN needs to expand its focus and learn to deal with external as well as internal threats, but, as long as the close military dependence on the Western powers remains, "no ASEAN country sees regional military cooperation as a substitute for security links with external powers," merely as an additional safety device meant to reduce the region's dependence on the West over time.[22] Additionally, a Northeast Asian security structure, possibly growing out of the Six Party talks, is needed that can address specific problems like North Korea's nuclearization that destabilize the region.[23]

In sum, given the multi-faceted nature of security threats in the post-Cold War era in Asia-Pacific, countries in the region need to take multiple measures to promote stability. First they need to find a way to keep the U.S. strategically involved and thereby prevent regional hegemony and an arms race. Simultaneously, they need to make use of existing institutions like ASEAN and ARF to assure the peaceful management of territorial disputes and engage in mediation to keep conflicts from escalating. And they need to give rise to a Northeast Asian security institution that can deal with security challenges in that sub-region. Pursuing these strategies, over time, countries in the region then are also likely to bring about multiple levels of governance with varying degrees of commitment that are better suited to deal with today's security challenges.

Since ASEAN occupies such a prominent place in the literature on Asian security, before turning to an explicit comparison between Europe and Asia, the next section briefly scrutinizes ASEAN which might best be described as a "security regime" that is gradually moving toward a "security community."[24]

As a security regime, ASEAN seeks to "significantly reduce, if not eliminate, the likelihood of war by securing adherence to a [discernible] set of [principles], norms and rules that constrain the conflictual behaviour of the regional actors in relation to one another."[25] To meet the requirements of a security community ASEAN would have to go further and develop "institutions and practices strong enough and stable enough to assure for a 'long' time, stable expectations of 'peaceful change' within its population."[26] More specifically, ASEAN would have to develop such measures as "norms concerning the non-use of force; contingency-planning against any other members within the grouping; formal and informal dispute settlement mechanisms," etc.[27]

Although ASEAN has come a long way and, similar to what has happened in Europe, has promoted regional stability via enlargement and bringing former enemies into cooperative arrangements, "persisting bilateral tensions, territorial disputes, militarization, and the conflict-creating potential of regional economic linkages undermine the claim of Southeast Asia to being a viable regional security community."[28] What we continue to see is a gradual, piecemeal approach to cooperation where the norm of non-interference constrains policy options, and where undesirable behavior by a member therefore often goes unpunished.

COMPARING APPLES AND ORANGES?

As many scholars caution, comparing Europe and Asia may be like comparing apples and oranges.[29] Factors like democracy, equality and institutions which have helped to stabilize the European continent for numerous decades are either non-existent, much weaker, or of a fleeting nature in Asia. Here each country tells its own history and, instead of taking meaningful steps to overcome their divisive past, East Asians largely behave in a self-interested manner. While the Europeans, early in the aftermath of World War II, began to build institutions to transcend animosities and reduce the likelihood of opportunistic behavior, East Asians, until fairly recently, for the most part, have been dragging their feet.

Just because international relations theorists have studied Europe for centuries, in and of itself this is no justification for applying western concepts, theoretical frameworks, and ideas to the East. In fact, to superimpose "Eurocentric ideas," onto Asia can easily lead one to deduce erroneous conclusions and to generate dubious predictions.[30] Just because something is true for Europe, does not necessarily make it so for Asia and it appears that, when it comes to institution-building, Asian leaders and policy-makers have consciously rejected western models of multilateralism.[31] Instead of "legalistic and fast-track modalities of institution-building," Asians seem to prefer incremental cooperation as well as "a high degree of discreetness, informality, pragmatism, expediency, consensus-building, and non-confrontational bargaining styles."[32]

And yet, there are similarities between Europe and Asia. The Franco-German axis, for example, in many ways resembles the Sino-Japanese one. Just because China and Japan have made less progress transcending their historical legacies to date does not imply that they could not draw useful lessons from

France and Germany's experience. On the contrary, one would expect Asia to seek insights from the European success story, analyze what led to it, and duplicate those measures that promise positive results for Asia.

LESSONS TO BE DRAWN FROM THE PROCESS OF EUROPEAN SECURITY INTEGRATION

Drawing on the European experience, next this chapter shows how the process of European security integration provides useful lessons that may inform a similar process in the Asia-Pacific region. Three factors in particular are considered crucial in promoting stability in Europe: reconciliation efforts, the inclusion of former enemies into security structures, and tying the U.S. closely to European security efforts.

European history is of importance to Sino-Japanese relations, especially when it comes to "dealing with the past and the question of guilt."[33] Although Japanese officials repeatedly have asked their neighbors for forgiveness for Japanese atrocities, these acts did not achieve the desired results, "because they were not fully internalized by Japanese society as a whole."[34] This is largely because Japan's apologies thus far have appeared "ad hoc and made grudgingly under international/regional pressure," but also in part because China has seen diplomatic utility in refusing the apologies.[35] Or, put differently, contrary to what happened in Europe where shared history helped to promote reconciliation, the steps taken thus far by China and Japan (war crimes trials, postwar reparations, peace treaty)—and to a lesser degree by China and Taiwan, and Japan and South Korea—have been "flawed and incomplete."[36] Hence the history problem resurfaces and, to this day, in many top-level meetings the Chinese admonish their Japanese counterparts never to forget Japan's wartime record.[37]

In all fairness it has to be said that, in recent years, several reconciliation efforts have been made by Asian nations that do signify a step in the right direction. To name but a few, the written apology Japan's Prime Minister Keizo Obuchi issued to South Korea's President Kim Dae-Jung in 1998 clearly deserves mention. Also, as already alluded to above, following his electoral victory Taiwan's President Ma Ying-jeou reached out to Beijing in an effort to normalize economic relations with the mainland and to reiterate reassurances to the Chinese Communist Party that the Kuomintang (KMT) would not seek de jure independence.[38] And, with respect to Sino-Japanese relations, the two countries have experienced a period of rapprochement under Prime Ministers Shinzo Abe and Yasuo Fukuda, leaving the dark days of their predecessor Junichiro Koizumi and his repeated visits to the controversial Yasukuni Shrine behind. In the first speech ever given by a Chinese premier to the Japanese Diet, on April 12, 2007, Wen Jiabao thus publicly acknowledged Japan's apologies for its aggression in Asia and called for reconciliation and cooperation. More recently, during his "warm spring" visit to Japan, May 6-10, 2008, Chinese President Hu Jintao, expressly stated that cooperation between the two countries should be expanded and should include consultation on foreign and security issues, exchanges between people, increased trade, greater cooperation with respect to energy and the environment, food safety, and a solution to territorial disputes.[39] And, even though during a speech at Waseda University on May 8, 2008, Hu reminded the Japanese of their war history, expressing his hope that history will be viewed as "a textbook for all to learn from,"[40] at the same time, he mentioned Japan's postwar development assistance to China, thereby drawing attention away from the war and onto positive Japanese postwar behavior.[41]

Even though some Chinese believe that Japan has apologized enough, most Chinese still feel strongly that Japan has to come to terms with its past and "face up to history" to aid in the normalization of relations between the two countries.[42] As long as "a sizeable segment of the population feels little remorse and vehemently opposes any apology," [43] "conservative elements in Japan...ma[ke] frequent efforts to deny the history of Japanese aggression,"[44] numerous Japanese continue to believe that their country's "purpose for invading its neighbors was...entirely noble" (freeing Southeast Asia from Western colonizers), and "cabinet ministers march to the Yasukuni Shrine to pay tribute to Japan's war dead," China's resentment and mistrust of Japan is unlikely to diminish.[45] Until serious change comes about, the Chinese can be expected to maximize their political utility by playing the "history card."[46]

For reconciliation to succeed, however, China also needs to do its part. The Chinese need to be willing to accept an apology from Japan and need to move away from their patriotic education that, to this day, portrays Japanese as villains. That is, the Chinese have to be willing to bury the hatchet and let go of the past.

More concretely, it can be hypothesized that steps that were essential in bringing about reconciliation between Germany and its neighbors such as the issuance of a formal apology, monetary compensation, the preservation of memory, the creation of trust, etc. will also matter greatly to Greater China and its neighbors. Since I scrutinized German and Japanese reconciliation efforts elsewhere, it here suffices to stress that transcending historical divisions is not only important in and of itself, but that reconciliation entails three essential elements—remembrance, restitution, apology—all of which need to be addressed for reconciliation to be successful and the quarreling parties to be able to move on.[47] Under the best of circumstances, an apology can provide a framework within which groups may rethink their past and reevaluate the present.[48] At a minimum, transcending historical legacies would facilitate security cooperation among Greater China and its neighbors. Working toward eliminating/mitigating distrust would construct a less hostile environment in which to promote cooperation.

Aside from reconciliation, what also mattered greatly in the European case was the inclusion of former enemies in newly created security structures. Germany and France took important initial steps to promote cooperation between the two countries in the aftermath of World War II with the founding of the ECSC which was much more than a free trade agreement. By pooling resources that are used in the production of armaments such as coal, iron and ore, France wanted to make sure Germany could not rebuild its military uncontrolled. Similarly, the discussions surrounding the creation of a European Army (European Defense Community) were meant to prevent independent German rearmament. And, when the French National Assembly failed to ratify the EDC Treaty in 1954, the United Kingdom—by promising to station British troops on the European continent—took the lead in bringing Germany into the western defense system, first into the Western European Union and, shortly thereafter, NATO.

As discussed above, in the aftermath of the Cold War both the EU and NATO, similarly, brought Central and East European countries into already existing institutional structures to reduce the likelihood that these countries might pose a threat in the future. With countries like Russia and Ukraine, as well as new neighbors to the East and South, special partnerships were created.

Europeans view the incorporation of former enemies into common institutions as crucial because they understand that being a member of a particular environment, and adhering to certain principles, norms, and rules, over time, builds trust and does not only change interests but can also change identities. Case in point Germany and France who, as members of the same institutions for over half a century, learned to trust each other so that war between the two is virtually inconceivable now. (Another example of the institutionalization of trust between former enemies is Germany and Poland but, given the more recent nature of this cooperation, it is not yet as deep as the relationship established between Germany and France).

A similar process is conceivable for Greater China and its neighbors in the long term. Even if there are no deeply shared values at this time, it is conceivable that there are certain ideas, norms, principles such as non-interference in domestic affairs, non-use of force, respect for sovereignty, etc., that many, if not all, actors in the region should be able to agree on. Keeping in mind that Asians, for the most part, value social over legal norms and prefer informal over formal contacts, the objective should be to solidify norms and rules, build trust, respect and tolerance and thereby, with time, modify "acceptable standards of behavior."[49] Or put differently, since, as Wendt argues, anarchy is socially constructed, it should be possible to overcome it.[50] Much like Germany which, having addressed its historical legacies and "by building a new, shared identity with former enemies," has been able to "transcend, at least in part, [its] Germanness," Asians, in due time, should be able to shed their "divisive Asianness."[51]

A final factor that was instrumental in bringing stability to the European continent was the role played by the U.S. in promoting security. Once the Europeans (by signing the Dunkirk and Brussels Treaties) had demonstrated their willingness to do more for their own defense, and the threat stemming from the Soviet Union had changed from being political to military in nature, the U.S. started secret North Atlantic Treaty talks and gave rise to NATO which protected Western Europe against the USSR throughout the Cold War. That is, the U.S. was willing to be tied to the European continent and encouraged institution-building in the region ever since. After initial hesitation—fearing that the creation of a European Army could take too long—the U.S. gave its support to the EDC, a few years later to the European Economic Community (now the EU), the Conference on Security and Cooperation in Europe (CSCE now OSCE) and, since the end of the Cold War, to a revamped and enlarged NATO.

Whereas the U.S. played an important role in giving rise to regional institutions in Europe, in Asia by contrast, the U.S., "due to a complex mix of political, material, institutional and identity factors," created bilateral (hub and spokes) alliances.[52] The only multilateral security effort it joined in the region, SEATO, it did so hesitatingly and without conviction, thereby contributing to its demise. The big question now is whether, given the changes in the post-Cold War environment, the U.S. as the dominant power in the Asia-Pacific region is likely to promote multi-layered, multi-tiered arrangements that would assure the diffusion of power among multiple actors and therefore enhance stability.

Before speculating about plausible future security scenarios, one multilateral institution created in July 1994 to safe-guard peace deserves special mention, the ASEAN Regional Forum (ARF). Conceptualized by its founders as the principal forum for security cooperation in the region, the ARF's goal is to address uncertainty in the post-Cold War environment. Comprised of 27 countries, the ARF is based on ASEAN-style diplomacy (non-interference in the internal affairs of states, non-use of force, pacific settlement of disputes, consensus decision making, a preference for non-binding and non-legalistic approaches) and displays minimal institutionalization, thus setting it apart from the above discussed European security structures.[53] The 1995 ARF Concept Paper envisions a "three-stage, evolutionary approach" ... "moving from confidence building to preventive diplomacy and, in the long term, towards a conflict resolution capability."[54] Thus far, the ARF has made progress in the area of confidence building, but efforts to develop mechanisms for preventive diplomacy and conflict management are still at an embryonic stage. More specifically, the ARF discourages the use of force to settle disputes, but makes no provision for common action to punish an act of aggression.[55] Among the measures proposed by ARF are a regional arms register, the exchange of defense white papers and observers during military exercises.

The ASEAN Regional Forum engages in both "first track" (official) and "second track" (unofficial) diplomacy. The former are typically attended by Foreign Ministers, whereas scholars, members of Think Tanks, government representatives not acting in their official capacity, as well as other individuals and organizations attend "second track" meetings on regional security issues. Examples of the latter are the Northeast Asia Cooperation Dialogue (NEACD) founded in 1993 or the Council for Security Cooperation in the Asia Pacific (CSCAP) founded in 1994.[56]

In sum, as a result of their history, Asians do not part with aspects of their sovereignty easily and prefer to begin cooperative efforts by building trust, respect, and tolerance through regular talks and then gradually advance to more ambitious goals. Institutions like ASEAN, the ARF and CSCAP play a central role when it comes to creating a sense of community and it is hoped that regular interactions will diminish distrust, keep problems manageable, and over time will give rise to more sophisticated security arrangements that are capable of dealing with serious problems. It is thought that, the more Greater China and its neighbors know about each other, the greater the likelihood that they might be willing to change their interests and preferences. What matters most in institutional settings is the suspicions they remove and the norms they create over time.[57]

Strategic instability is a real concern in the region and, as the Six Party talks most recently have shown, much like the Europeans in the aftermath of World War II, Asians slowly seem to comprehend that they need to include their most likely adversaries in cooperative security structures, rather than to ally against them. The specific form such arrangements will take in the years to come is still up for grabs. One possibility may be the ARF which, bringing both Japan and China into one institutional framework, promotes greater transparency. By virtue of its highly specific nature, however, the ASEAN Way may not be the best solution for the wider region.[58]

At present, different future security scenarios are plausible. There appears to be consensus that the bilateral alliances that have helped to stabilize the region ever since the end of World War II should remain in place, but that they should be modified and complemented with additional security structures. It needs to be stressed that the emphasis is on *complement* since "multilateralism is not expected to replace...time-tested bilateral mechanisms for regional conflict management" that have served the region well.[59]

However, given that more mileage may be gained from the creation of new institutional arrangements capable of solving specific problems in the region, it may be time for an additional trilateral structure, or a Northeast Asian security institution based on something like the Six Party talks.[60] Japan these days, clearly, seeks to prevent China from becoming a hegemon and tries to tie it firmly to regional institutions.[61] China, at the same time, seeks to prevent Japan's remilitarization, and both countries favor an active U.S. role in the region. Depending on the specific security issue to be addressed, it may make sense to broaden security negotiations and bring in additional countries such as North and South Korea, Russia, India, etc.

The parties involved in East Asian security matters understand that institutions do not represent a magic cure. Due to the benefits outlined above, however, institutions are a step in the right direction. By promoting greater transparency they can reduce the degree of uncertainty actors confront in an anarchic environment and, by using carrots and sticks, can reward desirable behavior and punish undesirable one.

If there are any lessons to be gleaned from Europe, it is that Greater China and its neighbors need to come to terms with their divisive past, transcend remaining obstacles to cooperation, and reap the benefits associated with greater integration. In the end, the European success story is largely about the institutionalization of trust on numerous levels and the removal of hurdles to cooperation. A three-pronged strategy of reconciliation, incorporation of former enemies in security structures, and tying the U.S. to the continent, allowed the Europeans, gradually, to build trust and redefine their identities such that Germans and French, or, for the most part, Germans and Poles, no longer think of themselves as enemies but allies.

Since there are differences between Asia and Europe, the security structures that will be developed in Asia are unlikely to be mirror images of their European counterparts. And yet, many Asian countries are already pursuing multi-level security strategies so that, what we see in Europe today—a system of multi-level governance—is a likely target for Asians in the long run. The time horizon matters greatly here. Presently, it may be correct to describe Asia's security architecture as "fractured," but, this is unlikely to be the end stage.[62] Various future scenarios (a North East Asian Security Regime; a Pan-Asian Security Community; a Multilateral U.S. Alliance System; a Multidimensional Asian Security Mechanism) seem plausible,[63] and one might forecasts that, over time, "different types of coordination among regional states, including bilateral, multilateral and minilateral or subregional, [will be] placed in a layered, hierarchical manner, to help maintain overall security in the region."[64] The exact form these new security provisions will take is still to be determined. Whether security structures will be arranged hierarchically, or whether we will see numerous centers of power (heterarchy), is still up for grabs. What can be said with certainty is that Greater China and its neighbors will continue to reassess their security provisions, that they will give rise to new security arrangements to deal with post-Cold War challenges, and that by institutionalizing trust, over time, much like in Europe, they will create a multi-level security structure that, once identities have been redefined, hopefully, will make war among them unthinkable.

NOTES

* Portions of this paper have been presented at the annual meeting of the International Studies Association in San Francisco in March 2008, and at "The Greater China in an Era of Globalization" conference at the Chinese University of Hong Kong in July 2008. The author is grateful for valuable feedback received there as well as from Professor Akio Takahara at the University of Tokyo. The author would also like to thank the Georgia Tech Foundation for its financial support.

[1] Lisbet Hooghe and Gary Marks, "Unravelling the Central State, But How? Types of Multi-level Governance," *American Political Science Review* Vol. 97, 2003, pp. 233-43.
[2] For an in-depth discussion of these three elements, see Caroline Rose, *Sino-Japanese Relations: Facing the Past, Looking to the Future?* New York: Routledge Curzon, 2005. For a comparative study of reconciliation efforts in Germany and Japan, see Katja Weber and Jonathan Huang, "East Asian Security Revisited in Light of the European Experience," (paper under review).
[3] This section draws on Katja Weber, *Hierarchy Amidst Anarchy: Transaction Costs and Institutional Choice*, New York: SUNY Press, 2000, chapters 5 and 6.

[4] C. G. D. Onslow, "West German Rearmament," *World Politics*, vol. 3, No.4, 1951, p. 467.
[5] See the UK, Sweden and Denmark who exempted themselves from the Euro zone.
[6] Until recently, when it became absorbed by the EU, there was also the Western European Union.
[7] See Mark Webber, Stuart Croft, Jolyon Howorth, Terry Terriff and Elke Krahmann, "The Governance of European Security," *Review of International Studies*, Vol. 30, 2004, p. 11.
[8] Ibid.
[9] Jolyon Howorth and John Keeler, eds., *Defending Europe: The EU, NATO and the Quest for European Autonomy*, Palgrave MacMillan, 2004.
[10] Mark Webber, et. al, "The Governance of European Security," p. 20.
[11] Emil Kirchner, "The Challenge of European Union Security Governance," *Journal of Common Market Studies*, Vol. 44, No. 5, 2006, p. 948.
[12] Mark Webber, et. al, "The Governance of European Security," p. 25. For a discussion of a multi-level governance approach in the context of the European Union's Neighborhood Policy, see Michael Smith and Katja Weber, "Governance Theories, Regional Integration, and EU Foreign Policy," in Katja Weber, Michael Smith and Michael Baun, eds., *Governing Europe's Neighborhood: Partners or Periphery?* Manchester: Manchester University Press, 2007.
[13] See Mark Webber, et. al, "The Governance of European Security," p. 7; and Emil Kirchner, "The Challenge of European Union Security Governance," pp. 951 and 964.
[14] Victor D. Cha, "The Dilemma of Regional Security in East Asia: Multilateralism Versus Bilateralism," in Paul F. Diehl and Joseph Lepgold, eds., *Regional Conflict Management*, Oxford: Rowman & Littlefield Publishers, 2003, p. 108. For a more recent discussion of the U.S. alliances—collectively referred to as the "San Francisco System"—see William Tow and Amitav Acharya, "Obstinate or Obsolete? The U.S. Alliance Structure in the Asia-Pacific," *Australian National University Working Papers*, 2007/4.
[15] http://www.state.gov/r/pa.ho/time/lw/88315.htm.
[16] Amitav Acharya, *Regionalism and Multilateralism,* pp. 31 and 59.
[17] Ibid., p. 110.
[18] Ibid., pp. 85-7.
[19] William Tow and Amitav Acharya, "Obstinate or Obsolete?" p. 3. Note that the authors conceptualize the successor strategy of "hub and spokes" as *alliance mutuality* which they define as "those collective or shared interests and values that cut across different alliances, particularly bilateral ones, to reinforce cooperation throughout an entire network of alliances" (p. 27). Over time they see alliance mutuality evolving and giving rise to a *convergent security strategy* which entails a "managed transition from a regional security system based predominantly on exclusivist bilateral security arrangements to one based predominantly on multilateral security arrangements" (p.32, emphasis in the original).
[20] Victor D. Cha, "Lecture on East Asian Security," *Center for International Strategy, Technology and Policy*, Georgia Tech, Feb. 20, 2008.
[21] Amitav Acharya, Regionalism and Multilateralism, p. 149.
[22] Ibid., p. 119.
[23] Victor Cha, "Lecture on East Asian Security."
[24] Amitav Acharya, Regionalism and Multilateralism.
[25] Ibid., p. 34; also see Robert Jervis, "Security Regimes," in Stephen Krasner, ed., *International Regimes*, Ithaca: Cornell University Press, 1983.
[26] Amitav Acharya, *Regionalism and Multilateralism*, p. 29. For in-depth studies of security communities, see Karl Deutsch, Sidney Burrell, Robert Kahn, Maurice Leem Jr.,

Martin Lichterman, Raymond Lindgren, Francis Lowenheim, and Richard van Wagenen, *Political Community and the North Atlantic Area: International Organizations in the Light of Historical Experience*, Princeton: Princeton University Press, 1957; and Emanuel Adler and Michael Barnett, eds., *Security Communities*, Cambridge: Cambridge University Press, 1998.
[27] Amitav Acharya, Regionalism and Multilateralism, p. 158.
[28] Ibid., p. 170.
[29] See Aaron Friedberg, "Ripe for Rivalry: Prospects for Peace in a Multipolar Asia, *International Security*, vol. 18, No. 3, Winter, 1993-1994, pp. 5-33; also see Christopher Hemmer and Peter Katzenstein, "Why is There No NATO in Asia? Collective Identity, and the Origins of Multilateralism," *International Organization*, vol. 56, No. 3, 2002, pp. 575-607; and David Kang, "Getting Asia Wrong. The Need for New Analytical Frameworks," *International Security*, vol. 27, No. 4, Spring 2003, pp. 57-85.
[30] David Kang, "Getting Asia Wrong."
[31] Amitav Acharya, *Regionalism and Multilateralism*, p. 252.
[32] Ibid., pp. 15-16 and 254.
[33] Karl Kaiser, "European History 101 for Japan and China," *Internationale Politik* (Transatlantic Edition), vol.7, No.3, Summer 2006, p. 90.
[34] Ibid., pp. 91-2.
[35] Shogo Suzuki, "Responsible Scholarship in Sino-Japanese Relations." Paper presented at the International Studies Association Conference, Chicago, IL, March 2, 2007, p. 9.
[36] Caroline Rose, *Sino-Japanese Relations*, p. 11.
[37] Ranbir Vohra, *China's Path to Modernization. A Historical Review from 1800 to the Present*, New Jersey: Prentice Hall, 2000, p. 299.
[38] In return, Premier Wen Jiabao has made clear that, if Taiwan is willing to recognize the "one China principle," negotiations can proceed. Whereas for Beijing this means "Taiwan is part of China," Ma interprets this as "mutual non-denial"—"neither side will deny the existence of the other." See Willy Lam, "Ma Ying-jeou and the Future of Cross-Strait Relations," *China Brief*, vol. 8, no.7 March 28, 2008, p.2. Also note that Hu Jintao in a meeting with Lien Chan, honorary chairman of the Kuomintang Party, on April 30, 2008, urged Taiwan to cooperate with the mainland on four principles: "building mutual trust, laying aside disputes, seeking consensus and shelving differences." See Xinhua News Agency April 30, 2008; reprinted as "Welcome, Mr. Zian Zhan," *World Affairs Board: International Conflict and Geopolitics*, p.1; http://www.worldaffairsboard.com/political-discussions/44350-welcome-mr-lian-zhan.html.
[39] Yuan Jing-Dong, "China and Japan Tiptoe into a 'Warm Spring,'" *Asia Times* online http://www.atimes.com/atimes/Japan/JE13Dh01.html and Yuan Jing-Dong, "Spring Time in Sino-Japanese Relations?" *OpinionAsia: Global Views on Asia* http://www.opinionasia.org/article/print/460.
[40] Bhaskar Roy, "Sino-Japanese Relations: Did "Warm Spring' Visit End With a Cold Sprinkle"? *South Asia Analysis Group*, paper no. 2703, 14 May, 2008 http://www.southasiaanalysis.org/%5Cpaper2703.html.
[41] See comment by Liu Jie in an interview by the Sasakawa Peace Foundation titled "A New Starting Point: What Can Be Done to Build Better Japan-China Relations"? in *Voices*, Newsletter of the Sasakawa Peace Foundation, No. 57, vol.1, 2008, p.2.
[42] Caroline Rose, *Sino-Japanese Relations*, p. 108.
[43] Nicholas D. Kristof, "The Problem of Memory," *Foreign Affairs*, vol. 77, No. 6, November/December 1998, p. 39.
[44] See Xinbo Wu, "The Security Dimension of Sino-Japanese Relations: Warily Watching One Another," *Asian Survey*, vol. 40, No. 2, March/April 2000, p. 297. Of

course here one might question how important these conservative elements are in today's Japanese politics.
[45] Nicholas Kristof, "The Problem of Memory," p. 40.
[46] For an analysis of the steps taken thus far by Japan to settle its historical legacies, see Katja Weber and Jonathan Huang, "East Asian Security Revisited." Also see Peter Gries, *China's New Nationalism: Pride, Politics, and Diplomacy*, Berkeley, University of California Press, 2005, chapter 6 for an insightful discussion of the "Sino-Japanese Apology Diplomacy."
[47] See Katja Weber and Jonathan Huang, "East Asian Security Revisited."
[48] Elazar Barkan and Alexander Karn, "Group Apology as an Ethical Imperative," in Elazar Barkan and Alexander Karn, eds., *Taking Wrongs Seriously: Apologies and Reconciliation*, Stanford: Stanford University Press, 2006, p. 7.
[49] See Peter Katzenstein and Nobuo Okawara, "Japan and Asian-Pacific Security," in J. J. Suh, Peter J. Katzenstein, and Allen Carlson, eds., *Rethinking Security in East Asia. Identity, Power, and Efficiency*, Stanford: Stanford University Press, 2004, p. 120; and Peter Katzenstein, *A World of Regions: Asia and Europe in the American Imperium*, Ithaca: Cornell University Press, 2005, p. 148.
[50] Alexander Wendt, "Anarchy is What States Make of It: The Social Construction of Power Politics," *International Organization*, vol. 46, No.2, Spring 1992, pp. 391-425.
[51] Richard Ned Lebow, "The Memory of Politics in Postwar Europe," in Richard Ned Lebow, Wulf Kansteiner, and Claudio Fogu, eds., *The Politics of Memory in Postwar Europe*. Durham: Duke University Press, 2006, p. 30.
[52] Peter Katzenstein, *A World of Regions*, p. 58.
[53] Members of the ARF are the ten ASEAN member states, ten ASEAN Dialogue Partners (Australia, Canada, China, the EU, India, Japan, New Zealand, ROK, Russia and the US), one ASEAN observer (Papua New Guinea), as well as the DPRK, Mongolia, Pakistan, East Timor, Bangladesh and Sri Lanka (Dept. of Foreign Affairs and Trade, Australian Government http://www.dfat.gov.au/arf/, p.1.
[54] Ibid.
[55] Amitav Acharya, Regionalism and Multilateralism, p. 190.
[56] For a discussion of three further venues for multilateral security dialogue—ASEAN +3, the Shangri La Dialogue, and the East Asia Summit—see Nick Bisley, "Asian Security Architectures," in National Bureau of Asian Research's *Strategic Asia*, 2007/08, pp. 355-57.
[57] Alastair Iain Johnston and Paul Evans, "China's Engagement with Multilateral Security Institutions," in Alastair Iain Johnston and Robert S. Ross, eds., *Engaging* China. The Management of an Emerging Power, London: Routledge, 1999, p. 264.
[58] Amitav Acharya, *Regionalism and Multilateralism*, p. 12; and Nick Bisley, "Asian Security Architectures," p. 352.
[59] Amitav Acharya, Regionalism and Multilateralism, p. 194.
[60] Nick Bisley, "Asian Security Architectures," p. 361-2; and Victor Cha, "Lecture on East Asian Security."
[61] Michael Jonathan Green, "Managing Chinese Power: the View from Japan," in Alastair Iain Johnston and Robert S. Ross, eds., *Engaging China. The Management of an Emerging Power*, London: Routledge, 1999, p. 165.
[62] Nick Bisley, "Asian Security Architectures," p. 359.
[63] Ibid., pp. 360-66.
[64] Kuniko Ashizawa, "Japan's Quest for Regional Order-Building: Quo Vadis?" Paper presented at the International Studies Association Conference, Chicago, IL, March 2, 2007.

Chapter 10

Development—Great and Small: "Greater China," Small Caribbean Islands and Offshore Finance

William Vlcek*

INTRODUCTION

Globalization is frequently represented with a figure displaying increased international financial flows, increased global trade or the increased density and penetration of telecommunication networks. Little noted in these grand portrayals for the overwhelming influence of neoliberal capitalism following the end of the Cold War has been the collection of small jurisdictions that are nodal points scattered across the transnational network of global capital. These jurisdictions host an offshore financial center (OFC), by design or through historical circumstances, that in turn facilitates not only financial flows but also arbitrage with the legal and regulatory regimes of other jurisdictions. As but one example, the number two source for foreign direct investment (FDI) to China in 2006 was the British Virgin Islands (BVI), the same was true in 2005 when it was also the number three recipient for overseas direct investment from China (behind Hong Kong SAR and the Cayman Islands). This very curious circumstance involves the OFC and its international business company (IBC) registry as a critical component in the circuits of capital flowing in and out of China. Notwithstanding the extensive and varied literature on FDI and China, the role and function of these offshore centers are not well represented. Offshore financial centers are pivotal to investment throughout Greater China (Mainland, Hong Kong SAR, Macao SAR, and Taiwan) as reflected in the ranking of the BVI as a source of FDI to Mainland China and consequently to the international political economy, for China is widely identified as the predominant destination for direct investment outside of the membership of the Organization for Economic Co-operation and Development (OECD).[1] For the purposes of this analysis, an offshore financial center is understood to be a jurisdiction that possesses a legal and regulatory regime designed to facilitate the international financial activity of non-domestic capital.

The use of the term jurisdiction recognizes that both sovereign (Bahamas) and non-self-governing/semi-sovereign (British Virgin Islands) territories host an OFC.[2]

The National People's Congress (China) enacted a new tax law, the Enterprise Income Tax Law, with effect from 1 January 2008 and it is expected to change the dynamics of foreign investment in China because it will equalize corporate tax rates between domestic-owned corporations and foreign-owned corporations at the national level. Foreign investment no longer will receive some of the preferential tax treatment that has helped to encourage the increasing amounts of FDI that have entered China over the past two decades.[3] The impact from the new law extends beyond foreign firms investing in China, for it also eliminates the differential tax rate that was one motivation for domestic capital to make a "round trip" visit to some foreign location in order to change its national identity and return to China as *foreign* capital.[4] A variety of sources identify the fact that *foreign* direct investment in China is to some extent *domestic* capital that has been re-routed through offshore locations in order to conceal its domestic origin and return to China as FDI.[5] One consequence of this fact is that any claims about development in China that are grounded on gross figures for FDI into China should be regarded with caution. If the activity of round tripping is not accounted for in a meaningful way conclusions about *foreign* investments in China are only tentative because of the failure to distinguish between the domestic and foreign beneficial interests behind these investments.[6]

The fact that recognized OFCs are present in the list for the top ten sources of FDI to China certainly supports the contention made concerning round trip capital. It must be agreed, however, that the use of a corporate vehicle registered in an offshore jurisdiction equally serves the investor from North America and Europe as much as it does the investor from China. For the Chinese investor the motivation behind these maneuvers is clearly a desire to benefit from the preferential tax treatment accorded FDI as compared to the constraints placed on domestic investment. For the case of other investors, this tactic similarly provides the opportunity for tax minimization. Consequently, the British Virgin Islands was second on the list of sources for FDI to China behind Hong Kong in 2003 where it was joined by the Cayman Islands and Bermuda in the list of the top ten sources.[7] In 2007, Hong Kong was still the leading source of FDI to China, together with the offshore jurisdictions of the British Virgin Islands (#2), Singapore (#5), Cayman Islands (#7), Samoa (#8), and Mauritius (#10) in the list for the top ten sources of FDI to China.[8] (See Table 10.1 for data on selected FDI sources to China during the period 2000-2005.)

Before looking at the relationship between OFCs and Greater China it is important to have a clear understanding for what qualifies as FDI. Foreign investment comes in several forms, including the purchase of equity shares in a domestic firm, debt instruments (bonds) of a domestic firm, and providing capital to a domestic firm for investing in the local markets. These activities are generally representative of foreign portfolio investment, whereas direct investment is more specific.

Foreign direct investment is net inflows of investment to acquire a lasting management interest (10 percent or more of voting stock) in an enterprise operating in an economy other than that of the investor. It is the sum of equity capital, re-investment of earnings, other long-term capital, and short-term capital, as shown in the balance of payments.[9]

The World Bank's definition is based on the international standard established in the International Monetary Fund's Balance of Payments Manual, however, the data collected and reported by China uses 25 percent as the criterion to determine foreign ownership and therefore whether or not an investment is recorded in its statistical yearbook as FDI.[10] Note here that the "foreign" characteristic of the definition involves the residence of the investing person (natural or legal) as one that is different from the residence of the corporate entity receiving the investment.[11] The challenge that arises from the use of an OFC to host an investment vehicle is the fact that its national identity becomes that of the OFC in which it is registered. The next section of the chapter looks at the development and role of offshore financial centers, with special reference here to those located in the Caribbean. The third section of the chapter looks at the emergence of Hong Kong SAR as an offshore center within Greater China. The fourth section offers an analysis of round trip capital in these capital flows. The final section concludes with the development implications of this relationship between Greater China and the Caribbean.

ORIGINS OF THE OFFSHORE FINANCIAL CENTER

Clearly, in a nautical sense the word "offshore" describes some object (ship, oilrig, rock, or island) located at a distance from the coast of a larger island or mainland (continental) territory. One definition located the emergence of the term offshore in the lexicon of international political economy with the development of the Eurodollar markets in the post-war Europe, describing it as an unintended consequence of the economic recovery driven by the Marshall Plan. The etymology of "offshore" provided by the Oxford English Dictionary referred to an *Economist* article from the 8 May 1948 issue—"The 16 nations will be provided with 'off-shore' dollars for buying from Germany."[12] The reconstruction of Europe (along with the Soviet Union and Japan) necessitated large capital flows, at the same time new international financial (Bretton Woods) institutions were established to control and regulate international financial flows. The desire for profit and to operate without the constraint of the new regulations led multinational firms to use offshore banking services.[13] Within the City of London, for example, banks were permitted to accept non-Sterling deposits from non-residents. Consequently, these financial institutions accepted deposits in U.S. dollars that they then lent onward, however, they maintained a separate set of books for such transactions because they were not subject to the regulatory review of the Bank of England.[14] The result was that these non-Sterling accounts for non-UK residents existed in a "fictive" space treated as independent of the sovereign territory of the United Kingdom and therefore beyond the regulatory oversight of domestic authorities.[15] Essentially, the transaction existed in an "offshore" location that permitted depositors to avoid any regulations or taxes that would be enforced when repatriating dollars to the U.S., or when converting them into the depositor's home currency.

More recently, offshore finance has been associated with the technological advancements and geographic dispersion of telecommunications as a support structure in global capital mobility. Since 1960, telecommunication technologies have dramatically changed the operation of the financial services industry. Initially via satellite links and subsequently through an expanding global infrastructure of high-speed, large bandwidth fiber optic cabling and secure telecommunication networks these technologies have enabled an explosion of near-instantaneous linkages among international financial centers. While this technological development has been treated as one facet of globalization, its impact is merely several factors greater than the pre-existing structure that supported inter-state finance before 1960.

More fundamental to the operation of international markets historically was the construction of a network of telegraph cables throughout the world during the second half of the 19th century. The extension of telegraphic connections via submarine cables connecting Europe to North America, the Caribbean and beyond, expanded business activity because of the increased timeliness of information. For example, when the General Council of Martinique contracted with the local telegraph company for a regular news dispatch, current wholesale sugar prices from European and American markets specifically were requested. "The French islands needed this information, especially wholesale prices, in order to compete in the cut-throat sugar business."[16] As Paul Hirst and Grahame Thompson observed on this aspect of globalization, the difference in the world economy between the transmission of market information by sailing vessel versus its transmission by electricity "is really one of a kind" in a way that the difference between a telegram and an e-mail is not. The reduction in transmission time from weeks to hours was considerably more important for markets than was the reduction from hours to minutes.[17]

Indeed, Bill Maurer argued that the origin of the Caribbean offshore financial space was an "unintended consequence" of these early trans-Atlantic telegraphic connections between Europe, the United States, and the Caribbean. He reached this conclusion from observing the continuity between the location of Caribbean financial centers and the telegraph/telecommunication nodes of Cable and Wireless in the Caribbean.[18] Early telegraph links were progressively upgraded as new technologies emerged, first with telephone trunk lines and then fiber optic cables. As a result, when financial firms went looking for locations to establish branches and subsidiaries outside of their onshore home jurisdictions they found these Caribbean islands already satisfied their communication requirements. As discussed below, the circumstances for Hong Kong's development as a financial center within Greater China are similar. It was the primary location for British investment into China and part of the British Sterling area, consequently Hong Kong developed and maintained extensive financial and telecommunication links with London.

The use of offshore financial services as an economic development strategy emerged in conjunction with formal decolonisation in the 1960s. Among the first jurisdictions in 1967 was the current exemplar of an offshore financial center, the Cayman Islands, while in late 1966 *The Sunday Times* (London) contained an article titled "Bahamas: the tax-free haven."[19] The phenomenon of offshore finance as an economic development strategy was already recognized in the 1960s, for example in supporting a case made to create an offshore financial center in New Hebrides (now Vanuatu) in 1970.[20] A government interdepartmental working group in London produced the report "British Dependent Territories and the Tax Haven Business" in 1970. It listed the "established tax havens" as the Bahamas, Bermuda, British Virgin Islands, Cayman Islands, Gibraltar, Hong Kong and Montserrat; it also identified a number of "potential tax havens": the British Solomon Islands (now the independent Solomon Islands), Gilbert and Ellice Islands (now Kiribati and Tuvalu, respectively), St. Helena and the Turks and Caicos.[21] The rationale for choosing to establish an offshore financial center as an economic development strategy is straightforward, an OFC provides a low-impact, high-gain approach to economic development. It is low impact to the jurisdiction because it does not consume large quantities of local resources nor compete with local businesses. At the same time the OFC is high gain due to the rents collected in the form of license fees and the employment opportunities created that require higher skill levels and education than those needed in the tourism industry as a sector for economic development in a small island economy.[22]

While the popular media image of an OFC may be that of a tropical island "tax haven," it should be recognized that an OFC provides many avenues for regulatory arbitrage beyond just taxation.[23] The OFC may also provide facilities for mutual (hedge) funds, captive insurance and re-insurance firms, trust companies, and shipping registries, as well as IBC registries. Moreover, in the context of this analysis of Greater China, offshore finance and FDI, there is the fact that routing an investment through an OFC also serves to transform the national residency of the investment. The IBC or special purpose vehicle holding the investment capital will possess the national identity (citizenship) of the jurisdiction hosting the registry. This feature helps to explain the BVI as a leading source of FDI for China, as the ultimate origin of the investment capital is concealed behind a veil established with the use of an IBC. At the end of 2006, there were 774,573 active companies registered in the BVI while the Cayman Islands reported a registry of over 83,000 active companies.[24]

HONG KONG SAR—AN OFC FOR GREATER CHINA

The business practice of incorporating firms offshore for use in Greater China emerged for reasons beyond simple regulatory arbitrage, which is the use of a foreign regulatory regime to work around any perceived limitations or constraints in a domestic regulatory structure.[25] The history of the role of offshore financial centers for business activity in China parallels the history of the opening of the modern Chinese economy. Mainland China began to open up to the world economy and foreign investment in 1979. At this point in time Hong Kong provided the financial interface between the Mainland and the world. Hong Kong already possessed a well-developed financial center and it provided the skills and expertise with financial services and intermediation that were lacking in the centrally-directed socialist economy of the Mainland. In October 1978 there were 851 offices for licensed banks, 234 registered firms approved to accept deposits, and offices for 104 foreign banks.[26] With the end of the Sterling Area in 1972, formal currency exchange controls in Hong Kong also ended, yet even before 1972 there were no controls on the exchange of U.S. dollars and other major currencies, only on Sterling, a situation that echoes the development of London as a financial center in the 1950s.[27] Catherine Schenk argued that it was this light regulatory approach toward foreign currency exchange, combined with the growing banking industry, which led to Hong Kong's emergence as an important financial center.

> The crucial determinant of Hong Kong's competitive position as an international banking center was the freedom from onerous regulation that weighed on regional and global financial centers elsewhere. Hong Kong's unusual position straddling the sterling area and dollar area allowed its banks to offer unrivalled services in the otherwise tightly controlled Bretton Woods international monetary system.[28]

The situation changed in 1982 with the announcement that Hong Kong would revert to China in 1997. As a defensive measure against expropriation and nationalization, many Hong Kong firms relocated their corporate domicile (registration) to other jurisdictions, in many cases OFCs with familiar legal systems including the BVI and the Cayman Islands. Yun-Wing Sung reported that 60 percent of all Hong Kong-listed firms had relocated their corporate registration by mid-1993.[29] As seen in Table 10.2, in 2004 the British Virgin Islands held 29 percent of Hong Kong SAR's position for all inbound direct investment while it was the destination location for 45 percent of the outbound direct investment position (Table 10.3).

The relationship between FDI and OFCs is not unique to China, though the existing political economy of China's state-directed market economy serves to promote its greater prevalence in China than is found in other developing or state-regulated economies. OFCs in the Caribbean and Pacific connect with the informal financial markets in China that were studied by Kellee Tsai, as well as with the structures of FDI analyzed by Yasheng Huang.[30] The categorization of Hong Kong SAR as an OFC has been challenged by Y. C. Jao, who argued that Hong Kong SAR is neither a tax haven, nor an offshore financial center. Central to his argument is an emphasis on the fact that academic authors making the case that Hong Kong SAR is an OFC fail to quantitatively support their position.[31] In this instance, however, the discursive power of naming exceeds that of arguments presenting quantitative assessments for the purpose and status of financial operations in Hong Kong SAR. Rather, the attribution and categorization of Hong Kong SAR as an OFC by the Bank for International Settlements (BIS), the International Monetary Fund (IMF), and the Financial Stability Forum serves as an indicator for an international community of policymakers, NGO activists and bureaucratic tax administrators that view Hong Kong SAR as an OFC.[32]

For this analysis the identification of a jurisdiction as an OFC is independent of the tax regime (which was Jao's main point of disagreement) and emphasizes rather the use of the jurisdiction for arbitrage while significant assets in the financial sector are of foreign origin. Thus it is an intersection of the BIS criteria for the designation of an OFC and the underlying issue in the use of IBCs to obscure identity and beneficial ownership.[33] Just as important, as already noted, is the use of an IBC registry in a jurisdiction possessing strong property rights and the agglomeration of skill sets to facilitate fast and efficient creation of a corporate vehicle. A major influence on the successful OFC is also reputation and political climate, amply reflected by the relocation of corporate registrations away from Hong Kong on the announcement of the territory's return to China. Reputation matters, as represented by the use of international blacklists for the noncooperative jurisdiction in order to discipline co-operation with the Financial Action Task Force's (FATF) anti-money laundering regime.[34] Balanced against this international perspective one can offer the absence of Hong Kong SAR (among others) from the OECD's tax competition project list of harmful tax regimes, while the European Union (EU) presently is attempting to establish negotiations with Hong Kong SAR on the matter of account holder information exchange for its Directive on the taxation of savings interest.[35]

From a policy perspective there is a similar resistance to the application of the "offshore" label to Hong Kong SAR. In this case, the problem expressed involves the connotation of the term, its use by media and critics as a form of shorthand to suggest the presence of illicit and illegal financial dealings.[36] Connected with this perspective was a complaint over categorizing all OFCs as one homogenous group, irrespective to their size, location, or compliance with the standards created by the OECD, FATF and other international bodies.[37] These concerns are valid with respect to public and industry perceptions of the Hong Kong SAR financial center or any other OFC, again it is a matter of reputation. From an analytical perspective seeking to understand and explain global capital flows and the economic relationships between small jurisdictions and Greater China, however, this policy concern fails to contribute to that understanding.

As already suggested, the use of OFCs to gain access to preferential tax rates in China and to reduce the risk from expropriation are not the only reasons for their significant presence in the FDI league table for China. There are a number of other legal and political reasons motivating the efforts made to obscure beneficial ownership for FDI in this fashion. One legal reason was that FDI, or more specifically the firm created or controlled via FDI, also received preferential treatment with respect to property rights until 2004.[38] Another motivation was the need or desire to obscure the jurisdiction of origin on the part of Taiwanese investments. Initially, the preferred jurisdiction for incorporation of an IBC by Taiwanese investors was Hong Kong, but with the imminent return of Hong Kong to the Mainland these firms also re-domiciled their corporate registration. As the politics of relations between Taiwan and the Mainland ebb and flow, the impetus to obscure the source of the investment may change;

nonetheless the routing of Taiwanese investments via an OFC serves to further cloud the true picture of FDI flows into the Mainland.[39] The next section further investigates the implications of this activity.

FDI FROM THE CARIBBEAN, A ROUND TRIP VISITOR FROM CHINA?

Rough estimates for the size of round tripping as a factor in FDI flows to China have ranged from 10 to 50 percent. At the same time, Edward Chen suggested that Chinese government measures instituted after the Asian financial crisis succeeded in reducing "unauthorized capital flows" and, consequently, the round trip activity.[40] Yet the World Bank would still suggest in 2002 that round trip capital continued to account for 17 percent of FDI to China, developing this estimate from the net errors and omissions data reported on China's balance of payments figures.[41] Alternatively, an IMF working paper argued that FDI inflows were not so much a case of round tripping, but rather it was more likely that they were "flows from sources such as Japan, Taiwan Province of China, and the United States that are channelled through such offshore financial centres in order to evade taxes in the source countries."[42] There is no question that this conclusion is valid, but it then raises the question as to why significant FDI originating in Japan and the U.S. has not been routed through an OFC, FDI levels that locate Japan at position three and the U.S. at position five on the list of top ten sources of FDI to China in 2005 and 2006. In sum, the nature of FDI into China and direct investment out of China argues that these various estimates do not capture the full complexity of the situation.[43] The challenge to measure capital flows into Mainland China continues, with a substantial increase in the first half of 2008 that led *The Economist* to write that "China is being flooded by the biggest wave of speculative capital ever to hit an emerging economy."[44]

The bi-directional nature of direct investment captured in Tables 10.2, 10.3, and 10.4 demonstrate the complexity of financial relations in Greater China and the difficulty confronting attempts to distinguish round trip capital from foreign investments that are avoiding taxes. Tables 10.2 and 10.3 display direct investment flows in and out of Hong Kong SAR because most analysts feel that a substantial portion of Hong Kong SAR's received investment moves on to yet another location, including Taiwan.[45] Thus these flows should be considered as additive to the data on Mainland China in Table 10.1 towards constructing a picture of direct investment for Greater China. Another point to keep in mind is that direct investment from China to Hong Kong SAR may not in turn flow out of Hong Kong SAR as direct investment, but it may instead be converted into a different financial instrument.[46] This situation may be suggested by the fact that Mainland China was the number two source/destination for direct investment from Hong Kong SAR, while the number one source/destination was the BVI. It was not the same situation for Mainland China, which has the Cayman Islands as its leading destination for direct investment in 2005 and 2006, followed by Hong Kong SAR and the BVI. Admittedly, some part of the investment capital sent to Hong Kong would remain there as its final destination, but that is not the case for the BVI, the Cayman Islands or the Bahamas. It would be expected for those initial destinations that the investment capital traveled on to yet another jurisdiction.

As indicated by the IMF analysis, there are a number of sources for FDI to China routed through an OFC. The first is domestic capital from China that returns as FDI after successfully circumventing capital controls to exit China in the first place (one example is through over-/under-invoicing practices). The second source could be that it represents profits acquired from other foreign investments made by Chinese firms that are then reinvested as FDI in China. A third possibility is that it represents investments from other locations (e.g. North America or Europe) which are using the OFC in order to minimize their corporate income tax at home.

Part of the difficulty with measuring round trip capital, in any context, is the fact that as with any illicit/illegal conduct, it strives to remain clandestine. Anecdotal reports indicate the space of possibility available for citizens to avoid the enforcement of capital controls. For example, a story in *The Economist* in November 2007 discussed the case of a Hong Kong entrepreneur taking advantage of the arbitrage possibilities with petrol and stock share prices between Hong Kong and the Mainland.

> The 43-year-old Hong Kong resident operated a black-market foreign-exchange business with an outlet in Hong Kong, four branches on the mainland, and a client list that included China National Petroleum and Sinopec, two state-run monoliths. Her firm handled transactions worth more than $1m a day.[47]

The raid on her firm and her arrest were connected to efforts by the central bank to stop the transfer of illicit funds across the border to Hong Kong. The need for such a "crackdown" at this time would seem to contradict the conclusion of one analysis that the effectiveness of China's capital controls regime "remain substantially binding."[48] Evidence on the ground (as it were) does not match the empirical results from available formal banking data. Consequently, efforts to definitively measure round trip capital flows will remain incomplete and any results tentative.

CONCLUSION

The important point to take away from this analysis is that the role of the offshore financial center *as* economic development for small jurisdictions has an under-recognized role *in* economic development. Widely seen as a location for tax arbitrage, the OFC also provides the facilities for risk and identity (nationality) arbitrage. This latter aspect is accomplished here through a veil placed over the national identity of investment capital that cannot be seen as operating in Mainland China (investment from Taiwan for example). It also has reduced the risk for a total loss of assets in the event of nationalization/ expropriation as a result of a government policy change. While the potential for such a significant reversal is diminishing, the concern over nationalization was one motivating factor behind the large scale relocation of corporate registrations from Hong Kong to the BVI and elsewhere in the early 1990s.

The analysis presented here does not involve questions of FDI with regards to host/home country impacts or the contribution of FDI to economic development, that debate will be left to other researchers.[49] Rather, the argument here is to appreciate the *location* of OFCs in these flows of global capital, including capital flows other than FDI.[50] This approach is in contrast to an empirical study of "The determinants of Chinese outward foreign direct investment" which did not include any of the jurisdictions that host an OFC (with the notable exception of Hong Kong and Singapore).[51] Given the presence of three other OFCs in the list of significant destinations for Chinese outward direct investment, the methodology used in that analysis fails to incorporate a significant portion of Chinese outward direct investment (Table 10.4). On the one hand, the use of an OFC for outward direct investment does obscure the intended destination and use of the investment capital. This fact is just as applicable for the assessment of Chinese direct investment to Hong Kong, which is very likely to be used as onward direct investment from Hong Kong. On the other hand, failing to acknowledge the involvement of these conduits for ODI limits the usefulness of the study's conclusions because it analyzed only part of the total picture of China's FDI. The fact that public knowledge of the ultimate destination for a significant amount of Chinese direct investment is not available in turn must be acknowledged as a potential constraint for effective policy analysis and recommendations.

The Caribbean nexus in particular is utilized to minimize corporate taxation in either (or both) home and host jurisdictions. Preferential tax treatment was one motivating factor that attracted FDI flows to China, as well as one factor behind the presence of the round trip capital that is concealed in these flows. The use of IBCs by firms and individual investors residing in North America, Europe and Japan to convey investment capital to China helps minimize their home jurisdiction tax obligations. Admittedly, the full complexity of these financial relationships between jurisdictions is not captured by the preceding discussion, which is limited to the aggregate figures reported at a national level. Moreover, the role of FDI in the processes of economic development, for China, India, and other developing states, is widely researched, while the contribution of FDI flows using an IBC domiciled in an OFC also serves to benefit economic development in these locations. The fees collected by the IBC registry explain the motivation of the British Virgin Islands and others to host the registry, as well as their efforts to maintain a reputation for integrity and respectability. The focus in this analysis has been with the Caribbean OFCs, however, Table 10.1 includes widely recognized offshore centers from throughout the world, reflecting the point that while the most significant investment flows may use the Caribbean centers, this phenomenon is global in nature. Further research and analysis is necessary in order to broaden our understanding for the role of the IBC and offshore financial centers in direct investment and global capital movements more generally.

Table 10.1 Selected Source Jurisdictions for FDI to China (U.S.$ millions)

Jurisdiction	2001	2002	2003	2004	2005
Asia	29,613.26	32,569.97	34,101.69	37,619.86	35,718.89
Hong Kong SAR	16,717.30	17,860.93	17,700.10	18,998.30	17,948.79
Macao SAR	321.12	468.38	416.60	546.39	600.46
Malaysia	262.98	367.86	251.03	385.04	361.39
Philippines	29.39	186.00	220.01	233.24	188.90
Singapore	2,143.55	2,337.20	2,058.40	2,008.14	2,204.32
Taiwan	2,979.94	3,970.64	3,377.27	3,117.49	2,151.71
Africa	329.77	564.64	617.76	775.68	1,070.86
Mauritius	305.63	483.69	520.98	602.32	907.77
Europe	4,483.98	4,048.91	4,271.97	4,798.30	5,643.10
Liechtenstein			2.29	47.80	2.86
Luxembourg	28.78	13.53	175.43	28.78	142.00
Monaco				1.88	0.04
Switzerland	205.44	199.80	181.34	203.12	205.88
North America	5,096.85	6,490.32	5,161.35	4,977.59	3,729.96
Bermuda	207.20	478.42	398.20	422.77	214.00
Latin America & Caribbean	6,308.91	7,549.79	6,906.57	9,043.53	11,293.33
Bahamas	59.60	89.90	87.87	48.00	74.67
Barbados	12.14	16.11	24.46	31.29	97.01
British Virgin Islands	5,042.34	6,117.39	5,776.96	6,730.30	9,021.67
Cayman Islands	1,066.71	1,179.54	866.04	2,042.58	1,947.54
Dominica	0.78	0.38		0.35	1.02
Jamaica	1.23		0.10	3.60	1.00
Panama	57.84	46.46	32.83	35.92	42.91
Turks and Caicos		0.80	0.57	1.27	3.50
St Kitts - Nevis			14.00	10.57	6.23
St Vincent and the Grenadines	0.29			1.27	1.66
Oceanic & Pacific Islands	1,014.78	1,417.22	1,731.19	1,974.37	1,998.98
Cook Islands	7.28	3.88	2.51	6.37	4.57
Nauru	0.50	1.19	2.58	7.00	0.64
Samoa	543.21	879.47	985.72	1,128.85	1,351.87
Marshall Islands	7.79	6.68	11.02	15.43	45.80
World Total	46,877.59	52,742.86	53,504.67	60,629.98	60,324.59

Source: National Bureau of Statistics of China, *China Statistical Yearbook* (various years). NB - an empty field indicates data not available or that it amounted to less than U.S.$10,000.

Table 10.2 Position and Flow of Inward Direct Investment to Hong Kong SAR (HK$ 100 millions)

Jurisdiction	Inflow 2002	Position 2002	% of total	Inflow 2003	Position 2003	% of total	Inflow 2004	Position 2004	% of total
British Virgin Islands	594	7,794	29.7%	198	9,352	31.6%	627	10,293	29.2%
China	317	5,946	22.7%	380	7,701	26.0%	620	10,201	29.0%
Netherlands	103	2,049	7.8%	247	2,561	8.7%	88	3,072	8.7%
Bermuda	21	2,732	10.4%	-136	2,548	8.6%	89	2,722	7.7%
USA	-110	1,866	7.1%	220	1,876	6.3%	484	2,435	6.9%
Japan	153	1,414	5.4%	142	1,422	4.8%	109	1,482	4.2%

Singapore	64	735	2.8%	-99	580	2.0%	32	871	2.5%
UK	86	558	2.1%	45	481	1.6%	182	700	2.0%
Cayman Isls	-687	449	1.7%	29	531	1.8%	65	618	1.8%
Canada	99	192	0.7%	2	199	0.7%	51	291	0.8%
Australia		445	1.7%						
Others	115	2,044	7.8%	36	2,351	7.9%	303	2,533	7.2%
Total	755	26,223		1063	29,604		2651	35,219	

Source: National Bureau of Statistics of China, *China Statistical Yearbook* (2006).
NB - The Hong Kong Monetary Authority has maintained a peg of 7.80 Hong Kong dollars to the U.S. dollar since 1983.

Table 10.3 Position and Flow of Outward Direct Investment from Hong Kong SAR (HK$ 100 millions)

Jurisdiction	Outflow 2002	Position 2002	% of total	Outflow 2003	Position 2003	% of total	Outflow 2004	Position 2004	% of total
British Virgin Islands	101	11,483	47.6%	248	12,703	48.2%	1368	14,021	44.7%
China	1243	8,430	34.9%	599	9,312	35.3%	1448	12,116	38.7%
Bermuda	-49	768	3.2%	-28	884	3.4%	267	1,297	4.1%
UK	36	205	0.8%	46	473	1.8%	49	553	1.8%
Japan	-171	119	0.5%	10	152	0.6%	284	421	1.3%
Singapore	43	260	1.1%	21	300	1.1%	45	342	1.1%
Panama	22	390	1.6%	-91	242	0.9%	-27	286	0.9%
Thailand	26	208	0.9%	-7	216	0.8%	32	248	0.8%
USA	72	322	1.3%	-94	204	0.8%	31	226	0.7%
Malaysia	50	279	1.2%	-28	242	0.9%	15	222	0.7%
Cayman Isls		279	1.2%						
Others	-11	1,387	5.7%	-247	1,638	6.2%	50	1,604	5.1%
Total	1362	24,129		429	26,367		3561	31,336	

Source: National Bureau of Statistics of China, *China Statistical Yearbook* (2006).
NB - The Hong Kong Monetary Authority has maintained a peg of 7.80 Hong Kong dollars to the U.S. dollar since 1983.

Table 10.4 Significant Destinations for China's direct investment (U.S.$ millions)

Jurisdiction	Net ODI 2004	Net ODI 2005	Net ODI 2006	Accumulated Net ODI at end of 2006
Total	5,497.99	12,261.17	17,633.97	75,025.55
Hong Kong SAR	2,628.39	3,419.70	6,930.96	42,269.91
Cayman Islands	1,286.13	5,162.75	7,832.72	14,209.19
British Virgin Islands	385.52	1,226.08	538.11	4,750.40
United States	119.93	231.82	198.34	1,237.87
Republic of Korea	40.23	588.82	27.32	949.24
Russia	77.31	203.33	452.11	929.76
Australia	124.95	193.07	87.60	794.35
Macao SAR	26.58	8.34	-42.51	612.47
Sudan	146.70	91.13	50.79	497.13
Germany	27.50	128.74	76.72	472.03
Singapore	47.98	20.33	132.15	468.01
Bahamas	43.56	22.95	2.72	17.52

Source: National Bureau of Statistics of China, *China Statistical Yearbook* (2007, 2006).

NOTES

* The author wishes to thank The Leverhulme Trust for the Research Fellowship that facilitated the presentation of this research at the ACPS conference *"Greater China" in an Era of Globalization,* Chinese University of Hong Kong, 14 - 15 July 2008.

[1] United Nations Conference on Trade and Development, *World Investment Report - FDI from Developing and Transition Economies: Implications for Development,* Geneva: United Nations Publication, 2006, p. xvii.
[2] William Vlcek, *Offshore Finance and Small States: Sovereignty, Size and Money,* Basingstoke: Palgrave Macmillan, 2008, pp. 18 - 25.
[3] With a few exceptions involving the environment, public infrastructure and technology transfer, see KPMG Huazhen, "PRC Enterprise Income Tax Law," at http://www.kpmg.com.cn/en/virtual_library/Tax/PRCtaxLawBook.pdf (accessed on 31 August, 2007).
[4] Louise de Rosario, "China's FDI merry-go-round," at http://www.fdimagazine.com/news/fullstory.php/aid/215/China%92s_FDI_merry-go-round.html (accessed on 30 June, 2007).
[5] Shaun Breslin, "China and the Political Economy of Global Engagement," in Richard Stubbs and Geoffrey R. D. Underhill, eds., *Political Economy and the Changing Global Order,* Oxford: Oxford University Press, 2006; Edward K. Y. Chen, "Hong Kong as a Source of FDI: Experience and Significance," in Shujiro Uranta, Chia Siow Yue, and Fukunari Kimura, eds., *Multinationals and Economic Growth in East Asia: Foreign direct investment, corporate strategies and national economic development,* London and New York: Routledge, 2006; Yun-Wing Sung, *The Emergence of Greater China: The Economic Integration of Mainland China, Taiwan and Hong Kong,* Basingstoke: Palgrave Macmillan, 2005; Jing Zhong, "Offshore financial centers affect cross-border capital flow in China," at http://en.ce.cn/Insight/t20040607_1016937.shtml (accessed on 28 June, 2004); Friedrich Wu, "Chinese Economic Statistics—Caveat Emptor!," *Post-Communist Economies,* Vol. 15, No. 1, March 2003; Yasheng Huang, *Selling China: Foreign Direct Investment during the Reform Era,* Cambridge: Cambridge University Press, 2003.
[6] United Nations Conference on Trade and Development, *World Investment Report (2006),* pp. 114 - 15; World Bank, *Global Development Finance: Financing the Poorest Countries,* II vols., vol. I, Washington, D.C.: IBRD/World Bank, 2002, p. 41; Geng Xiao, "Round-Tripping Foreign Direct Investment in the People's Republic of China: Scale, Causes and Implications," ADB Institute, Tokyo, 2004 at http://www.adbi.org/files/07_roundtrippingfdi_prc.pdf (accessed 25 September 2007).
[7] de Rosario, "China's FDI merry-go-round."
[8] US-China Business Council, "Foreign Investment in China," at http://uschina.org/public/documents/2008/02/2008-foreign-investment.pdf (accessed on 20 February, 2008).The identification of Singapore as an OFC here may be subject to debate, however, this point will not be explored further in this chapter.
[9] World Bank, *World Development Report 2006: Equity and Development,* Washington, D.C.: The World Bank and Oxford University Press, 2005, p. 304.
[10] Huang, *Selling China,* p. 5. Hong Kong meanwhile follows the World Bank/IMF convention of 10%, which further increases the difficulties with disaggregating round trip capital out of FDI flows between Hong Kong and China. National Bureau of Statistics of China, *China Statistical Yearbook,* vol. 25, Beijing: China Statistics Press, 2006, p. 973.

[11]International Monetary Fund, *Balance of Payments Manual*, 5th ed., Washington, D.C.: International Monetary Fund, 1993, p. 86.

[12]OED, "OED online," at http://athens.oed.com/ (accessed on 16 December, 2002).

[13]Sol Picciotto, "Offshore: The State as Legal Fiction," in Mark P. Hampton and Jason P. Abbott, eds., *Offshore Finance Centres and Tax Havens: The Rise of Global Capital*, London: Macmillan Press Ltd., 1999.

[14]Gary Burn, "The state, the City and the Euromarkets," *Review of International Political Economy*, Vol. 6, No. 2, Summer 1999.

[15]Picciotto, "The State as Legal Fiction."

[16]Daniel R. Headrick, *The Invisible Weapon: Telecommunications and International Politics, 1851 - 1945*, New York: Oxford University Press, 1991, pp. 54 - 56.

[17]Paul Hirst and Grahame Thompson, "The Problem of 'Globalization': International Economic Relations, National Economic Management, and the Formation of Trading Blocs," *Economy and Society*, Vol. 21, No. 4, 1992, p. 366.

[18]Bill Maurer, "Islands in the Net: Rewiring Technological and Financial Circuits in the 'Offshore' Caribbean," *Comparative Studies in Society and History*, Vol. 43, No. 3, 2001, p. 469.

[19]United Kingdom. Public Record Office, "Tax havens," London: 1967 - 1969. I refuse to use the term "tax haven," in part because it carries normative assumptions about the role and purpose of taxation in society. More to the point in this analysis, my insistence on the use of "offshore financial center (OFC)" serves to re-emphasize and underscore the distinct territorial separation between jurisdictions and their sovereign right to establish independent legal structures governing finance, trade, and taxation. Moreover, it highlights the fact that the OFC has developed into far more than a simple location for tax avoidance. This viewpoint remains applicable for the Hong Kong SAR and the non-independent Caribbean jurisdictions in that they are constitutionally self-governing in these areas.

[20]United Kingdom. Public Record Office, "Investment Industry in New Hebrides," London: 1973 - 1974, p. Folio 2.

[21]United Kingdom. Public Record Office, "Tax Havens in Cayman Islands," London: 1973, p. Folio 1.

[22]William Vlcek, "Why Worry? The Impact of the OECD Harmful Tax Competition Initiative for Caribbean Offshore Financial Centres," *The Round Table: The Commonwealth Journal of International Affairs*, Vol. 96, No. 390, June 2007.

[23]On this point, the repeated reference to "tax havens" in the literature on FDI in China serves to obscure the fact that tax minimization is not the only reason to use an international business company incorporated in an OFC to route FDI into China. The British Virgin Islands, the Cayman Islands and other OFCs have developed specialist capabilities in the efficient creation and maintenance of corporate entities and represent jurisdictions with stable political systems and a legal tradition of strong property rights. See Rose-Marie Belle Antoine, *Commonwealth Caribbean Law and Legal Systems*, London: Cavendish Publishing Limited, 1999.

[24]BVI Financial Services Commission, "Statistical Bulletin," British Virgin Islands, 2006 at http://www.bvifsc.vg/ [accessed 18 July 2007], 3; Economics and Statistics Office, "Annual Economic Report 2006," George Town, Grand Cayman, 2007 at http://www.eso.ky (accessed 20 April 2008), 35. "Active" is understood here to mean that all fees are paid and the registration is current, and not that the firm is actively engaged in any current business transaction or relationship.

[25]For a summary of one such use as reported by the Asia Development Bank, see Asia Development Bank, "Report and Recommendations of the President to the Board of

Directors on Proposed Equity Investment Credit Orienwise Group Limited (Project Number: 38908)," at http://www.adb.org/Documents/RRPs/PRC/38908-PRC-RRP.pdf (accessed on 28 August, 2007).
[26]Y. C. Jao, "The Rise of Hong Kong as a Financial Center," *Asian Survey*, Vol. 19, No. 7, July 1979, p. 675.
[27]Jao, "The Rise of Hong Kong as a Financial Center," p. 684, footnote 20; Catherine R. Schenk, "The Origins of the Eurodollar Market in London: 1955-1963," *Explorations in Economic History*, Vol. 35, No. 2, April 1998.
[28]Catherine R. Schenk, "Banks and the emergence of Hong Kong as an international financial center," *Journal of International Financial Markets, Institutions and Money*, Vol. 12, No. 4-5, October-December 2002, p. 338.
[29]Sung, *The Emergence of Greater China*, p. 26.
[30]Kellee S. Tsai, *Back-alley Banking: Private Entrepreneurs in China*, Ithaca: Cornell University Press, 2002; Huang, *Selling China*.
[31]Y. C. Jao, "Hong Kong as a Financial Centre of China and the World," in Lok Sang Ho and Robert Ash, eds., *China, Hong Kong and the World Economy: Studies in Globalization*, Basingstoke: Palgrave Macmillan, 2006.
[32]Bank for International Settlements, *BIS Quarterly Review: International banking and financial market developments*, Basel: Bank for International Settlements, June 2007, p. Table 6a; Ahmed Zoromé, "Concept of Offshore Financial Centers: In Search of an Operational Definition," International Monetary Fund, Washington, D.C., 2007; Working Group on Offshore Financial Centres, "Report of the Working Group on Offshore Centres," Financial Stability Forum, 2000 at http://www.fsforum.org/publications/publication_23_31.html (17 March 2003), 14. It may also be noted that Hong Kong SAR is a member of the Offshore Group of Banking Supervisors, see <http://www.ogbs.net/members.htm>.
[33] Monetary and Economic Department, "Guidelines to the international locational banking statistics," Bank for International Settlements, Basel, 2006 at www.bis.org (accessed 24 June 2007), p. 70.
[34]J. C. Sharman, "The Bark *is* the Bite: International Organisations and Blacklisting," Forthcoming.
[35]Organisation for Economic Co-operation and Development, *Towards Global Tax Co-operation: Progress in Identifying and Eliminating Harmful Tax Practices*, Paris: OECD Publications, 2000, p. 17; Adolfo Martin Jiménez, "Loopholes in the EU Savings Tax Directive," *Bulletin for International Taxation*, Vol. 60, No. 12, December 2006.
[36]It should be recognized that while illegal refers to an activity that is in violation of a jurisdiction's legal code, the illicit is an activity deemed by some as morally or ethically wrong, which is not otherwise in violation of a jurisdiction's legal code.
[37]Kevin Rafferty, "The biggest offshore centre of all," in Kevin Rafferty, ed., *Offshore Financial Services Guide 2005 - 06*, Hong Kong: Media Solutions2, 2005, pp. 23 - 26.
[38]Kellee S. Tsai, "Adaptive informal institutions and endogenous institutional change in China," *World Politics*, Vol. 59, No. 1, October 2006, p. 137.
[39]Sung, *The Emergence of Greater China*, p. 29.
[40]Chen, "Hong Kong as a Source of FDI: Experience and Significance," p. 133.
[41]World Bank, *Global Development Finance (2002)*, p. 41.
[42]Eswar Prasad and Shang-Jin Wei, "The Chinese Approach to Capital Inflows: Patterns and Possible Explanations," International Monetary Fund, Washington, D.C., 2005, 5.
[43]One wide-ranging effort is Xiao, "Round-Tripping Foreign Direct Investment in the People's Republic of China: Scale, Causes and Implications."
[44]"Hot and bothered," *The Economist*, 28 June, 2008, pp. 95-96.

[45] Sung, *The Emergence of Greater China;* Xiao, "Round-Tripping Foreign Direct Investment in the People's Republic of China: Scale, Causes and Implications."

[46]For an analysis of international portfolio investment and the probable impact of these transformations, see Nick Coates and Mike Rafferty, "Offshore Financial Centres, Hot Money and Hedge Funds: A Network Analysis of International Capital Flows," in Libby Assassi, Anastasia Nesvetailova, and Duncan Wigan, eds., *Global Finance in the New Century: Beyond Deregulation*, Basingstoke: Palgrave Macmillan, 2007.

[47]"The dambusters," *The Economist*, 22 November, 2007 at http://www.economist.com/finance/displaystory.cfm?story_id=10180842 (accessed 30 November 2007).

[48] Guonan Ma and Robert N McCauley, "Do China's capital controls still bind? Implications for monetary autonomy and capital liberalisation," Bank for International Settlements, Basel, 2007 at www.bis.org (accessed 10 October 2007), 22.

[49]On these points see Shujiro Uranta, Chia Siow Yue, and Fukunari Kimura, eds., *Multinationals and Economic Growth in East Asia: Foreign direct investment, corporate strategies and national economic development*, London and New York: Routledge, 2006; Harbhajan S. Kehal, ed., *Foreign Investment in Developing Countries*, Basingstoke: Palgrave Macmillan, 2004; John M. Mutti, *Foreign Direct Investment and Tax Competition*, Washington, D.C.: Institute for International Economics, 2003.

[50] Further analysis locating offshore financial centers in global capital flows is contained in William Vlcek, "A semi-periphery to global capital: Global governance and lines of flight for Caribbean offshore financial centres," in Owen Worth and Phoebe Moore, eds., *Globalisation and the Semi-periphery*, Basingstoke: Palgrave Macmillan, forthcoming.

[51] Peter J. Buckley et al., "The determinants of Chinese outward foreign direct investment," *Journal of International Business Studies*, Vol. 38, No. 4, July 2007.

Index